The Psychological World of

the Juvenile Delinquent

The Psychological World of the Juvenile Delinquent

BY

DANIEL OFFER

RICHARD C. MAROHN

ERIC OSTROV

BASIC BOOKS, INC., PUBLISHERS

New York

Library of Congress Cataloging in Publication Data

Offer, Daniel.
  The psychological world of the juvenile delinquent.

  References: p. 203
  Includes indexes.
  1. Juvenile delinquency. 2. Child psychopathology.
I. Marohn, Richard C., joint author. II. Ostrov,
Eric, 1941–   joint author. III. Title.
RJ506.J88033   618.9′28′58   78–53813
ISBN: 0–465–06674–7

CONTENTS

———————

CONTENTS

CONTENTS

PART IV
Appendices

PREFACE

The onset of adolescence is a critical period of biological and psychological change for the individual. Moreover it involves for many a drastic change in social environment as well. The adolescent years are highly formative for health-relevant behavior patterns such as the smoking of cigarettes, the use of alcohol or other drugs, the driving of automobiles and motorcycles, habits of food intake and exercise, and patterns of human relationship including high risk pregnancy and sexually transmitted disease. They are also critical for the formation of prosocial and antisocial commitments.

Recent advances in biological, behavioral, clinical, and epidemiological research have begun to clarify this great transition from childhood to adulthood. The conjunction of urgent social problems and new scientific opportunities make it likely that deeper understanding of this transition will be achieved in the next decade or two. The need is intense and poignant. The health, education, and social services are hungry for better information that could enhance our ability to treat these problems effectively and above all to prevent many of the disorders that arise in adolescence. This in turn would decrease the adverse impact of adolescent disorders on human suffering in adult life.

Adolescents are rapidly learning how to become adults. They can benefit from anticipatory guidance in respect to vital matters of human biology, health, disease, and behavioral adaptation. Before damaging patterns are firmly established, there is an opportunity to intervene helpfully. But to be effective in such efforts we need a deeper understanding of adolescents and how to reach them constructively.

Over many years, Drs. Offer, Marohn, and Ostrov have patiently and carefully sought to provide such badly needed information.

The methodology is based on a bridging of competence in clinical psychiatry with techniques of behavioral science. In this way, they are able to go beyond much earlier work in this field. Many investigations have been either (1) detailed case reports which are exceedingly difficult to generalize; or (2) well-designed studies whose primary data are so superficial that few useful conclusions can be drawn. Thus, the integrative nature of this research is especially significant.

Although the study does not have a control group as such, many of the interview schedules, psychological tests, and rating scales were used in Offer's previous research on normal adolescent populations (*From Teenage to Young Manhood,* Basic Books, Inc., 1975). There, he developed a baseline of normative behavior on one group of adolescents (middle-class, white, suburban, Protestant). In the present study, half of the delinquent population was comparable in socioeconomic characteristics to the normal population. This provides a useful perspective on the findings.

The authors are careful not to assert that the study represents the psychological profile of *the* juvenile delinquent. Rather, as cautious investigators, they believe they have described *one* population of psychiatrically disturbed delinquents. Whether they represent 20 or 30 percent of the delinquent population will be for future research to discover. But even if it is a minority of the delinquent population, it is a significant minority, and one that deserves thoughtful attention.

The study reflects six years of systematic observation. Keeping biological and social variables as nearly constant as possible, they delineate four distinct kinds of persons who enter the arena of juvenile delinquency. These are: (1) the impulsive delinquent; (2) the narcissistic delinquent; (3) the empty-borderline delinquent; and (4) the depressed-borderline delinquent.

Better classification will likely lead to better understanding of delinquency. This should, in turn, lead to alternative ways of helping the different kinds of persons. Indeed, Offer's group is already pursuing this course to explore therapeutic and preventive interventions for the future. These data, when ready, will help determine whether the different approaches (individual, family, or group therapy) do indeed make a difference. They represent a differentiated approach coming into wider use on the frontiers of mental health—i.e., serious attempts to determine what therapy is useful for whom in different phases of the lifespan.

Throughout the course of their work over the years, Daniel Offer and his late wife, Judith—a truly remarkable person whose loss is deeply felt—have sought with great dedication, sensitivity, and compassion a deeper understanding of adolescent problems. Such understanding is badly needed, deserves high priority in research, and holds authentic promise for alleviating much human suffering in the not-too-distant future.

DAVID A. HAMBURG, M.D.
President, Institute of Medicine
National Academy of Sciences

ACKNOWLEDGMENTS

The authors are grateful for the continuous support and encouragement of their project by the former and current directors of the Illinois State Psychiatric Institute, Dr. Lester Rudy and Dr. Jack Weinberg, and by Dr. Roy R. Grinker, Sr., former director of the Institute for Psychosomatic and Psychiatric Research and Training. We deeply appreciate the help given us by the staff of the delinquency unit at ISPI. They provided the patients with continuous excellent therapeutic care while never failing in the various research tasks we asked of them. We also acknowledge the invaluable support given us by the patients and their families. This book belongs to them as much as to us.

Specific contributions have been made by Dr. Kenneth I. Howard, who guided us through the maze of statistics, and by Ollie Knight, Jean Melton, and Marie Allison, our excellent secretaries who did far more than type. They kept the project in motion. Sallie Jaggar Hayes worked with us as editor during the final stage of the writing.

Our thanks also to the Illinois Law Enforcement Commission, whose grants #A–70–15 and 824 provided the main support of the research components of the program. Data analysis was started and the writing begun while the senior author was a Fellow at the Center for Advanced Study in the Behavioral Sciences at Stanford University. We appreciate the Center for the opportunity it gave us, the resources it provided, and for being the marvelous scholarly retreat that it is.

DANIEL OFFER
RICHARD C. MAROHN
ERIC OSTROV

Chicago, Illinois
January 1979

The Psychological World of

the Juvenile Delinquent

1

Introduction

This book describes the results of a five-year (1969–1974) research program [1] concerning disturbed juvenile delinquents and conducted by the authors—two psychiatrists and a psychologist—at the Illinois State Psychiatric Institute in Chicago. A great deal of research on this subject is being done by colleagues in the social sciences and by lawyers, but this study is primarily psychological. It has been our impression—indeed, our conviction—that there is a paucity of behavioral science research on juvenile delinquency which combines psychiatric and quantitative approaches. As psychiatrists and psychologists, we have our own bias, thought patterns, feeling tone, and techniques in doing research. We have not surveyed all the available data, neither have we been completely objective; rather, our methodology, data collection, analysis, and interpretation of the results are based on our personal and professional experience. But we believe our findings to be solid, and to be of help in the understanding of juvenile delinquency as a human phenomenon. While aware of our shortcomings, we urge the reader to realize that *no study* can give *The Answer*. Each study can add to our knowledge, so that in the future we may be able to integrate data drawn from bio-psycho-social research in order to increase our understanding of youth with both behavior and delinquency problems.

It is not our goal to review the historical background of juvenile delinquency other than to note that the phenomenon is not of recent origin. To compare with any degree of accuracy the incidence of juvenile delinquency across cultures, across time, and across social classes is all but impossible. The reason for this is simple enough. Different criteria are

3

used to label juveniles as delinquents in different settings and at different times. Certain middle- and upper-class juveniles are steered in the direction of mental health rather than in the direction of criminal justice, hence they are not part of any juvenile court study. The inner-city youth who has some (minor) delinquent problems is handled by law-enforcement agencies very differently than is the suburban youth (see, for example, Offer 1969). In other periods of time the rates of delinquency did not include the ghetto population at all. The police then circled the ghettos in metropolitan areas (not only in the United States; this was a universal practice), and ignored crimes that took place within their walls. Hence even the minimal epidemiological data available from the beginning of the twentieth century are slanted. The reader might ask: What about current FBI crime reports—are they not the most reliable sources we have? Do not writers, educators, journalists, and other interested intellectuals continuously tell us that the rate of all crimes (violence against people, violence against property, white-collar crime) has increased both for adults and for adolescents? It is a fact that there is no conclusive evidence concerning the purported increase in crime rates.

Our contention in this book is that we do not have enough hard data to know whether the rate of juvenile delinquency has gone up, gone down, or stayed relatively the same. Our law-enforcement system is not giving us a reliable yardstick to which we can compare, for example, the rates in suburban Chicago, rural Kentucky, and Harlem. Nor are there comparative studies across time that answer the question of whether the rate of juvenile delinquency has increased during the past one hundred years. The little evidence we do have seems to suggest that society's tolerance for violence has decreased; i.e., there may actually be fewer violent acts against others. The immediate reaction is to exclaim: But look at all the murders in Detroit, New York, Chicago! Look at the "increase" in violent acts performed by teenagers, etc., etc.! We indeed suggest that once all the epidemiological factors are taken into account we will be perplexed, without a definite answer at hand. The FBI controls for such obvious factors as the increase in population, the percentage of youth compared to other age groups, the number of attempted violent crimes which do not end in actual violent crimes, and other (nonviolent) crimes as compared to the violent ones. But the FBI cannot control who reports what on whom; it does not control the percentage of autopsies on suspicious deaths in smaller communities where the local physician tends routinely to write "heart attack."

There is also the matter of awareness. Law-enforcement techniques have undoubtedly improved tremendously in the past hundred years, as have communication techniques. Until relatively recently we did not know how many "justifiable homicides" took place in the South and the "Wild West." What about the labor clashes at the turn of the century? How would the many who were killed then be classified today? Spiegel (1971) points out that during the draft riots of the Civil War and the First World War many more people were killed than the relatively few killed during the protests of the Vietnam war years. Are we not becoming more aware of the various abuses within our family systems and, as a result, less tolerant of them? Whether the abuser is a child, parent, wife, or husband, prosecution is much more conscientious today. Does that mean that the phenomenon did not exist fifty or a hundred years ago? Such a suggestion would seem preposterous. But our tolerance for such physical abuse and violence has definitely decreased. As a result of our awareness that the problem of physical abuse exists, we have set up intervention programs and therapeutic approaches. But how does society deal with juvenile delinquency?

First, the phenomenon must be defined. It is a *behavior* by a *juvenile* in violation of the laws or values of the prevailing society. It can be very serious (murder, violence against other humans); serious—but less so (violence against property which belongs to others: robbery, theft, destruction, etc.); less serious and tending to be more self-destructive, but still defined as delinquent (truancy, runaways, sexual activity without physically hurting another human being, and drug abuse).

It is important to stress that we define the preceding as "delinquent," whether or not the behavior has come to the attention of the law-enforcement agencies, the schools, the helping professions, or the parents. Since delinquency is a behavior, it can be caused by a variety of syndromes. Its etiologies have been described as biological (Lewis and Balla 1977; Wender 1971; McCord 1968), sociological (Shaw and McKay 1969; Cohen 1971; Glueck and Glueck 1962; Matza 1964; Short and Strodtbeck 1965; Thrasher 1936), and psychological (Aichorn 1935; Eissler 1949; Friedlander 1960; Johnson and Szurek 1952). Until recently the sociological and socioeconomic factors have been given a central role in explaining the etiology of such behavior. Most social scientists follow the tradition of Merton (1938, 1957), who stated that deviance (in our case, delinquency) stems from the frustration of the lower classes, living as they do within the context of a middle-class society. This is a limited point of view concerning normality as well as deviance (Offer and Sabshin 1974). As Reckless and Dinitz (1967) pointed out, it does not explain why not all lower-class adolescents become deviant and juvenile delinquents. It circumvents the issue of individuality and specific psychological variables

5

which we are addressing in this monograph. Studies of biological factors were only recently begun; the psychological ones were few and far between. They concentrated mostly on delinquents who found their way to the psychiatrist's waiting room, often with other characterological problems which were more serious psychiatrically.

As stated, the purpose of this book is to study the psychological factors of delinquency, and thus to contribute to a better understanding of the phenomenon. More correct comprehension of the diagnostic problems, better differentiation of the subtypes of adolescents with delinquent behavior would, of course, also help in therapeutic intervention programs. If, through a series of tests and interviews during the screening process, we can document those who would best benefit from which program, we may be able to help considerably more adolescents in the future.

Our goal in the project was to better understand a group of disturbed juvenile delinquents. We wanted to be able to generalize our findings to a larger group than the fifty-five subjects we examined. Needing some uniformity in the study, we eliminated delinquents with obvious brain damage (epilepsy, severe mental retardation), acute or chronic psychotic states or schizophrenia, and the seemingly healthy who did not want or need intensive psychiatric care. We intentionally accepted only chronic offenders who had performed serious offenses against the law; our subjects did not include juveniles with minor offenses. We chose adolescents who acted violently against others (attempted murder, assault and battery with an intent to injure), who were involved in drug abuse, prostitution, larceny, armed robbery, theft, property destruction, incorrigible truancy and/or running away. The reason selected subjects were hospitalized and not cared for in an open setting or an outpatient clinic had to do with the psychiatric and legal realities of the setting. Because our patients needed a locked door in order to be treated, we do not know how many cases the juvenile court would have referred to us, or whether we could have really studied them, under conditions of minimum security. As it was, we lost some subjects because we were not operating a prison (see, for example, Marohn et al. 1973).

In 1970, at the beginning of the study, we stated our hypothesis (Ostrov, Offer, and Marohn 1972):

There were different types of juvenile delinquents. Specifically, we hypothesized that there were two major classes of delinquents: juvenile delinquents whose behavior resulted from an underlying (and unidentified) depression, and juvenile delinquents whose impulsive behavior was caused by an underlying character disorder. The character disorder may have been psychopathic (i.e., deficient superego development), or immature (i.e., poor ego development).

In actuality, we found four dimensions, each of which can be typified by a particular kind of delinquent:

1. The Impulsive
2. The Narcissistic
3. The Depressed Borderline
4. The Empty Borderline

Four case examples will be presented, each exemplifying one of the preceding four dimensions.

It is our firm belief that the types of juvenile delinquent whom we have studied are frequent visitors to our halls of justice. Some of them want to be caught (Alexander and Staub 1956); others are caught because they do not know how to avoid it; still others are caught by chance. Some are never caught and continue their delinquency into adult criminal behavior. That the group we studied is not a population selected at random is self-evident. The question we raised and which continues to haunt us is: whom in the adolescent population do they represent? (And can we prove it?)

Based on our experience with this study population, and on our professional role as consultants, teachers, and diagnosticians of adolescent psychiatry, we can state that this indeed is a group of disturbed adolescents who utilize the acting-out route as a convenient way of expressing their innermost feelings. They do not impress us as the glamorized delinquents of fiction. They are dramatically different from the normal adolescents studied previously (Offer 1969; Offer and Offer 1975). They do not remind us of Cohen's (1971) delinquent boys, nor of other studies of gang delinquency. They are reminiscent of the group studied by Baittle and Offer (1971); in that project, Baittle's in-depth interviews with some members of a gang in Chicago pinpointed their psychopathological problems and conflicts.

It is, therefore, our conviction that by better understanding these fifty-five juvenile delinquents we will have learned much about the psychology of delinquency itself, its etiology, its treatment, and ultimately its prevention. We are fully cognizant of the other forces impinging on youth in today's society. Whether it is economic opportunity, educational influences, or biological givens, all are of extreme importance in the eventual integration of our knowledge into one open system. In this monograph the task we have set for ourselves is much more modest: a better understanding of the psychology of juvenile delinquency.

We have tried to understand a group of people who lived very difficult lives and experienced an inordinate amount of suffering. Part of their response to the world was delinquent behavior, but we wanted to study more than this; we wanted to examine the people who were exhibiting this behavior, and to learn of their world and their feelings. In doing so, we did not set up a detailed psychological experiment. Nor did we try to predict the behavior of masses of people. Instead, we used a methodology derived by one of us from earlier studies of normal adolescence, and the clinical and quantitative skills possessed by all of us. The study of normal adolescence involved in-depth psychiatric interviews, ratings, and quantitative methodology through which we were able to capture the psychological world of the normal teenager (Offer 1969; Offer and Offer 1975). We hoped to be able to use a similar methodology on a very different group of individuals in order to penetrate their psychological world.

In this book we thus find a variety of approaches designed to grasp the phenomenology of the delinquent teenagers with whom we had contact. We studied the cognitive functioning, the families, the emotional status, and the behavior of the teenagers through a variety of means, and subjected the resultant data to quantitative procedures. In doing so, we did not pretend to capture every aspect of the environmental experience or biological makeup which might pertain to the delinquent behavior of these individuals. We are aware, for example, of the powerful sociological influences on human behavior. To understand and predict the delinquent behavior of aggregates of people, sociological variables are essential. From the point of view of the individual delinquent, these sociological variables are part of their world. Our concentration on the psychological aspects of the delinquent's world was not to the exclusion of biological or sociological variables. Our reason for screening out the biological variables and methodologically factoring out [2] the sociological variables was not to make a statement that these variables are irrelevant; rather, we were using a statistical procedure which highlighted psychological variables which, while still reflecting biosocial factors, have a useful and autonomous explanatory power of their own. In this case the interrelationship of psychological variables provides us with psychological dimensions for study which are valid for understanding the phenomenology and assisting the treatment of the individual delinquent. In brief, the fact that we place heavy emphasis on many aspects of the delinquents' psychological functioning is not a denial of the validity of biosocial forms of thinking. It is only an affirmation of a way of regarding the delinquent experience which is valid for individual phenomenology. Other ways of looking at delinquency are valid for understanding groups of delinquents from another point of view and for other purposes.

8

NOTES

1. The results of the model therapeutic program are described by Marohn et al. (1979).

2. The model we used assumed that interrelationships between psychological variables are a function of sociological as well as conceptually more purely psychological influences. For example, older adolescents may feel better about themselves than younger adolescents do while at the same time older adolescents may be less impulsive. If we did not control for age, self-image and impulsivity might appear to be related in the sense that one leads to the other directly. However, in fact, in any one age group these psychological constructs may not be related. Factoring out demographic variance gave us a residual matrix wherein psychological variables interrelationships are related less to demographic influences and more to correlations on a psychological level only.

PART I

THE PROJECT

Subjects and Method

Background

The difficulties of doing juvenile delinquency research can be illustrated by discussing a relatively simple model often used for this purpose: the investigator first identifies youthful perpetrators of crime, and then contrasts them along various dimensions with their law-abiding counterparts. Results are said to indicate the concomitants of delinquency. Once identified, these concomitants can presumably be used to point to causes of delinquent behavior which, in turn, can be modified or removed, thus eliminating the problem. The paradigmatic and probably the best study along these lines was that of the Gluecks (1950), who used a wide variety of instruments to compare five hundred delinquents and five hundred nondelinquents; the subjects were carefully matched to ensure that differences in extent of criminal behavior formed the critical differentiating factor between the groups. On the basis of observed differences, the Gluecks (1970) proposed a way to predict who would become delinquent, and ultimately proposed a way to prevent delinquency.

While apparently simple and relevant, this paradigm can be criticized on various methodological grounds. For example, the concept that juvenile delinquents form a readily identifiable class of people is open to question. To be more concrete, studies like that of the Gluecks use incarcerated delinquents as their target group; it is not obvious, however, that incarcerated juvenile delinquents are representative of all juvenile delinquents. Instead, in light of the evidence of bias with respect to who gets arrested and who gets remanded to correctional facilities (see chapter 1) and the likelihood that many juvenile delinquents are never caught, the chances are strong that apprehended adolescents are an atypical sample of the juvenile delinquent population as a whole. An alternative way of identifying delinquents is to ask them, in effect, to label themselves using self-report questionnaires (Short and Nye 1957; Nye and Short 1957; Kulik, Stein, and Sarbin 1958). But this procedure also contains pitfalls since there is evidence that subjects either minimize or exaggerate their previous delinquency to an appreciable degree when completing self-report delinquency check lists (Fabianic 1972, Gold 1966; Clark and Tifft 1966). To sum up this point, studies which contrast delinquents and nondelinquents suffer from an inability to specify the actual populations to which the results pertain. Often it is not certain whether the "delinquents" are in fact more delinquent than the nondelinquents, or if they are, whether that is the only pertinent difference between the groups. Studies which are most questionable contrast groups which are not matched demographically—usually apprehended lower-class delinquents with middle-class control groups. Such findings pertain as much, if not more, to social-class differences as to any purported differences between delinquents and nondelinquents.

A related point is that comparing delinquents and nondelinquents can be useful only to the extent that delinquents more or less homogeneously and uniquely possess qualities (or reflect circumstances) which nondelinquents do not. As was just noted, depending on how "delinquent" is defined, the one attribute common to all delinquents as opposed to nondelinquents may be that the latter were never apprehended; so defined, qualities or circumstances unique to delinquents could simply be correlates of that one overarching communality—the fact of having been caught. Another possibility is that all criminals, properly labeled, share at least a propensity toward action. This propensity would not be unique to criminals, but at least it would characterize the vast majority of this group.

The chances are good, however, that aside from characteristics or circumstances associated with having been caught or having a tendency toward external action, few features of life space are uniquely associated with delinquents as a whole. The reason is that the causes of juvenile delinquency may be as diverse as the numerous theories that have been adduced to explain this phenomenon. For a number of years data have existed which indicate that delinquents should not be regarded as a homogeneous group but instead, for meaningful assessment, should be subdivided along various behavioral, attitudinal, and sociological dimensions (Hewitt and Jenkins 1946; Jenkins and Glickman 1947; Peterson, Quay, and Tiffany 1961; Quay 1964). Many delinquent/nondelinquent comparisons ignore these significant intradelinquent distinctions, making it much less likely that meaningful delinquent/nondelinquent differences will be found. In light of the evidence presented by Jenkins, Peterson, and Quay, a more useful model would involve identifying subgroups of delinquents and nondelinquents, and comparing these subgroups by means of selected variables or dimensions.

Another difficulty is that even if meaningful subgroups of delinquents and nondelinquents are compared and a sample of delinquents chosen that is reasonably representative of the population to be studied, the problem would remain of selecting relevant dimensions for analysis. Sociologists have an easier task in this regard than do scientists working at the psychological level. The relevant sociological variables are fairly simple to identify and to measure. Lander's (1954) research provides as good an illustration as any. In that work, he correlated delinquency rates with various other census tract statistics and described the significant associations. Alternatively, he could have compared the economic and residential backgrounds of delinquents and nondelinquents and described significant differences. Workers at the psychological level, however, are confronted by a much wider array of variables for potential study, and are less clear about the relevance, validity, and reliability of possible variables than are sociologists. Actually, as Schuessler and Cressey (1950) have described, many of the psychological variables used to compare delinquents with nondelinquents have been of dubious validity and stability. A pressing problem in this area is that the delinquents' current functioning with respect to some psychological measures could reflect the fact of having been identified and treated as a delinquent. Careless performance on a Porteus Maze (Porteus 1945) and poor self-image might be thought of in this context, though evidence now exists which indicates that Porteus Q-scores can predict recidivism rates (Roberts, Erikson, Riddle, and Bacon 1974), and self-image predicts susceptibility to delinquency over the course of several years of study (Reckless, Dinitz, and Murray 1956).

To summarize these points, studies contrasting delinquents and nondelinquents are beset with numerous problems including sample choice, difficulty in matching target and control groups, internal heterogeneity of delinquent and control groups, and the problem of selecting reliable, valid, and relevant variables, especially on the psychological level.

In this research, we chose to study intensively a small, but theoretically important, sample of juvenile delinquents. We sought to bring psychiatric depth to the investigation of delinquency without sacrificing the quantitative methodology of the psychologist or the perspective of the sociologist.

In doing so, we tried to allow for the effects of demographic factors while using psychological variables such as cognitive controls which are demonstrably reliable and valid. Furthermore, we explored the possibility of psychological subtypes within our delinquent sample and supplemented official and self-reports regarding delinquent behavior with quantification of observations of delinquent behavior in vivo. Nevertheless, we are aware that this study, like others before it, has its own methodological limitations and presents results which are more suggestive than conclusive.

Our framework for this inquiry was the longitudinal research project on normal adolescent males by Offer (1969) and Offer and Offer (1975). In that investigation the Offers brought new meaning to the concept of "normal" adolescence and established the precedent for conducting intensive yet quantitative research with teenagers. In practice, the Offers used a variety of sources of information including the teenager himself, his parents and teachers, and psychiatrist-interviewers, along with a range of data-gathering techniques including rating scales, projective tests, and psychiatric interviews. The data obtained were gathered repeatedly over an eight-year period leading, as the culmination of the work, to a factor analysis and a cluster analysis which delineated three normal developmental routes through adolescence. When the Offers then described subjects typical of those associated with each route by using in-depth case histories, they exemplified the approach of combining clinical, psychiatric, and quantitative methodology.

By essentially replicating this methodology, we hoped to gain two things. First, we wished to extend the Offers' success in delineating one kind of adolescent adaptation, namely normality, to another kind, juvenile delinquency. Second, we anticipated being able to compare findings about delinquents to analogous data regarding the Offers' normal, demonstrably nondelinquent teenagers.

Our first task was to choose a sample of delinquents upon whom to concentrate our efforts. Since the project's design called for intensive, multifaceted, and prolonged investigation, we needed a setting where this kind of work would be both possible and equitable. We also wished to study a group of delinquents whose members, theoretically, it was important to understand in greater depth. To fulfill these two considerations the intensive treatment program at the Illinois State Psychiatric Institute (ISPI) seemed particularly suitable: for one thing, in-depth study fitted well with the concern for complex understanding of the individual expected in an intensive treatment center, and for another, the treatment provided in such a center formed an equitable quid pro quo for the extensive research participation to be asked of subjects and parents. As to the importance of this sample, we were aware that we could not demonstrate that these subjects were representative of all delinquents. Nevertheless, we believed that they represented an important subclass of adolescent lawbreakers, since they manifested repeated and severe delinquency problems and more or less significant emotional disturbance.[1]

The psychological variables chosen for study either had been demonstrated by the Offers to have relevance to adolescent adaptations or, as in the case of cognitive style variables, were known to be reliable, valid, and meaningfully related to type of behavioral adaptation. Other factors were studied by means of instruments which had been specifically created for this study, such as the Adolescent Behavior Check List (ABCL) described later. Following the methodology used by Offer and Offer (1975), plans were made to consider the delinquents not just as a homogeneous group vis-à-vis normal controls, but to explore psychological dimensions of delinquency and, if possible, to define subtypes of delinquents which in turn could be contrasted with subtypes of normal adolescent coping.

The Subjects

The research project was piloted on two inpatient delinquents beginning in January 1969, and formal data collection began in July of that year. Data collection ended with the discharge of the last research subject in November 1974. During that period ninety-three subjects were screened for possible admission to the program. Sixty-six of them were accepted for admission; the twenty-seven rejected could not meet one or more criteria for admission—either they were overtly brain damaged, epileptic, grossly retarded, or psychotic, or they were not delinquent or in need of hospitalization. Six of those accepted did not come into the hospital for one reason or another, most of them because they were placed in another facility while marking time on the project's waiting list. Five more of the sixty-six did not complete the minimum requirements for inclusion in the final sample: four left the hospital early—one because he was psychotic and grossly inappropriate for the program, one because he successfully eloped from the hospital, and two because they physically attacked staff members and were administratively discharged; the fifth noncompleting patient and her parents refused to cooperate with the research, and data was insufficient to warrant her inclusion in the final sample. This subject was the only patient, at screening and thereafter, who refused to take part. The final sample therefore comprised fifty-five delinquent adolescents.

Patients accepted at screening were somewhat—but not significantly—younger than those rejected; acceptance rates for males and females, blacks and whites, were almost identical.[2] Among the fifty-five inpatient delinquents (see Table 2.1) were thirty-eight whites and seventeen blacks, thirty males and twenty-five females; the mean age of this sample was fifteen years six months, while the median age was fifteen years five months. Subjects came from a wide range of social-class backgrounds: seven (13 percent) from the highest social class according to Hollingshead's (1965) five-level classification; twelve (22 percent) from class two; seven more from class three; nineteen (35 percent) from class four; and ten (18 percent) from class five. Twenty-nine of the subjects came from intact homes, seven had been adopted, and nineteen came from one parent only, or one parent-one stepparent, family structures.

Subjects were recruited for the program by means of letters sent out on two different dates (Fall 1969, 1970) to potential referral agencies and private psychiatrists. The letters specified that treatment would be offered to delinquent adolescents between the ages of thirteen and seventeen who were in need of hospitalization and who were not retarded, brain damaged, psychotic, or epileptic. In practice, referrals came from a variety of sources: twenty-six of the subjects accepted were referred by probation officers or other court or corrections personnel; the remainder were re-

TABLE 2.1

Demographic Attributes of the Final Sample
(Fifty-five Juvenile Delinquents)

Sex		Race		Social Class[a]				
Males	Females	Blacks	Whites	1	2	3	4	5
30	25	17	38	7	12	7	19	10

Mean Age: 15 years, 6 months (S.D. = 14 months)
Median Age: 15 years, 5 months

Number from intact families: 29
Number from one-parent families: 9
Number from one biological parent—one stepparent families: 10
Number from adoptive families: 7

[a]Based on Hollingshead 1965.

ferred by school social workers or counselors (seven); parents (six); social-work agencies (five); other hospitals (five); therapists in private practice (four); and the outpatient department of ISPI (two). They had shown a wide range of delinquent behavior including runaway, car theft, forgery, drug use, arson, shoplifting, breaking and entering, prostitution, and assault with a deadly weapon.

The Instruments

Data collection proceeded in three stages (see Table 2.2). The first took place during the screening process: the subject responded to two questionnaires and an interview, while the subject's parents replied to another questionnaire. During the last two-thirds of the project subjects were also given a complete battery of cognitive style tests during screening. Most of the data collection occurred during the second stage—the period of time corresponding to the subjects' stay in the hospital, especially their first thirteen weeks. The third stage occurred six months or more after the subjects' discharge from the hospital, at which time the subjects, if located, were asked to respond to a follow-up interview. Details of these data collection phases are given below.

The following instruments were used at screening:

a. *The Admission Questionnaire*: a semistructured interview schedule which provided a thorough review of the adolescent's history of antisocial behavior, his involvement with various institutions such as the courts or psychiatric facilities, and his peer-group relationships. Questions were precoded, and answers involving a yes/no or multiple-choice format were included in the code book.[3]

b. *The Offer Self-Image Questionnaire* (OSIQ): described in detail in Offer, Ostrov, and Howard (1977), this instrument taps adolescents' self-image in various areas important to the adjustment and psychology of the teenager. Its authors found the test to be reliable as well as valid in that it can significantly discriminate among normal, delinquent, and disturbed groups.

c. *The Delinquency Check List* (DCL): first described by Kulik, Stein, and Sarbin (1968a), this self-administered check list asks subjects to answer questions which pertain to "the extent of their participation in a broad range of misbehaviors"; cluster analysis has shown four dimen-

TABLE 2.2

Time of Collection of Data Used in the Study
(Fifty-five Juvenile Delinquents)

Time of Collection	Instrument	Source of Data
Initial contact for research purposes	Telephone intake form*	Referral source
During screening	Admission questionnaire*	Patient
	Parents' interview*	Parents
	Consent for research and treatment*	Parents, patient
	Videotape consent form*	Parents
	Offer Self-Image Questionnaire (OSIQ)*	Patient
	Delinquency Check List*	Patient
	Cognitive style tests	Patient
After admission:		
Day 1 and daily thereafter until discharge	Adolescent Behavior Check List*	Staff ratings
Day 1	Physical, neurological, laboratory examinations	Patient
Day 2	Likability scale (early)	All staff working with patient
Week 1 but before school began	Bender-Gestalt Test, Rorschach, Thematic Apperception Test, Wechsler Adult Intelligence Scale, Wechsler Intelligence Scale for Children	Patient
First Monday after day 1	Chromosomal analysis	Patient
First week	EEG	Patient
Week 2	Offer Parent-Child Questionnaire (OPCQ)* plus record of revealed differences	Parents
	Semistructured interview*	Patient
Week 3	Background questionnaire*	Patient
	Videotape interview*	Parents
Week 6	Videotape consent form	Two treatment staff and therapist
	Videotape interview*	Two treatment staff and therapist
Week 13	Therapist rating scale*	Therapist
	Teacher rating scale*	Teacher
	Likability scale (late)*	All staff working with patient
Six months or more after discharge:	Follow-up interview*	Patient
After all patients discharged:	Staff rating of impulsivity, psychopathy, and depression of the subjects*	Seven staff who had worked with patients throughout the project

*Available from the authors on request.

sions of antisocial behavior: delinquent role, drug use, parental defiance, and assaultiveness. Kulik et al. (1968*a*) also presented evidence that the DCL is reliable and valid. Though our administration of the DCL was necessarily nonanonymous, doubts about the validity of the answers are ameliorated, first by our assuring the subjects of the confidentiality of their answers and, second, by the fact that Kulik et al. (1968*b*) found that administering the questionnaire in nonanonymous conditions essentially did not change the subjects' rank along the various delinquent dimensions. Following their factor analysis, we used DCL data to generate five scores: a total score, and scores corresponding to each dimension of delinquency.

d. *Cognitive style tests*: these tests and the scores generated from them are described in detail in chapter 6. Briefly, four dimensions of cognitive control were tapped: field articulation, leveling/sharpening, constricted flexible control, and scanning. When possible, these tests were also given to a sibling within three years of the age of a given delinquent target subject; scores of the delinquents and siblings were then compared along these dimensions.

While the subject was responding to the tests and questionnaires during screening, parents were asked a number of questions relevant to the family's socioeconomic status, to their residential, occupational, legal, and psychiatric history, and to their view of the child's developmental history, especially with respect to the behavior that led to the current hospital referral. This schedule of semistructured questions, called the Parents' Interview, was the main source of data from parents during the screening process. Scores from this interview, corresponding to answers to precoded questions, were used in the code book.

After admission to the hospital, subjects were under intense clinical observation by the treatment staff. More formal and quantitative examination was made by using a number of different instruments, the most elaborate of which was the Adolescent Behavior Check List, (ABCL) first developed at Michael Reese Hospital by Fine and Offer (1965) and subsequently expanded and modified for use on the Delinquency Unit at the Illinois State Psychiatric Institute. As used in this project, the ABCL consisted of more than two hundred specific antisocial behavior items drawn from the original Fine and Offer list and from anticipations by various ISPI Adolescent Program staff members (before the first research patient was admitted) as to the specific antisocial behaviors they might expect from delinquents on an inpatient ward. Items were grouped according to the object of the antisocial behavior (staff, self, property, other patients, rules, visitors), and each item was listed and given a unique three-digit number. Members of the staff used the ABCL as if it were a dictionary by means of which they could translate any given patient's antisocial behaviors during any block of time into a set of three-digit codes. In practice, the staff responsible for patients over the course of a shift, an activity, or a school day filled out an IBM code sheet for each patient, writing in the appropriate ABCL numbers and a code for the location, time, and date of the behaviors observed. This procedure was followed after every shift, activities-therapy session, or school day during each patient's entire hospital stay.

Outside the staff's purview was a set of weightings for each ABCL item which reflected the severity of the antisocial act listed, derived from ratings made a priori by a panel of judges before data collection began. By compiling the code sheets for each patient over the course of hospitalization and putting the information on IBM punch cards, a complete record of the patient's daily antisocial behaviors throughout hospitalization was obtained and made ready for computer analysis. Using the antisocial behavior record and the a priori weightings, four scores were then generated for each patient—specifically one each for violence toward property, for violence toward others, for violence toward self, and for nonviolent antisocial behavior. Violence was defined as the exercise of force toward the end of either harming a person or other living being, or damaging property. The scores were generated using a computer program which scanned each subject's ABCL item record over that subject's first thirteen weeks of hospitalization [4] and calculated the frequency of occurrence of each item during that time. The computer was then instructed to multiply each item's frequency by its a priori severity of antisocial behavior weighting. The weighted totals were then added according to the authors' judgment, made before data analysis began, of which items reflected the use of violence and which did not, and, within the set of violent acts, which items reflected violence toward property, toward others, or toward self (see Table 2.3 for examples). The resultant scores thus summarized hundreds of different observations by a great variety of staff members. Reliabilities were calculated by use of an analysis of variance model "adjusted for anchor points" (Winer 1971). Reliabilities were moderate but satisfactory (see Appendix B).

During their first thirteen weeks of hospitalization, subjects were also rated according to a likability scale which consisted simply of a sheet of paper bearing the names of a subject and rater, and a 120-mm line with the words "very likable" at one end and "very unlikable" at the other. For each patient, every treatment staff member was asked to make a slash intersecting the line at a point corresponding to the extent of his

TABLE 2.3

Examples of Adolescent Behavior Check List Items Included in Scales Reflecting Violence toward Property, Others and Self, and Nonviolent Antisocial Behavior

Violence toward Property:

    Patient overtly and destructively broke a piece of hospital property of considerable value, such as a window, chair, desk, or lamp.

    Patient caused actual damage to walls, doors, or other structural damage, e.g., by punching holes in the ceiling.

    Patient destroyed or broke a valuable personal item belonging to another patient.

Violence toward Others:

    Patient initiated an apparently unprovoked and violent attack on a staff member—slapped, punched, kicked, or bit in a way that revealed premeditation and an intent to injure.

    Patient punched, grabbed, bumped, or tripped a staff member in a consciously provocative manner.

    Patient threw an object dangerous enough to injure in an apparently unprovoked and premeditated attack on another patient.

Violence toward Self:

    Patient made an obviously serious suicide attempt by taking an overdose of medication.

    Patient engaged in disfiguring but not dangerous self-mutilation such as scratching or burning of the skin.

Nonviolent Antisocial Behavior:

    Patient eloped from the hospital without having permission.

    Patient refused to attend school.

    Patient was ten or more minutes late for a scheduled activity.

or her liking for that patient at that time. The number of millimeters from the left end of the scale indicated how likable the patient was to that staff member at the time the slash was made. The first likability rating of this type was made during the first two or three days of a patient's hospitalization, and the second after the first thirteen weeks of hospitalization. For each patient, the staff's likability ratings at each of these two periods were averaged to yield separate "early" and "late" likability ratings.[5] Reliabilities using the ANOVA* model described above are shown in the Appendix. In passing, we may note that this analysis shows that likability can be simply and reliably measured and, to the extent that there is agreement across judges, that it is reflective of characteristics of the subject, not those of the individual evaluators of the subject.

Staff assessment of the patients was measured in several other ways.

* Analysis of Variance (ANOVA).

After approximately six weeks of hospitalization, two staff members chosen at random and the therapist of a given patient were interviewed on videotape using a structured format.[6] Staff comments about the subject and the interviewees' affect in general were then rated by observers who did not know the subjects, and these ratings were averaged across the three staff interviewed to generate video ratings for each subject.[7] Reliabilities (see Appendix B) on the ratings of staff affect were calculated by applying Cohen's (1968) Kappa statistic to ratings made by two independent raters of a sample of twenty videotaped interviews. Kappas ran from .41 to .77. The two ratings with Kappas below .65 were dropped, so that Kappas on ratings actually used ranged from .66 to .77.

Various staff members were also asked to rate patients on the Therapist Rating Scale and the Teacher Rating Scale. The former scale was rated after thirteen weeks of hospitalization—as the name suggests, by the patient's therapist [8]—while the teacher who felt he or she best knew the patient filled out the Teacher Rating Scale. These instruments were, aside from some minor word changes, identical with parallel instruments used and evaluated by Offer (1969) and Offer and Offer (1975) in studies of normal adolescents.

While the staff was providing the indicated information, data were being collected from the subjects themselves and from their parents, particularly during the first thirteen weeks of hospitalization. In this period the subjects were given the Semistructured Interview, in which they were asked by one of us (DO) to answer a number of questions which had been posed to the normal adolescents studied by Offer and which concerned values, attitudes, and behavior. The answers were rated by means of the same coding system described by Offer (1969). In addition, subjects filled out the Background Questionnaire, an instrument identical to one completed by the normal teenagers in Offer's 1969 study, and which asks subjects to affirm or deny statements relevant to parental attitudes and behavior and to the subjects' own values.

Each subject also received a complete battery of psychological tests.[9] If he or she was younger than sixteen he was given the Wechsler Intelligence Scale for Children (WISC; Wechsler 1949); if sixteen or older, the Wechsler Adult Intelligence Scale (WAIS; Wechsler 1955). Variables used were age-adjusted scale scores from either test. Also included in the test battery were the Rorschach Inkblot Test, the Thematic Apperception Test (TAT), and the Bender-Gestalt Test. The Rorschach was administered and scored according to Beck et al. (1961), and the TAT was administered in the manner described by Henry (1956). The Bender-Gestalt

Test was given in three phases: five-second recall, copy, and total recall (Hutt 1969). To date, TAT and Bender test results have not been formally scored and therefore were not used in our quantitative analyses. Rorschach scores were scaled in the manner described by Haggard (1973) and added to the code book in that form.

In addition to psychological testing, during their initial thirteen weeks of hospitalization subjects also were given an electroencephalograph (EEG), a buccal smear preparatory to chromosomal analyses, and a neurological examination. Neither the EEG, the subsequent chromosomal analyses, nor the neurological examinations revealed abnormalities in the great majority of the subjects. Chromosomal fracturing in the case of two subjects was probably due to the use of LSD. EEG abnormality was found in only one subject who had manifested no apparent history of seizures or abnormalities indicative of brain damage and showed no pathology indicative of brain damage in psychological testing.

During the subjects' hospitalization, their parents were studied in two ways: first, by the revealed differences technique in conjunction with the Offer Parent-Child Questionnaire (OPCQ), and second, by use of videotaped interviews of parents paralleling those used with the staff. The OPCQ and the method of its administration is described in chapter 4. The revealed differences technique (Strodtbeck 1951) involved asking parents, once they had completed the OPCQ individually and independently, to reach a common parents' answer to each OPCQ item; when their responses to a particular item had differed, as often happened, they were forced to cope with the task of resolving their differences. The ensuing discussions were taped and rated according to Bales's interaction categories (Bales 1970). These ratings were done by two independent raters and were found to be reliable by means of the following method. A tape was selected at random from the forty-two tapes available, and the one selected was scored according to Bales's (1970) system by the first rater. A second rater scored the tape independently and the results were compared with each other. Differences were so minimal that the two raters divided the remainder of the tapes for scoring. Results of the Revealed Differences procedure also generated scores reflecting power relationships in the family (which parent gave in the most) and the closeness of family communication (how closely each parent's view of the child's self-image matched that of the other parent and the child's own self-assessment). Using the videotaped interviews with the parents, other ratings were made using the same scales that were used with the analogous staff interviews.

The third phase of data collection involved obtaining follow-up data.

In our first attempt, we mailed a brief questionnaire to subjects and their parents six months after the subjects were discharged from the hospital. This questionnaire was greatly expanded six months after that initial attempt, and a staff member hired to spend half-time locating and interviewing former patients, using the expanded questionnaire. Some follow-up information was thereby obtained on 89 percent of the fifty-five patients in this study.[10]

One more aspect of this data collection took place after all the subjects had been studied in the hospital. At that time, six staff members, each of whom had worked with all fifty-five subjects in our final sample, were asked to rate the individual subjects on scales ranging from one to six regarding extent of impulsivity, psychopathy, and depression. These ratings were averaged to yield ratings for each subject. Impulsivity and depression ratings were retained for further analysis. The reliabilities of these ratings are shown in Appendix B.

Statistical Analyses

The data-gathering procedures described above generated hundreds of variables per subject studied (see Appendix A for a description of the variables included in the code book). Aside from specialized data assessments,[11] the overall plan was to seek relationships among the variables studied in order to establish meaningful subgroups of delinquents, following the path taken by Jenkins and Glickman (1947), Quay (1966), and Offer and Offer (1975). At the same time, we intended to compare the delinquent subjects with the normal teenagers studied by Offer (1969) in as many ways as possible, keeping in mind differences within both the delinquent and normal groups.

To identify subgroups of delinquents, we chose to factor-analyze key variables and to use the cluster analysis technique described by the Offers (1975). As a first step, forty variables were selected whose distribution and clinical saliency suggested that they might be effective and meaningful in differentiating delinquents from one another (see Appendix A). The next step was to factor-analyze the forty variables chosen. Given the demographic heterogeneity of our subjects we felt that relationships among the raw data would be as apt to reflect associations with demographic factors as much as intrinsic psychological relationships. The danger, in other words, was in generating factors, and ultimately clusters, that simply replicated demographic groupings such as males and females or blacks and whites. To cope with this problem, the residual error matrix formed by intercorrelations among the forty variables was factor-analyzed, after eliminating the variance due to age, sex, and social status (trichotomized into categories of upper white, lower white, and black) and their inter-actions. The residual-error matrix generated by MULTIVARIANCE (Finn 1972), a preprogrammed multivariate analysis of variance package, was used for this purpose, followed by the factor-analytic procedures out-lined by Howard and Gordan (1963). Upon examination, the authors found that the five-factor solution contained the most stable groupings (see Appendix C). One of the five factors (factor III) contained Ror-schach variables almost exclusively; this factor, it was decided, was an artifact of common test variance and was not further considered. The other four factors made clinical "sense" and could be described with the use of psychiatric and psychoanalytic terminology.

Subjects' scores for the four factors respectively were obtained by add-ing each subject's unweighted z scores on variables that constituted each factor (variables were considered part of a factor if they loaded highest, and loaded .40 or more, on that factor). The z scores for this procedure were formed by putting subjects in "cells" (two levels of sex by two levels of age by three levels of social status), subtracting cell means from sub-jects' scores and dividing by cell standard deviations. Next, we looked at subjects who were one standard deviation higher or lower than the total sample mean on each factor, and attempted to ascertain whether groups of subjects existed who were systematically high and low on certain com-binations of factors. What we learned paralleled Tiffany, Peterson, and Quay's (1961) finding that delinquents distribute normally across the space formed by various factor dimensions. With some exceptions, delin-quents could be found in almost all combinations of factors; no one factor or combination of factors contained numbers much different than would be expected given distributions formed by chance alone.[12] For this reason we decided to consider each factor as a separate dimension along which delinquents could be arranged on a continuum. Subjects scoring high (that is, one standard deviation above the mean) on one factor and not on the others were considered representative of delinquents whose psy-chological functioning is singularly notable along the dimension in ques-tion. Representative subjects among those with unipolar high scores were selected for detailed case history exposition.

Treatment of Juvenile Delinquents
Within a Hospital Setting *

As data collection progressed, our subjects also participated in a highly organized treatment program, integrating individual and milieu therapy. In order to understand the setting for our research, it is important to understand something of the treatment philosophy and program.

The idea that delinquents can be understood psychologically is not new. Freud (1905) found that certain character disorders and perversions are the reverse of psychoneuroses. The neurotic conflict is externalized via an alloplastic solution, and the problem becomes not one of internal pain or disabling symptoms but of conflict with reality, or some attempt to change the outside world or an outside relationship, or some form of discharge of the internal tension through behavior that is often delinquent or criminal in nature. The term "acting-out" referred to a similar process in a treatment context wherein the patient—instead of experiencing a neurotic conflict with the psychoanalyst and talking about it in the context of the treatment, and instead of remembering its roots and origins in the patient's childhood experiences and conflicts—behaves *outside* the analytic treatment situation in such a way as to prevent himself from experiencing the pain and to keep from remembering the original painful or traumatic experience.

Aichorn (1935) was impressed with Freud's teachings and, in his work with Viennese delinquents, attempted to interpret their delinquent behavior as an expression of unfilled wishes. He trained his staff to gratify these wishes, feeling that this would lead to the establishment of a neurotic conflict between the wish and a prohibition against the wish. The therapist would then begin to be utilized by the delinquent adolescent for the gratification of other infantile neurotic wishes, thus establishing a classical clinical transference situation in which the delinquent would repeat with his therapist the wishes, conflicts, fears, and prohibitions from early childhood. In analyzing and understanding this transference neurosis, the symptomatic delinquent behavior would disappear. Aichorn noted, however, with a certain kind of delinquent that no therapeutic relationship could be established. He also noted that if by chance a relationship was established with this kind of deliquent, the therapist was not being treated by the delinquent as a separate person but as an idealized part

* For a more complete statement see Marohn et al. (1979).

of himself; in other words, a narcissistic transference had been established. To the delinquent, the therapist often possessed certain ideal qualities that the adolescent either attributed to himself or hoped one day to achieve. Aichorn then found it necessary to try to work quickly with this kind of delinquent, and to rapidly establish a narcissistic transference bond in which the patient idealized the therapist. This work with the "juvenile impostor" foreshadows some of Kohut's (1971) later contributions, and some of our own work in dealing with disturbed delinquents and the narcissistic transferences they established with therapists and staff.

Alexander and Staub (1956) observed that certain criminals were motivated by a sense of guilt, often experiencing neurotic guilt because they felt their internal wishes, desires, or fantasies to be wrong and prohibited. Their criminal behavior was an attempt to draw punishment from the external world that would set their consciences at ease. An example well known to the police is that of the person who confesses to crimes he has not committed. The need in therapy is to uncover the psychological crime of which the person feels guilty and to attempt to remove the neurotic conflict. One of our own delinquent boys from a ghetto background had been sexually impotent, even though he bragged about his sexual exploits. To reassure himself of his masculinity he stole cars, but he would usually be caught because of his own actions—such as driving at night without headlights, driving the wrong way down a one-way street, or parking the car in front of the owner's house and repeatedly returning to make use of it. Therapy was directed at helping this boy to come to grips with his own sexual inhibitions.

Following Freud's formulation of character disorders being the reverse of psychoneuroses, Friedlander (1960) postulated that delinquent character disorders needed to be converted into neuroses by blocking the avenues for acting out discharge, thus attempting to create an internalized psychological conflict which could then be handled therapeutically. This stance is similar to Aichorn's, but the emphasis here is not on gratification of the infantile wish; rather is it an attempt to reverse the process by reinternalizing an externalized internal conflict, or by converting motor behavior to internal affect, thought, and fantasy.

In a similar vein, Anna Freud (1965) viewed delinquency as a failure of the socialization process; that is, as a failure of the child to internalize controls and limits which were initially applied externally by parents and other authority figures. She also noted, however, that some delinquency develops because of the chance availability of delinquent peer groups onto whom the adolescent may displace his libidinal investments while in the process of separating from childhood and parents. It is questionable whether delinquency ever develops by chance, or whether, indeed, the choice of peer groups is not related to the adolescent's psychological stage, level of development, or need for certain kinds of relationships rather than to neighborhood or culture. A youth may belong to a gang not because only gangs exist in his neighborhood and no other peer groups are available, but because gang membership and what the gang stands for resonates with his own values, psychological defenses, ways of coping, and wishes and fantasies.

This focus on delinquent value systems and problems in superego or conscience development is emphasized in the work of Johnson and Szurek (1952), who described a number of delinquent children who were responding to and gratifying the unconsciously transmitted deviant urges and wishes of their seemingly upright parents. Bird (1957) also developed a paradigm of the delinquent child responding to the unconscious communication of the parent's wishes while having developed no psychological skills to cope with his own internal wishes. This commonly described formulation for delinquent behavior is often uncovered in family therapy. The father of one of our boys, for example, expounded at length on having taught his son to be polite and compliant with the police because, if he were a "gentleman," he might be excused by the police when they caught him some night on the streets after curfew. Furthermore, he boasted, he taught his son never to steal anything of consequence—taking a car battery was o.k., but stealing a car was absolutely forbidden. He noted that his son reminded him very much of his own father, pointing to a generational tradition of delinquent patterns.

Glover (1960) distinguished two kinds of delinquents: the structural and the functional. The structural showed significant but not psychotic psychopathology both before and after adolescence, though not necessarily of a delinquent nature; while the functional, during the adolescent maturation process, experienced a temporary psychic imbalance which resulted in delinquent behavior. Baittle and Kobrin (1964) utilized this formulation in their study of a delinquent gang, noting that the leaders of the gang were structural delinquents and occupied a place in the community power structure just below the top. They suggested that family strivings to achieve in a delinquent sociocultural milieu manifested themselves in fairly stable character pathology in the offspring, while children from other families took part in delinquent gang activity simply because of the need to work through and discharge maturational tension. The work of Baittle and Kobrin is a good example of the possibility of integrating psychoanalytic and sociological data.

Blos (1962) offered a variety of psychodynamic explanations for delinquency, beginning with the difficulties encountered in separation/individuation. He also described children with precocious ego development who are exquisitely sensitive to the cues and needs of adults, and who learn how to maneuver and manipulate quite successfully in the interpersonal world. He noted that the adolescent's propensity for action language is intensified and verbal modes of communication are minimized in the delinquent, and that in any delinquent act one must look for the symbolic communication of the delinquent's underlying wish or conflict.

Redl's (1966) contributions to this field revolved around the vicissitudes of ego development and ego functioning. He underlined the importance of a psychodynamic understanding of the delinquency in an attempt to engage the child therapeutically, and constantly emphasized the importance of the schoolteacher and child-care worker in assessing and modifying delinquent behavior. Another approach came from Winnicott (1973), who focused on the early and primitive object hunger for the mother who was once possessed but later lost, and whom the delinquent hopes to recapture through his behavior. Winnicott sees this solution as a sign of hope, since it indicates that the delinquent is still searching, has not given up, and may indeed include the therapist in his search.

From the beginning of the present study in 1969, the problem of juvenile delinquency has been attacked on two fronts. A book written by R. C. Marohn and the unit staff (D. Dolle-Molle, E. McCarter, and D. Linn) describes in detail the model therapeutic program which they developed over the years 1969–1977 (see Marohn et al. 1979), while this book details another aspect of the study—the search for psychological etiology. What are our subjects like? What about their family life and their communities? If we offer them the best psychiatric care we can give, will that affect their recidivism and the course of their future lives? In order to view our findings in better perspective, a brief summary of the essential therapeutic philosophy is given below.

The Therapeutic Alliance

The psychological types described in chapter 3 never appear in "pure form." They should be understood, however, since our studies show that these contributing factors seem to be operative in all socioeconomic groups regardless of race, sex, or age, and they add a psychodynamic perspective to understanding and working with the delinquent adolescent.

For many teenagers delinquent activity, including drug and alcohol usage, are attempts to defend against psychotic fragmentation and to maintain some kind of self-cohesion. The delinquency or the frantic activity may serve to establish boundaries, to distinguish between inside and outside, and may be attempts to deal with devastating feelings of emptiness. But the impulsive behavior of some delinquents may indicate that a fragmentation has already occurred and that the adolescent is simply behaving rather than thinking, having lost his boundaries and being no longer able to distinguish between inside and outside, between thought and action. Many of the violent teenagers we have seen are not behaving destructively because of hostile urges, but rather are experiencing transient periods of psychotic-like disintegration in which their assaults on others indicate that they have been overstimulated and traumatized, and that they are discharging tension. Their random motor behavior is much like an infant's temper tantrum or uncontrollable crying (Marohn, 1974). We have noted that in many instances the intense affectionate longings stirred up in psychotherapy, and often in the milieu, may lead to increasingly serious and escalating violent behavior as the adolescent disintegrates and his transference wishes become more and more intense.

In working with the adolescent delinquent who tends to experience and to express his problem in deviant or unacceptable behavior, many psychotherapists have difficulty in establishing a therapeutic alliance, and in distinguishing such an alliance from a transference. Adolescent patients rarely develop a transference neurosis toward their therapist, and this is particularly true in a delinquent. Conversely, a negative transference is not to be equated with resistance or with an untreatable patient. An inexperienced psychotherapist may be only too eager to terminate with one of his treatment cases because he confuses the absence of a therapeutic alliance with a negativistic, deprecating, critical, disparaging patient. The therapist cannot understand that the patient's negative transference arises from the patient's disillusionment because an idealized parent has failed to materialize. All too often, we have seen compliant adolescent patients who conform to the requirements of the psychotherapy and milieu situation and yet, after discharge, principally because no therapeutic alliance had ever indeed been established, are unable or unwilling to continue in psychotherapy. It is also true that some adolescents leave therapy because the therapist served certain developmental functions for the patient. Just as it is part of the adolescent process to separate from the relationships of childhood, so too maturing adolescents detach themselves from therapeutic alliances characterized by infantile ties. Yet, at least with the kinds of adolescents we have observed, considerable ego support and external control is required before the delinquent adolescent can engage in a therapeutic alliance; many missing or deficient functions must be provided by the staff, or the patient must be relieved of a number of psychological tasks in order for him to invest in the psychotherapy relationship. Staff support is required to enable the adolescent to begin to identify symptomatic behavior and to initiate the process of introspection. It is thus vital to understand the question of negative transference and the difficulty presented when one confuses it with an absent or derailed therapeutic alliance.

Narcissistic Transference

A similar problem is the confusion between a narcissistic transference and resistance. The patient's idealization of a therapist must be distinguished from the reaction formation or denial of aggression or hostility. There are therapists who are not comfortable being idealized and who frequently attempt to search for the hostility lying beneath the positive valence. Merger transference may also frequently be experienced as "resistance" in which the therapist is being utilized as a self-object and not experienced as a separate person. Consequently, interpretations about missing the therapist after an interruption usually cause a violent reaction by the patient, not because the patient is "resisting" the meaning of the interpretation, but because the interpretation is incorrect. The patient did not miss the therapist in the sense that he experienced the loss of another person; rather, the patient fragmented or disintegrated, and attempted to restitute or reconstitute himself through various forms of behavior and other symptomatology because an important function not at all related to the person of the analyst or therapist had been taken from him.

Traditional models of psychic functioning utilized in psychoanalytic thinking, such as the repression-barrier model of the unconscious, preconscious, and conscious systems or the structural or tripartite model of ego, id, and superego, are not very useful in understanding the difficulties of many of these patients. Better is a self-object model which postulates that certain psychic functions, particularly those of self-soothing, are missing, and that self-objects are utilized to complete deficiencies of the self-system. The absence of the therapist thus poses a threat to the integrity of the self-system. The patient who continually expects the therapist to like the same kind of movies that he does, and then is continually frustrated and disillusioned when he learns otherwise, is not attempting to identify with the therapist; he requires similarities in the therapist because certain activities of the therapist are needed to mirror the patient's grandiosity and to bolster his faltering self-esteem. It clearly misses the point to misinterpret this as a patient attempting to identify with the therapist, whom he may have perceived as an aggressor in an attempt to resolve oedipal conflict; such interpretation or conceptualization may not only create difficulty in the therapeutic relationship, but also may be experienced by the patient as a lack of empathy and a painful narcissistic injury.

An additional way in which narcissistic transference and resistance may be confused is that in some cases resistance is not an inertia that needs to be overcome by interpretation, but is an important and necessary defense against the fragmentation that might be caused by the kind of overstimulation experienced by some patients when the therapist accurately empathizes with their needs.

Countertransference

"Countertransference" problems also interfere with the establishment of a therapeutic alliance, and an awareness of them is particularly vital in work with adolescents. It is important to distinguish between true countertransference reactions by the therapist to the patient, derived from unresolved transferences from the therapist's own early life, from affective reactions of a more neutralized nature to the transference of the patient. An example of a true countertransference would be a therapist's difficulty in handling an adolescent's rebellious attempts at individuation, actions which create for the therapist a blind spot and make it difficult for him to recognize that the patient's flouting of authority has its roots in psychological conflict. On the other hand, irritation and anger at a patient's persistent attempts to challenge and ridicule the authority of the therapist is an expectable and useful reaction which can give the therapist some clue to the meaning of the patient's behavior. It need not be evidence of countertransference, though the manner in which the therapist behaves in response to such feelings and to such a challenge may have countertransference aspects.

We notice countertransference problems arising at times from the therapist's own narcissistic fixations, which may cause him to reject the patient's idealizations or to distance himself from mirroring or merger, but which can also cause him to encourage idealization, mirroring, or conformity in order to avoid a patient's anger or his attempts at differentiation and autonomy. A patient's "resistance" and the therapist's belief that the patient is "fighting" him is frequently a misinterpretation; the adolescent is utilizing the therapist as a self-object, and the therapist is incapable of empathizing with this intense deficit and need of the patient. It is difficult to empathize with this situation because one is not treated as an independent and autonomous being, but rather as an object to be possessed, manipulated, dominated, and used.

Often the therapist believes that a patient is resisting his interpretations when the interpretation actually is not being resisted in the sense of defending against an id impulse, but rather the interpretation itself is "incorrect." The interpretation may not be imprecise, inaccurate, or wrong in content, but it may not be directed at the level at which the patient is functioning. Interpretations need to be made on the basis of current experience in the analysis of the treatment situation. Therapists frequently understand, and correctly so, that whatever the patient talks about in a session has some relevance to the transference; this is not to say, however, that when a patient talks about an external event the feelings about that event or the experience of that event have been stimulated by transference strivings. On the contrary, bringing the event into the session has some transference implications and, more often than not, a therapist is more successful when he talks about the event having its parallels in the analytic or therapeutic relationship; but he usually fails when he attempts to convey the idea to the patient that the *real* meaning of the event lies in the transference experience. The patient is unable to accept these interpretations, not because he is resisting the emergence of an instinctual impulse or the transference phenomenon, but because he has enough reality testing to know that there is a real life outside the treatment relationship and that the therapist's focus is simply wrong. And an adolescent needs to cling fervently to his reality testing.

Another difficulty experienced by therapists, particularly in the beginning phases of their training, is the need to avoid entirely the implications of transference. Many therapists prefer to view the therapeutic experience as one that can be understood only in terms of cognitive theory; still others state explicitly that certain kinds of patients, such as schizophrenics, are to be viewed primarily and solely as suffering from biological or biochemical disorder and that their communications have no real meaning and do not require attention. Beginning therapists in particular have considerable difficulty in accepting the transference experience. They often respond with "I am not that important," "There is nothing wrong with her," or "I don't like him." The first position often results from the fact that the therapist's own narcissism has not been attenuated sufficiently; the transference idealization thus is experienced by the therapist as a reality experience rather than as a phenomenon emanating from the patient's past and not really based on the worth of the therapist. On the other hand, therapists who require narcissistic feeding may not reject the transference idealization of the patient, but may also accept such a transference as a reality, enjoy it, seduce the patient into subtle reinforcement of the therapist's needs, and never come to grips with the transference distortions. Finally, the therapist who rejects the patient may be doing so either because the transference is anxiety ridden for the therapist himself, or because the transference is of such a nature that it does not reinforce certain of his needs. The patient is then experienced as an impossible or difficult human being.

Problems in the Therapeutic Process

Our own work suggests the existence of four major dimensions in the functioning of nonpsychotic delinquent adolescents typified as follows: the *depressed borderline,* the *impulsive,* the *narcissistic,* and the *empty borderline.* A preliminary survey would indicate that each type may present different problems in the establishment of a therapeutic alliance. While ordinarily a depressed patient is characterized by a low energy level yet desires treatment to relieve himself of suffering, an adolescent who is acting out delinquently in order to relieve himself of depression may find it difficult to engage in therapy because painful affect precipitates the need for action and distancing. The narcissistic personality disorder may defend himself from engagement with a therapist in order to avoid self-esteem fluctuations or personal injury. The impulsive adolescent will find it difficult to tolerate a transference of any nature, and will need to discharge through action rather than to engage in verbal interactions. The borderline, because of his need for merger and self-object relating to prevent fragmentation, may readily engage in a therapeutic alliance which will be fraught with many delicate problems as one attempts to forestall psychotic regression. The adolescent who seeks out or initiates treatment with a clearly demonstrable potentiality for a therapeutic alliance is becoming more common, but is still not seen as often as we would like it. Adolescents often require an external ego support in order to engage in a therapeutic alliance. Quite obviously, at the outpatient level, such external functions are provided by parents or family in either collateral or family therapy work.

Questions about dropouts from therapy continue to plague us and, even though at follow-up most of our patients are doing well, they have discontinued outpatient therapy within three to six months after discharge. At first glance it would appear that no therapeutic alliance existed; yet these patients evidence the internalization of a therapeutic process. And so one is left with the distinct possibility that the discontinuation of the therapy relationship is the result of a developmental separation. But it may also be incomplete work which can only be completed in adulthood; it is now temporarily suspended because of the unavailability of external ego and self-object support outside of the hospital setting. Parallel problems occur in the supervision of psychiatric residents in working with such patients. Considerable support by the full-time permanent staff and by the supervisors is required to sustain the resident in the challenges and demands of his work with our delinquent adolescent patients. The emergence of a transference may be so frightening to the therapist that the patient, sensing such insecurity, may choose to leave treatment rather than persist. Or, as mentioned before, the therapist may be buffeted by depreciation and challenges in experiencing a negative transference; he may choose to see this as resistance and prefer to terminate with the patient. Such responses indicate an overwhelmed and frightened therapist, and require a considerable amount of empathy and support from the permanent staff. Because of the transferences that the staff themselves experience toward physicians—even novices—and because of the resident's common difficulty in accepting help from professionals of other mental-health disciplines, this supportive alliance is not easily accomplished. The relationship with the supervisor cannot be limited to psychotherapeutic material, but needs also to embrace the entire process of being a member of a staff.

Most hospital treatment programs that deal with behavior disorders, particularly in adolescent behavior, attempt to convert behavior or "acting-out" into some kind of an internalized conflict. One assumes that the behavior is symbolic of underlying psychic conflict, or that it represents a discharge defense against the experiencing of such psychic conflict. In Freud's sense, then, this is true "acting-out"—that is, behaving instead of remembering.

Others, such as Kohut, would take the position that the delinquent or antisocial or acting-out behavior is not necessarily symbolic of a conflict because, in fact, there exist deficiencies of psychic structure. Some patients may in fact have regressed to a stage of psychological functioning in which they are capable of no distinction between inside and outside, or between thought or feeling or action. So the task of the hospital program is either to convert true neurotic acting-out behavior into internalized neurotic symptomatology, or to provide an externally sufficient psychic structure to compensate for psychological deficits so that the person can achieve in the hospital setting a homeostasis without needing to resort to discharge behavior in order to reestablish his psychological equilibrium.

In either event, it seems that the primary task in treating the delinquent adolescent is to help him develop a capacity for self-observation and introspection. In many instances the adolescent defends against this process because introspection would lead to psychological pain, to the sadness and grief of the depressed delinquent, to the empty devastation of the borderline delinquent, or to the painful hurt feelings of the narcissistic delinquent. Other adolescents have no capacity to experience affect or to think and to fantasize, but move immediately from stimulus to behavioral response;

they need to learn to delay and concurrently to think about their internal psychological world. This task characteristically confronts the impulsive delinquent whose cognitive style and way of experiencing the world is devoid of introspection—not defensively, but developmentally.

And so it is that staff members serve as external egos or self-objects, providing externally those psychological functions which the delinquent lacks internally, and helping to set limits on his behavior—to delay, to plan, to anticipate, to soothe himself, to modulate the intensity of his experiences, to look inside himself, to identify affect, to assuage hurt feelings, to organize fragments, and to clear up confusion.

Our experience is that virtually any adolescent, regardless of socioeconomic status or race, is capable of participating in meaningful insight-oriented psychotherapy. He may need to be taught how to introspect and how to identify affect; he may need help in focusing on those behaviors which are indicative of psychological conflict or psychological deficiencies; and he may need help in tolerating, modulating, and mastering the intensity of a transference experience—but he can gain insight. It may not be insight into the roots of his oedipal competition, though that indeed is possible, but it may be insight into the fact that when he tries to hit someone it is because he is angry; when he is angry it is because his feelings have been hurt; and frequently his feelings are hurt because he anticipates that other people will view him and treat him the same way as he views himself—worthless.

To take the position that certain delinquents, because of their cultural backgrounds, cannot participate in this kind of psychotherapy—erroneously labeled "white middle class"—is to deprive many adolescents of the very help they need, and is indeed a subtle, or perhaps not so subtle, form of racism and class discrimination. Ultimately the kind of psychological structure building and personality restructuring that we hope to achieve is accomplished in the individual psychotherapy relationship, building upon the ideas of the therapeutic alliance and transference. However, delinquents are not initially ready for psychotherapy and need a period of preparation.

The Present Program

In our own program the ward staff is trained to identify those deviant behaviors which indicate that the delinquent, as he relates to the basic structure of the hospital program, is experiencing some kind of psychological breakdown or conflict. Such behaviors are then identified and targeted—they are marked with red flags—and the staff member attempts to work with the adolescent, insofar as the latter is psychologically capable, to try to understand the meaning of his behavior. With some subjects that may represent simply the recognition or acceptance of the idea that something went wrong. With others it may be considerably more complex, and involve the understanding that something of the clinical transference is being displaced into the hospital milieu. In any event, the ward staff performs extremely important preliminary and preparatory functions in helping the adolescent begin to recognize that all behavior has meaning and can be psychologically understood. At the same time, the therapist is advised of certain occurrences on the unit, and both patient and therapist are expected to spend some time together talking about these issues.

Traditionally the psychodynamically oriented therapist holds that he is to deal with the material brought to him by his patient; in our experience, teenagers rarely bring all their concerns verbally into the treatment setting, although they often express their problems behaviorally. But we have noticed in working with delinquent adolescents that they may also express their problems behaviorally on the unit, viewing it as an extension of the treatment room and the therapy session and fully intending that the omnipotent and omniscient therapist be aware of and able to deal with all behavior. On the one hand, one could view this as an idealizing transference response. But, on the other, it makes sense psychologically since we are dealing with structurally deficient adolescents who have little capacity to contain their psychological work within the confines of a treatment hour. Were they able to do so they would not be inpatients, but would be capable of engaging in outpatient psychotherapy. As a result, we do expect the patient and the therapist to deal with certain kinds of targeted behavior in the treatment setting. This is reenforced not only through interventions by the ward staff and by the therapists' focusing on significant behaviors; it is also emphasized in the weekly team meetings which the therapists, but not the patients, attend and which attempt to integrate data from various observational points of view with the data of the individual psychotherapy sessions. In addition, a weekly progress review occurs at which each teenager's behavior is reviewed with him and he is reminded, in the presence of the therapist, of the psychological work that needs to be accomplished.

The administrator-therapist split is a modality of intervention in a number of hospital programs. Our belief is that the therapist needs to have a certain amount of administrative control in working with the delinquent, but we have found that giving the therapist absolute control over the patient's treatment is fraught with considerable difficulty. Consequently, subject to the direction of the chief of the unit, our therapists are part of a team which plans and administers the hospital management of the adolescent delinquent. The therapist thus is viewed as part of the administrative decision-making process who, like the parent, is capable of exerting some control over the adolescent's life. At the same time, the adolescent is not presented with the myth that all treatment occurs in the individual therapy session. We would expect, of course, that as treatment progresses the individual therapy becomes more and more important. But initially the groundwork for a meaningful individual psychotherapy experience is laid by the kinds of interchanges and confrontations, limit-setting and feedback, and attempts to help the adolescent introspect as these occur daily in the living unit, in shop, in the gymnasium, or in school.

The philosophy and process of treatment with delinquent adolescents is complex. One must be creative and flexible in understanding the delinquent act. One must work diligently to establish a therapeutic alliance with an adolescent, capitalizing on those psychological functions which the adolescent so desperately craves in the treatment relationship, and not being embarrassed by his idealization or frustrated by his negativism. One must understand the nature of the adolescent's grandiosity and his tendencies to idealize or deidealize the significant adults in his life. And one must provide a supportive, safe, and therapeutic milieu in which individual therapy is sown, nurtured, and allowed to bear fruit. The task is arduous, but the harvest, in those good seasons when it occurs, can be bountiful.

Transition and the Maturation Process

The treatment of the juvenile delinquent has had inconsistent and unpredictable results. In 1934 and 1940 the Gluecks studied one thousand Boston delinquents and found an 88 percent recidivism rate, despite community "treatment." They noted that delinquency seems to decline with maturation, and that by age twenty-nine the recidivism rate had dropped to 48 percent. Carrol and Curran (1940), in contrast, reported a follow-up study of three hundred delinquent boys who were treated in a hospital setting, and found a success rate of some 67 percent.

Some studies (Powers and Witmer 1951) have shown that treatment reduces the seriousness of subsequent criminal acts, while others (Morris et al. 1956) have shown that little change in adjustment occurs beyond the age of eighteen, and that female delinquents have a poor prognosis. McCorkle et al. (1958) found that treatment in a residential center helps, but Robins (1966) showed that maturation does not cure a once-established pattern of psychological behavior.

The several reports of Shore and Massimo (1966, 1969, 1973) on follow-up studies at two-, five-, and ten-year intervals demonstrated the effectiveness of treatment for delinquent boys; change was minimal, however, once a positive or negative direction was noted at initial follow-up. They concluded that adolescence is an ideal time for therapeutic intervention before identity consolidation occurs.

Persons (1967) showed that a delinquent who is amenable to treatment will improve, just as Garber (1972) had shown that the healthier adolescent patient stays a shorter period of time in the hospital and does better at follow-up. Other studies have shown that a new program is initially effective, but that its effectiveness wanes with time.

The sophisticated studies of the California Youth Authority (Warren 1976) have reported that the outcome is favorably affected by the level of interpersonal maturity and proper matching with a therapist. In his review of follow-up studies, Martinson (1974) concluded that no definitive treatment intervention has been found which reduces recidivism, that good follow-up studies are scarce, and that reported results may lead one to conclude either that a stronger commitment to a therapeutic approach is necessary, or that the belief that delinquency is a "disease" which must be "treated" needs to be rethought.

One year following discharge, we began to contact the fifty-five delinquent subjects who formed the core of the research population. Eighty-nine percent of our subjects were eventually interviewed some twenty-one months after discharge. The data showed that our average subject had been arrested 1.7 times, had spent 1.5 months in a correctional facility, and twenty-one days in a mental hospital. Thirty-nine percent had used no drugs, in contrast to 18 percent on admission, and 28 percent had used only marijuana. Twenty-six percent had used heavy drugs such as psychedelics, speed, uppers, or downers, in contrast to 63 percent at admission. Seven percent used heroin, in contrast to 19 percent at admission. At follow-up, 85 percent used no alcohol or used it only moderately, while 15 percent used alcohol to the point of drunkenness; these figures at admission were 15 percent and 41 percent, respectively. Half of our subjects had been rearrested and half had not been arrested at follow-up, in contrast to the 95 percent who had been arrested prior to referral; of those rearrested, half were status or minor offenses and half were felonies. According to the follow-up interviews, 79 percent of our subjects felt positive or very positive about themselves, 9 percent were ambivalent, and 11 percent were negative or very negative about themselves.

In addition to the research interviews, we have had numerous further contacts with our core population as well as with all the other delinquents we have treated. Most of the research patients have been provided with some form of therapy since their discharge. For many of them, termination from the hospital is a stormy and disruptive time. For others, it appears to go smoothly, but later, though a therapeutic alliance seems to have been established, the adolescent may drop out of outpatient therapy quickly— usually within three months. Initially this seemed to indicate a failure in establishing a therapeutic alliance: the adolescent had, indeed, not yet been ready for discharge. On further contact, however, we found that these patients have been doing quite well, and have quite obviously internalized something of the treatment program. What becomes clear is that part of the adolescent maturation process, which had been derailed and was again reestablished due to our therapeutic efforts, leads to separation from the hospital and from the therapist. The latter now becomes part of the adolescent's earlier life, and must be left behind as maturation presses on.

Relationships Between the Research and Treatment Staffs and Patient Cooperation

There is no question that most of the data gathering described earlier would not have been feasible without the cooperation and support of the treatment staff. From the onset of the research project to its termination, clinical personnel made suggestions, filled out rating scales, and participated in videotaped interviews. The story of the working alliance between the research and treatment staffs on the Juvenile Delinquency Unit at the Illinois State Psychiatric Institute was largely one of mutual support and cooperation, but there were some persistent themes of conflict and tension.

The largest involvement of treatment staff with the research project concerned their ongoing completion of ABCL forms. In addition to writing routine clinical notes, treatment personnel had to take time out after each shift or activity to go through the ABCL book to check which codes, if any, should be reported. While staff members were usually conscientious and invested, the tendency at first was to underreport behaviors and, later, to use the "216" code, a catch-all item reflecting any antisocial behavior "not described above"; its use, of course, saved having to look up more specific codes in the ABCL book. This tendency to underreport behaviors or use "216s" was especially notable when the raters did not have group support in doing the ABCLs, a circumstance which occurred when a staff member was alone on a night or weekend shift. This problem was handled by one of the researchers (EO), who periodically checked nursing notes for reportable behaviors and compared them with the ABCL codes for the shift in question to see if the codes accurately reflected the behavior noted. Discrepancies were discussed with the staff, who began to see the need for greater attention. In time most staff members learned the most common ABCL codes by heart, and many would joke about a certain patient doing an "029 again today." There were appreciative comments on the detailed and systematic observation of patient behavior which was ensured by use of the form. Nevertheless, continuous filling out of the ABCL required time and effort, and on certain occasions, when under pressure, there was an underlying annoyance at having to complete this task, a feeling often expressed toward research personnel in the form of good-natured griping.

Similar feelings pertained to other research tasks given to the staff. Likability forms, for example, were distributed and collected at staff meetings; most of the staff usually seemed at least as pleased by the attention paid them as they were displeased at having to complete a form which took only a few seconds, yet some of them filed the form away and had to be cajoled repeatedly before they would pull it out and mark it. Similarly, there were times when the researcher had a defensive and even apologetic manner when he announced the need to process a form on a newly admitted patient; it is unclear how much this attitude contributed to the staff's reluctance to complete the form, or how much it encouraged their feeling of being overburdened by research demands, but it indicates the mutually experienced feelings of overwork. Reluctance to complete this form seemed related to staff members' assessment of their priorities with high priority on direct work with the patients, and low priority on paperwork.

The videotaped interviews caused more uneasiness. Though we explained to staff members that the focus of the research was on the delinquent subjects and not on the staff, the fact that they, and not the subjects, were being videotaped made many staffers feel that the investigation was centering on them as individuals. Jokes were periodically heard about the possibility that staff meetings were being secretly videotaped, or that concealed cameras and recorders might be taping conversations in the employee cafeteria. Another source of occasional tension concerned scheduling patients to undergo research testing. The usual reason for such tension was the intense program load of patients in the Delinquency Unit which, on occasion, caused research testing to interfere with routine treatment activities, once again raising questions of priorities. At one point, those clinical activities which could be displaced by research on a one-time basis were actually spelled out; usually, however, "bumping" was avoided by the research staff's efforts to use the few lacunae in patients' schedules as testing times.

The patient length of stay caused periodic conflicts between research and treatment staff. For purposes of our investigation, we had specified that most patients should stay four to six months, not longer. Greater duration of in-hospital residency, we pointed out, would unwarrantedly prolong the data-collection phase of the project, or would result in an unacceptably low number of subjects in our final sample. As people who became committed to long-term treatment of juvenile delinquents, some clinical staff resented the six-month limit and the pressure to conform to it; they conceded the necessity of discharge from the research point of view, but complained that they felt termination often to be premature and questionable. An eventual compromise specified that two patients could be "long term" at any one time and would be so designated, while the other patients on the unit would be treated within the six-month limit.

Probably the greatest tension between research and treatment staff arose over some aspects of the treatment program. One researcher saw certain treatment practices as undesirable—or at least questionable. When these feelings were made known in staff meetings, for example, the researcher was viewed as an interloper who could talk glibly and ill-advisedly because he was not out there on the "firing line." This dispute is best exemplified by a situation when the researcher saw a patient being placed in restraints apparently because she refused to lower the volume on her radio. He criticized this sequence of events at a staff meeting, drawing resentment from the treatment personnel; they said that he did not understand the need of setting limits, maintaining structure, and preventing escalation through early intervention. To quote the ward staff, the researcher should "trust us to do our jobs just as we trust him to do his." Needless to say, these arguments did not erase the feelings involved. Rather a modus vivendi was established which had the research team collecting its data and the clinical staff conducting therapy with minimum mutual interference.

Other problems stemmed from the respective positions of the senior and coprincipal investigators. The senior investigator was associate director of a program located in a prestigious private hospital, while the research was conducted in a state facility, albeit probably the most renowned psychiatric hospital in the state system. The state hospital staff at times seemed to feel they were being used to promote the prestige of the private hospital: they were doing all the work, but ultimately the private hospital and the senior investigator would get most of the credit. The coprincipal investigator shared some of these feelings, but was also helpful in easing such tensions. He pointed out to the treatment staff that the research gave a sense of purpose and vitality to the program, and helped to justify in the eyes of state budgetary personnel a very expensive course of treatment. He added that the skill and knowledgeability of the senior investigator and the resources of the private facility helped to make the research project possible and to mobilize a considerable amount of ISPI support. Although many of the treatment staff felt pleased by their indirect association with the private hospital, feelings of being used and of rivalry were never completely assuaged.

The dual position of the coprincipal investigator as chief of the unit and as one of the people responsible for the research led to further complications. Treatment staff looked to him as their chief, and expected his support of their concerns. Concurrently, research expectations were ultimately channeled to ward staff through the coprincipal investigator's authority. This duality of positions personalized many of the conflicts described in the preceding paragraphs, intensifying feelings even more as issues about the chief's preferences, loyalties, and commitment came into play.

Throughout the research project, one aspect of data collection which gave little cause for concern was the cooperation of subjects and their parents. Despite the fact that our subjects were emotionally disturbed and delinquent, almost all cooperated fully with research tasks, some of which (like the schematizing test) are quite boring to take. Parents were equally amenable to participation. The approach used with both patients and parents—that we were studying teenagers who had gotten into trouble with the law and that we would appreciate their working with us—did elicit full cooperation from the majority of those approached. Most patients and parents seemed to like the idea that they were making a contribution and, like the staff, savored the attention they were receiving. Some patients even asked to be tested when their involvement was delayed, apparently feeling slighted that they had not as yet been approached. On the other hand, as already mentioned, one young female subject and her parents refused to be involved, and she was therefore not included in the final sample. Another subject threatened not to take the cognitive style battery after his sibling already had spent several hours doing so. That subject was told it would waste his time and ours if he took only part of the battery and not the rest. Perhaps predictably, his response was to take every cognitive style test but one, and then refuse to take the last one. He was returned to his room for the routine "study hour." The next day, for whatever reasons—perhaps because of guilt or staff verbal feedback—the patient apologized and offered to take the last test. Of course, he was immediately taken to the cognitive style laboratory and the battery was completed that day. In the greatest number of cases, however, patients and their families gave research staff their full cooperation and the atmosphere that prevailed was one of mutual respect and liking.

It is impossible, of course, to assess how much the desperation of parents to get help for their delinquent children influenced their tendency to cooperate with the research. The treatment program generally took the position that failure to meet certain expectations, such as regular sessions with the social workers, would result in a child being seriously considered for expulsion from the program. Parent participation in the research was generally expected, and its failure would cause serious question of their commitment to the overall treatment program. Obviously, then, the staff's attitude about involving the parents in all aspects of the program helped to support parental and subject cooperation in the research.

At this time it is questionable whether our stand regarding participation would be tenable, due to recent thought about research ethics. Our feeling was that patients had a duty to participate in a research endeavor that was physically nonintrusive and that overlapped clinical information-gathering to a large degree; furthermore, we felt that an unwillingness to participate in the research—a failure, in other words, of the research alliance—portended very poorly for the success of a treatment alliance. How this reasoning would stand up to the scrutiny of present-day hospital research committees is an open question.

From a wider perspective, research and treatment staff were partners in an excellent inpatient program for delinquent adolescents. Treatment staff provided the occasion and often the resources for data collection. Research staff provided a sense of importance, a sense of transcending immediate concerns for long-term gains. That is not to say, however, that relationships between these endeavors were free of tension; instead, the atmosphere that prevailed was more or less uneasy, more or less mutually admiring, and mutually supportive.

Comment

When everything is said and done, the theories understood, and therapy techniques described, what remains is the cultural and societal place of the psychotherapist and the researcher. In some social groupings in America, the psychotherapist and the researcher are accepted commodities: people to consult for help or answers. In other social settings, such as inner-city minority groups, the psychotherapist and the researcher may be viewed with suspicion and mistrust: tools of the established middle class and hence, not to be trusted. Often the inner city youngster and the mental health professional never meet as witness the fact that for similar behavior (e.g., theft or drug abuse) teenagers are treated differentially; the lower-class adolescent is much more likely to be incarcerated, while the suburban adolescent is more likely to be referred for therapy. Many police officers, teachers, judges, psychiatrists, and parents tend to support these options.

The psychotherapist contributes something unique to our understanding of all youths' needs and to our ability to fulfill them. It is a perspective which is different from that of parents, teachers, peers, community leaders, or other interested adults. It is a perspective that enriches and gives meaning to research data, and itself is reciprocally enriched.

Evaluative research on the outcome of psychotherapy is sorely needed. The few research projects on outcome are retrospective in nature (e.g., Hartmann et al., 1968; Garber, 1972). There are no prospective research reports on outcome in psychotherapeutic work with adolescents. We feel that one of the priority areas in clinical research over the next decade is evaluative research which will help us to understand the process, the psychodynamics, the theories, and simply, the outcome of psychotherapy.

NOTES

1. It is not certain whether severely delinquent subjects studied by others (Shaw, 1930; Cohen, 1955; Sutherland, 1955; Sykes and Matza, 1957; Block and Niederhoffer, 1958) are disturbed as well. In that sense, this study is a step toward elucidating psychological factors in severe delinquency.

2. Comparisons among subjects who were admitted to the program and completed the data collection protocol; subjects who were admitted but did not complete the protocol; and subjects who were not admitted also revealed no significant differences with respect to Offer Self-Image Questionnaire scores or Delinquency Check List scores.

3. Forty variables among those generated by these instruments were selected for factor analysis. The selection process is described briefly later in this chapter (pp. 26–27), while the specific variables chosen and the instruments from which they were taken are shown in Appendix A.

4. Four subjects did not stay thirteen weeks, but were included in the project because, in other respects, data collection for them was complete. Scores were generated for these subjects by taking the shortest total length of hospitalization for this group (nine weeks) and, using subjects who did stay thirteen weeks or longer, generating a regression equation associating nine- and thirteen-week ABCL totals. This equation then was used to predict short-term subjects' thirteen-week ABCL totals based on their nine-week totals.

5. Three subjects did not receive "late" likability ratings because they were discharged prior to their thirteenth week of hospitalization.

6. Subjects' probation officers and arresting officers also were interviewed when possible. These data have been scored and will be discussed in other publications.

7. Interviews regarding two subjects were inaccessible due to the incompatibility of the earliest tapings with newer equipment.

8. If there had been a change of therapist during that time, as sometimes happened, the therapist who had seen the patient longest was asked to do the rating.

9. One of the authors (EO) did approximately half the testing; one or the other of three additional clinical psychologists did almost all of the remainder of the testing. Each psychologist scored his or her own protocols in consultation with the others, using standard scoring procedures.

10. Information about one subject who refused to participate in the follow-up study was obtained from her former outpatient therapist (with that subject's consent).

11. Specialized data analyses are described elsewhere in this book; e.g., the statistical procedures used to demonstrate the relationship between impulsivity and violence are described in chapter 5.

12. Actual numbers were: with respect to factor I, five subjects had z scores one standard deviation or more higher than the mean on that factor only; three subjects were high only on factor II, six only on factor III, and seven only on factor IV. That is to say that twenty-one subjects were high on one dimension alone. Seven subjects were high on two factor dimensions; no subjects were high on three or on all four. Twenty-seven subjects were not high on any dimension. Assuming a normal distribution and independence of the factor dimensions, we would expect by chance, using the binomial expansion, twenty-six out of fifty-five subjects not to be "high" (that is, in the top sixth of the distribution) with respect to the various factor scores; twenty-one to be high on one factor only; six to be high on two factors; one to be high on three; and none to be high on all four. As can be seen, the actual and theoretically expected distributions are almost identical.

PART II

RESULTS

3

Four Psychological
Subtypes*

Introduction

In this chapter we will discuss in detail four case examples, each typifying one factor analytic dimension. The four examples were selected from among those subjects who were one standard deviation or more higher than the mean on one but no other of the four factors elicited by our factor analytic procedures (see chapter 2). The cases that follow thus comprise the four subjects among the fifty-five delinquents studied who best elucidate the results of our factor analyses. Brief summaries of the psychodynamics of each case follows:

1.   The *impulsive* delinquent shows more violent and nonviolent antisocial behavior than do delinquents representing the other types. He is considered quite disturbed by his therapist, socially insensitive by his teachers, and unlikable and quick to act by most hospital staff members. Yet he seems to have some awareness of his need for help. His delinquency derives from a propensity for action and immediate discharge.

2.   The *narcissistic* delinquent sees himself as well adjusted and not delinquent. Parents and staff, however, recognize his difficulties in adapting, and characterize him as resistant, cunning, manipulative, and superficial. He denies problems, only makes an appearance of engaging in

* Section prepared with the assistance of Mary Feczko, Ph.D.

therapy, exaggerates his own self-worth, and through his delinquency, tends to use others for his needs, especially to help regulate his self-esteem.

3. The *empty-borderline* delinquent is a passive, emotionally empty, and depleted youngster who is not well liked, is sometimes an outcast, at other times needy and clinging, and whose future seems pessimistic. These adolescents behave delinquently to prevent psychotic disintegration or fusion, and to relieve themselves of internal desolation.

4. The *depressed-borderline* delinquent shows initiative in school, is liked by the staff, and tries to engage therapeutically with staff members. Relationships with parents lead to strongly internalized value systems; these delinquents show a considerable amount of guilt and depression from which delinquent behavior serves as a relief; but they also show an anaclitic need for objects to which they cling and for which they hunger. They also lead to strongly internalized value systems, and these delinquents tend to show structuralized or neurotic conflicts from which, again, delinquent behavior serves as a relief.

The Impulsive Delinquent

Precipitants of Hospitalization

Victor was a handsome, wiry, black Catholic boy, sixteen years old,* who presented himself as hypermature, self-sufficient, and always in control of the situation. He was not a particularly tall adolescent, and compensated for his lack of height by the use of a braced-up posture and a swaggering gait. His facial expressions seemed calculated to appear menacing; he would curl his lip, squint his eyes, and screw up his face.

Referred to the Illinois State Psychiatric Institute by his probation officer, Vic was incarcerated at a youth detention center at the time of original contact with the program. He reported great difficulty in "keeping my head" and maintaining an even temper, particularly at home. He claimed to need medicine to control his feelings, as he felt chronically and pervasively angry. After assaulting his mother and his younger sister with a broom he was placed in the youth home.

Both Vic and his mother dated the onset of significant problems to an accident that had occurred a year prior to his admission to the home. Vic

---

* The fact that a patient presented as a case example was black or white or male or female does not imply that patients in any one subgroup typically fell into one particular racial or gender category. On the contrary, our selection method ensured that there were likely to be patients of both races and sexes in each subgroup.

was visiting a girl friend in a nearby housing project when he was caught in the crossfire of two feuding gangs and was shot in the anterior chest. He sustained a spinal cord injury that left him paralyzed from the waist down, and was allegedly told that he would never walk again. He did not accept this prognosis, and claimed to have restored the use of his limbs through his own determined exercising. The contribution of physiotherapy to his recovery was never mentioned, but he did credit his mother and his younger sister with helping him. His investment was clearly in presenting his recovery as his own achievement, a mastery of his body through sheer determination and will. Two weeks after the accident he had regained some strength in his lower right leg, and in another two weeks he had regained the use of both legs and was discharged from the hospital.

At home he intensified his efforts to strengthen his legs by working out on parallel bars, lifting weights, and cajoling assistance from his mother and his siblings for passive leg exercises. During this recuperation period, the interaction within the family became intensely conflictual. In the year between his accident and hospitalization in the adolescent program Vic was arrested six times, all on his mother's complaint. Each of the arrests occurred at the culmination of similarly orchestrated fights which began with verbal insults, progressed rapidly to fistfights, and finally to assaults with household "weapons." The first four arrests were not adjudicated, the fifth resulted in six-months' probation, and the sixth saw Vic remanded to the detention center. The family's equilibrium had been severely disrupted by the accident. His dependency and anger, and his recurrent threats to avenge his accident by murdering his assailant, added intolerably to the stresses with which the rest of the family was already coping.

Vic reported that the same sister who helped him to exercise in the hospital would taunt him during his recuperation by calling him "nigger" and "cripple," and by noting that he was "the blackest in the family." His mother had a highly negative reaction to his increased dependency. He had functioned "as the man in the family," and had been increasingly independent and responsible until he was injured. Vic complained bitterly of the contradictory messages he received from his mother; she allegedly alternated between treating him as an adult and as a "helpless" child. His frustration and anxiety were directly acted out, with each argument resulting in an assault on his mother.

Developmental and School History

Vic was reported to have been a happy baby—the result of a normal labor and delivery. He was not a planned child, but his mother expressed contentment with his birth. She reported that he had completed his developmental milestones on time, but the social worker had some reservations about the reliability of the history.

Vic's father deserted the family when Vic was three years old, and he had no memories of him. His parents were never married. His mother had married and divorced, once each before and after her relationship with Vic's father. All of these relationships were brief, the longest lasting five years. The mother had no particular male friend during Vic's childhood, and the various fathers did not maintain contact with the family subsequent to divorce. The absence of any consistent and significant male figure in Vic's history is clear. Interestingly, his earliest memory concerned a visit to his uncle's farm in Alabama. He remembered milking cows with his uncle, and recalled how the tails of the cows swished across his cheek; he said that he cried when his uncle told him that he would have to return home up North, and that he felt very sad when that uncle died around his fifth birthday.

Vic's mother, Mrs. D., at one point stated that the family had first experienced problems with him when he was thirteen. However, the history documents numerous instances of aggressive and impulsive behavior prior to puberty. At eight, Vic was playing with matches (after having been previously punished for doing so), and ignited the family clothes hamper. The home and all their possessions were totally destroyed. As a preadolescent he stole fishing rods from a parked car, and assaulted a policeman with a brick when the officer tried to intervene in one of his fights. As a child, he reportedly enjoyed catching grasshoppers and breaking their legs. While involved in outpatient treatment at age nine, he was described as "nervous" and "easily frightened." His early school history is one of frequent transfers and repeated instances of acting-out and truancy.

With the onset of puberty, Vic became combative outside the home and intensely rebellious and belligerent within his family. His school noted some thirty major infractions of the rules during his preadolescent and adolescent years, including numerous brawls, continual truancy, and instigation of riots. His mother felt that she lost control of him at fourteen, when he became involved in the local gang. She felt that gang members encouraged his estrangement from the family, and reinforced his preoccupation with guns and violence. Victor reported that he had used an automatic rifle on several occasions. He also boasted of committing four episodes of armed robbery, and commented dispassionately that he enjoyed spending afternoons with his girl friend's older brother shooting at dogs. He said that he was intrigued with thcir struggle, even after they seemed to be dead.

Vic claimed to have first had sexual intercourse at the age of eight, and reported having had sex with numerous girls since that time. He saw intercourse as a healthier release of sexual tension than masturbation. At the time of admission, his sixteen-year-old girl friend was pregnant with his child. Their relationship, which was not an exclusive one, had lasted for three years, and he intended to marry the girl and support the child.

He was very much concerned with physical appearance and with grooming. Prior to high school he had been extremely heavy, and through rigorous diet and exercise (lifting weights two hours every day), he not only controlled his weight but built up his physique for football. He expressed great satisfaction with his body, and frequently wore excessively revealing clothes.

Family History

Vic was the third child born to Mrs. D., who was forty-two at the time of his hospitalization. She had five other children, three of them his half-siblings: Virginia, twenty-four, married and the mother of three; Alex, twenty-one, married and living outside of the home; Suzanne, fourteen, Vic's full sister and primary combatant; Liz, twelve, also his full sister; and John, seven years old, his stepbrother. Vic functioned, by all accounts, as "the man of the house," and was an extremely strict disciplinarian with his sibs. He complained frequently of his mother's leniency with them.

According to Mrs. D., her daughters had no difficulties, while all her sons had problems of some kind. Alex had been arrested for armed robbery and was incarcerated, although later acquitted. John was involved in outpatient treatment (and allegedly was receiving medication), after having made a serious suicidal gesture. Unlike Alex and Victor, John seemed to be excessively passive and self-punitive, and was reported to be a frequent victim of assaults.

Mrs. D described herself as being high-strung and continually anxious. When upset by her children, she frequently would "fly off the handle," engage in heated battles, only to retreat later to her room with a headache. She suffered from hypertension, was being treated in outpatient psychotherapy for her nerves, and reported the daily use of mild tranquilizers. She saw herself as a very strict parent, but this was not corroborated by her children.

Her own childhood was marked by continual separations, desultory care, and poverty. She was born in the rural South to parents who were not wed, and her father died shortly after her birth. She lived with her mother until she was three; from the age of three to ten she lived with a great-aunt and uncle, from ten through thirteen with an aunt, and from thirteen through seventeen with still another aunt and several cousins. She saw little of her mother after she was three, and when she was ten her mother died. She remembered brief periods of prosperity followed by stretches without enough food or clothing.

At seventeen she married her first husband, partly to escape her home at that time; the marriage lasted five years. Her first husband had no contact with the family after the divorce, and soon she began to live with Vic's father. This relationship lasted four years until she moved from the South to Chicago. Vic's father chose to remain behind and he, too, lost contact with the family. Three years after the move Mrs. D. remarried, and five years later this marriage also ended in divorce.

Test Findings

Vic's performance on the OSIQ was characterized by extreme scores; he tended to feel that statements either described him perfectly or did not apply to him at all. He was fairly consistent in his view of himself. He admitted to having great difficulty in controlling his anger, to worrying about his health, and to feeling ugly and unattractive at times. He repeatedly expressed a preference for solitude over companionship.

Psychological testing was completed at the time of admission. The summaries of the findings that follow were prepared subsequently, without access to clinical data or to a case description of any type. They report the psychologist's independent analysis of Vic's psychological functioning:

> Victor functions at an average level of intellectual achievement. His pattern of performance on both the structural and projective measures is characteristic of an unreflective, impulsive, action-oriented individual. He does have a keen, accurate grasp of social situations—a talent he may utilize sociopathically. Concept formation is generally commensurate with his intellectual level; however, he tends to be very concrete. His independent creative thinking is primitive and unarticulated. He is severely deficient in imaginal capacities. Those ego abilities which have to do with active understanding and integration are severely impaired.
>
> Victor's emotional functioning is characterized by an almost complete defensive withdrawal—his style of dealing with the social world is by investing as little of himself as is possible. He is withdrawn and insensitive to his environment, and unaware of and unresponsive to his own inner needs. His withdrawal and his heavy use of repression and denial leave him rigid and anxious in his interpersonal relationships.
>
> Victor fails to elaborate in his responses any values, identifications or interests—a failure which further cripples his capacity to relate to others. Empathy, anxiety and guilt feelings are also conspicuously absent, indicating a basic callousness.

Victor's conception of the world seems to preclude the possibility of serious object attachments. Where he indicated emotional relationships between characters, he always designated himself as the recipient of affection which he was unable to return. Despite a superficial bravado, his sexual role is not well-established. His highly eroticized "macho" front shields concerns about weakness and inadequacy.

Diagnostic Impression: Psychopathic Character Disorder

Hospital Course

From the onset of his hospitalization, Victor carefully cultivated the tough-guy role. He wore clothes that revealed his muscular physique, walked in a menacing fashion, and proudly displayed the extensive scarring from his accident. He was insolent to the staff and verbally abusive to the other patients. He reveled in the acting-out of other patients, and promoted it. Once, when the social system of the unit shifted slightly due to new admissions, he mobilized the patient group to dress up as Ranger commandos. He engaged in countless power struggles with staff, and quibbled about the fine points of rules. He felt "accused" whenever asked to examine his behavior; yet he seemed to welcome altercations with the staff and appeared to be comfortable when haggling with them and provoking them. He would physically relax once limits were set on his behavior.

Vic was particularly likely to struggle with the staff when his peers were pressuring him for some sort of involvement. He was very much a loner. His interactions with the other adolescents were confined to the narrow range of either flirting or intimidation. The patient group frequently expressed fear of him. He pressured both male and female patients to have sexual contact with him during his hospitalization.

When staff members made some inroads with Victor and correctly interpreted some of his feelings, he became intensely anxious and complained of diffuse pain and of difficulty in sleeping. He attempted to distance himself through threats. He was furious that he had let down his guard, and he promised to "terrorize" for the rest of his life a staff member in whom he had confided. He showed this pattern of offensive hostility whenever he felt warmly toward any of the staff, and had particular difficulty in tolerating positive feelings about male staff.

In the school program, Vic was lethargic, and frequently somatized in order to justify poor performance. He was able to complete his work with encouragement, but held himself aloof from both the school staff and the other patients. He enjoyed more competence in occupational therapy, where he worked hard and compulsively, seeking out special instruction and generally excelling at his projects. His impulsiveness occasionally disrupted his performance in occupational therapy; when small details of his project went awry he would reject the project entirely, seeing the mistake as irreversible. In recreational therapy, too, he drove himself relentlessly, and complained of being cheated when he did not receive special instruction.

In individual treatment, he spent much time discussing his sexual prowess. He was indiscriminate in his choice of sexual objects, vacillating between courting one of the boys on the unit and flirting with the girls. He seemed to act out sexual feelings without conscious thought or control. He admitted to having had homosexual contact, but since he had always been the passive and recipient partner he felt that he was not truly a homosexual. A consistent theme throughout his hospitalization was excessive concern with his body. In his first therapy session he requested a circumcision "in order to cut down on germs." He discussed his potency continually, subscribed to male body magazines, and sent for a body-building kit. He claimed to be an "all star" in sports, and planned on a career in professional football. Vic seemed to have a narcissistic need to prove repeatedly that he was attractive, potent, desirable, adequate. Throughout all of his sexual acting-out, his own needs predominated over qualities or desirability. His need to mask his own feelings of inadequacy led him to constantly malign the masculinity of various staff members. He frequently talked of his impending fatherhood, and would denigrate the unmarried male staff.

Both staff and patients were frightened of his proclivity to physical expression of anger. During the first visit of his pregnant girl friend he became enraged, verbally abused her, and began to twist her arm before the staff could intervene. He also attacked his mother during her visits. On one occasion he refused to hand in a sharp piece of equipment; when it was taken from him and placed in the nursing station, he stormed the station and had to be placed in restraints. Confronted with an obstacle or a demand he could not meet, Vic would begin to curse and threaten, and would quickly escalate to physical violence. He was under intense pressure from both his girl friend and his family to quickly finish his business with the hospital and to reassume his responsibilities. He felt guilty about "letting his family down," and was both frightened and angered by the demands made upon him. He desperately wanted to be strong and to live up to his inflated notion of what constituted manhood; unfortunately, he equated strength with physical coercion.

It has been noted that Vic would act out aggressively when he was stirred by warm feelings for the staff. A similar pattern for Vic was to diffuse intimacy with the staff by sexual performance. Treatment inroads with him were often followed by sexual attention-seeking, as described in the following staff notation:

Sept. 2: Vic really ate up attention in the nursing station door for 2 hours tonight. Seeking staff contact.

Sept. 3: Wearing his pajamas under his clothes. Shaved his legs and nicked himself with razor. Keep tabs on his sexual behavior.

Vic's manner of discharge was analogous to the way he interacted throughout his hospitalization. Four days prior to his administrative discharge a relative was seriously wounded in much the same manner he had been, and Vic felt that he was urgently needed at home to somehow assuage this new familial difficulty. He immediately began to belittle patients and to hassle the staff. When he heard the next day that his relative's condition had deteriorated, he attempted to walk off the unit with one of his visitors. He could not tolerate his feelings of depression and anxiety. He told the other patients that he planned to hit a staff member in order to be discharged from the unit. As his anxiety rose, so did his acting-out. The next day he lit a small fire in the bathroom. He became quiet when firm limits were set, and ceased the testing. However, on the fourth day he awoke in a clearly agitated state, and paced up and down the hallway. He was visited by his mother, his sister, and his girl friend, and the question of who headed the household was discussed. This led to a violent argument, and the visit was terminated by the staff. Vic immediately tried to engage the staff in a verbal battle. When he got no response, he threatened, spat at a male staff member, and then physically attacked him, bruising him quite badly. He was administratively discharged after a three-month hospitalization.

Summary: Impulsive Delinquent

Victor, because of his impulsive behavior—both violent and nonviolent —was obviously disturbed, as was apparent to all who saw him. He was quite insensitive to the social needs of others and his unpredictability, high anxiety level, and propensity for aggressive outbursts characterized him as an impulse-ridden delinquent. He was not prone to delay or to modulate urges, to tolerate frustration, or to conceptualize, and he demonstrated a marked deficiency in fantasy life and a marked tendency to discharge through action.

The impulsive delinquent exemplifies a style well described by Shapiro (1965), in which there is no interposition between urge and behavior or motor discharge. Instead of motivations being discharged through thought or fantasy or work, the result is motor behavior. The impulsive style may be simply an habitual style, but it may also serve the defensive purpose of maintaining distance from painful affect and from disturbing interpersonal situations.

The Narcissistic Delinquent

Precipitants of Hospitalization

Kenneth E. was a good-looking, superficially charming, cherubic fourteen-year-old white youth who immediately attempted to ingratiate himself with staff and patients as a "likable little guy" who truly wished to reshape the course of his life. He was referred to the program by his mother's therapist. There had been considerable police involvement with his case, and it was clear at the time of the referral that Ken must either seek therapy or be involved with the correctional system. His delinquent acts included repeated check-forging, fire-setting, and stealing. Both his mother and Kenneth saw his problems as starting around age twelve. He transferred from public school to parochial school at his own request in some hope of being more accepted by his peers, but found himself ostracized at the new school; in an attempt to distinguish himself, he began to assume the role of the class tease and provocateur. At this time he forged some of his mother's checks and was, in fact, keeping a box of her blank checks under his bed. He stole shoes that did not fit him from a department store; was arrested for stealing a bicycle and a baseball glove; and was apprehended but not arrested for shoplifting.

When Ken was thirteen he was hired to walk a neighbor's dog and to feed the animal when its owners were away; he was paid by check, and he altered the figures to read eighteen dollars rather than the agreed figure of eight dollars. He repeated this tactic even after the neighbor had caught and confronted him with his previous forgery. Ken brutalized the animal —leaving the dog without food for three days and whipping it—until concerned neighbors notified the police.

His mother felt helpless and totally ineffectual in controlling her son. She considered herself to be a strict disciplinarian, yet in her attempts at control she frequently lost her temper, and great physical battles erupted between the two of them.

Developmental and School History

During her pregnancy with Kenneth, Mrs. E. reported that she had gained an excessive amount of weight that she never lost. She also developed kidney stones while pregnant, another difficulty which persisted throughout her later life. Despite these problems, labor and delivery were normal. All developmental milestones were on time. Mrs. E. reported chronic feeding problems with Ken—he consistently spit up his formula, and was fussy about solid food. At age two he went on a hunger strike which greatly alarmed his mother, but he quickly terminated it. His mother remembered him as being sickly throughout his infancy, with frequent respiratory infections and high fevers. Ken swallowed half a bottle of aspirin and his mother's kidney pills when he was three, and had to have his stomach pumped. Mrs. E. related numerous similar incidents—a broken arm, a broken wrist, severe cuts, falls, and the like. She felt that Ken was particularly accident prone.

Kenneth experienced problems in school from kindergarten on. He was shifted from one kindergarten to the other, as teachers complained vociferously that he was too disruptive and that he would do anything to attract attention. He allegedly pushed and shoved the other children, frequently hurting them, and destroyed their property and clothing. Mrs. E. was frequently called to school, and at one such conference it was reported that Ken, while bullying the children, would fawn over the teacher and tell her what a beautiful dress she was wearing and how pretty she was.

He seemed to calm down through the first and second grades; his mother was not summoned to emergency conferences, and his deportment and grades were satisfactory. His interpersonal behavior in school deteriorated rapidly, however, from the third grade on. Teachers once again complained of his antagonistic behavior toward his peers; he was described as impolite, disrespectful of the rights and property of others, domineering and aggressive with other children. By the fifth grade his academic performance also declined, and he neglected to bring home his report card while lying "very sincerely" about the novel grading procedures then being used by the school. In the sixth grade he requested transfer to a parochial school; his mother said that he hoped that the new school would afford him less difficulty in making friends and in keeping them.

It was at this time that Ken initiated his delinquent acts. He began with shoplifting and progressed to check forgery. He was frequently truant and broke curfew, yet Mrs. E. was incapable of curtailing his behavior. Ken was arrested five times for assault, stealing, vandalism, and forgery, but was never convicted. His mother took him for outpatient psychotherapy, but he neglected to keep his appointments. In addition to the delinquent acts noted, he was accused of harassing elderly people in his neighborhood. He reportedly rammed old women with his bicycle, and tormented an elderly man by name-calling and pelting him with rotten fruit until the man finally moved away.

Ken was then sent to another city to live with his natural father and his stepmother. He had looked forward to living with his father, but was bitterly disappointed at his father's involvement with his new family. Ken was continually at odds with his stepmother, and claimed that she forced him to spend his time outside the home and did not feed him sufficiently. Mrs. E. corroborated this account, saying that Ken had lost thirty pounds by the time he was returned to Chicago. Ken felt that his stepmother saw him as a threat to her marriage. He remained in Chicago with his natural mother for two months before she again sent him to live away from home, this time with her mother. Allegedly, Ken was doing well at his grandmother's until his sister Kelly, three years younger, joined the household. At that point, Ken began again to steal. He appropriated money from his grandmother and her friends, and shoplifted equipment from a sporting goods store. His grandmother sent him back to his mother.

Mrs. E. reported that from this time on she was tyrannized by Ken, that she had lost any vestige of control she might once have held. He bullied other children, lied, stole, and played truant. He was more unmanageable at home—he rammed his fist through a wall, blackened his sister's eye, and injured his mother's arm. He repeatedly hit his sister, and engaged in frequent sex play with her.

Family History

Mrs. E. was divorced from Kenneth's father when Ken was ten months old. His sister was fathered by another man, a fact that had never been shared with Ken; instead, he had been told that his parents divorced when he was three years old. Mrs. E. said that her marriage was filled with conflict, and that she had finally divorced her husband because he was totaly unreliable, a gambler, and a heavy drinker. She reported that he had been unemployed during most of their marriage.

Mrs. E. was a highly intellectual, college-educated woman who proudly traced her lineage to the original Pilgrim settlers. She was the daughter of an alcoholic lawyer father and a "long-suffering" mother. Her father had inherited money, so the family had been moderately affluent during her childhood. Her life-style drastically altered when her parents were divorced when she was in her early teens. Her mother then supported the two children by working as a saleswoman, and Mrs. E. recalled financial hardship during that time.

Although Mrs. E.'s income was moderate, she and her children presented themselves as being extraordinarily wealthy. Mrs. E. had been involved in outpatient psychotherapy for several years, and was aware on an intellectual, but not affectual, level of the "double messages" she gave

Ken. She expected him to be the "man of the house" as well as the mischievous little boy. He was cognizant of the contradictory expectations. He felt that he had to be a great person in order to "make up to mother" for what his father had been unable to give, but he fled the burden of this overwhelming expectation by acting out and fulfilling the other side of his mother's predictions. He admitted to feelings of longing for his father, perhaps hoping to be given a more secure and controlled environment.

The home environment was intensely stimulating to Ken's sexuality. Mrs. E. had been unable to control his sexual activity with his sister; this included jumping into the shower with her, getting into bed with her, lying on top of her. At some level Ken felt able to control all authority figures, and thus to get away with anything he desired. It was clear that he unconsciously entertained fantasies of winning the oedipal victory.

The history of Kenneth's father was reported by Mrs. E. and is, therefore, rather sparse. The father was eleven years older than his wife and was a college graduate. His mother died in childbirth and his father died five years later, leaving him to be brought up by his stepmother and maternal grandparents.

From the start of their marriage, the E.s experienced serious discord, usually involving money. Mr. E. reportedly changed jobs frequently, and freely speculated large sums of money on big business ventures. He worked in sales, media advertising, and similar fields. Mrs. E. described him as a "wheeler dealer" and as a heavy drinker. They were separated for two months in the year prior to Kenneth's birth, and his conception was an attempt toward a reconciliation. The attempt failed, however, and the parents divorced prior to Ken's first birthday. For the five years following the divorce the father's contact with the family was sporadic; he was allegedly unemployed and living in a commune. During this time he was arrested for robbing a bank, but the charges were dismissed. At the time of his remarriage, when Ken was eight, Mr. E. tried to reestablish his ties with the family.

Test Findings

On the OSIQ Ken presented himself as generally well adjusted, and answered in the moderate range. He painted the picture of a very self-confident young man who tried hard to excel and who was bothered by correction or criticism. He reported frequent episodes of feeling sad, and thinking that authorities sided with other kids rather than with him. The report from the independent psychological testing reads:

Kenneth's intellectual capacity is significantly above average and some of his abilities are clearly superior. The fact that Kenneth's performance skills exceed his verbal skills point up a characteristic need to externalize and "do things" rather than to consider his problems judiciously. The obvious depression on the subtest most sensitive to anxiety is indicative of Kenneth's consistent tendency to avoid, deny, and somehow minimize anxiety-arousing situations. He also diffuses the anxiety of the testing situation by continually "showing off," by smart-alecky joking, and by making disparaging comments to the examiner. Such behavior implies a need to forestall anxiety and to negate the seriousness of both the testing situation and his own personal problems.

Despite Kenneth's high intelligence, he has a basically weak integrative ability. This need to cling to areas of certainty may be reflective of a fear of error, and of the narcissistic need to always be right. He shows limited interest in seeking out the possible relationship and meanings inherent in concrete facts—which further highlights Kenneth's aversion to sustained introspection. His responses throughout the tests indicated grasps, though possibly superficial, of external social conventions and appropriate social behavior.

Kenneth's orientation to the world is largely egocentric, characterized by insistent demands for nurture, attention, and recognition. Not surprisingly, Kenneth overestimates his personal worth and adequacy. He likes to think of himself as a force to be reckoned with. He scorns older males and authority figures as unequal (if not impotent) competitors. These intensely rivalrous feelings suggest continuing oedipal preoccupations. Superficially he may appear quite charming as he utilizes a fine intelligence to gain social advantage and manipulate others. His capacities for empathy and mature object attachments are minimal—he is driven to establish dependent relationships which are focused on the satisfaction of his needs.

His anxiety tolerance appears to be low. He is potentially capable of impulsive behavior; but he is generally fairly adequately controlled. His impulsive behavior is most likely to be intermittent, and to be a subtle expression of hostility. His resentment is aroused by threats to his core dependency. He fears rejection and abandonment, particularly by women.

His strong affectional needs and the accompanying resentment are distressing to Kenneth, and he attempts to restrain them (and other anxiety-provoking emotions) by massive denial. He generally avoids dealing with problems by denying their existence or by projecting responsibility for his problems onto other people, or to forces or circumstances beyond his control.

Diagnostic Impression: Narcissistic Character Disorder

Hospital Course

On the unit, Ken alternated between compliance (attempting to impress the staff with his sincerity and desire to please) and hostility (trying to appear bored and above the whole situation). He was very much "on display," attuned to clothing, appearance, and to the social amenities. He saw himself as handsome, brilliant, and in control. He was manipulative, vigilant, and extremely clever in maneuvering interpersonal situations to his advantage—whether this ultimate end was to bolster his own self-esteem or to inflate his image in the eyes of other people. He was hypervigilant in interactions with others; observing others was crucially important to his successful manipulation of the environment. When threatened, he distanced himself from other people and from his own feelings, and defended himself by refusing to introspect, by denying persuasively. He was also quick to exonerate himself from any blame for his problems, and continually shifted this blame onto his mother, another authority, or other patients.

Beneath his omnipotent and manipulative stance, Ken experienced considerable depression, fear, and real affectional hunger. He would become dejected when his mother didn't visit. He expressed an infantlike fear of being abandoned, and complained of these thoughts plaguing him just before he fell asleep at night. He responded well to limits and to clearly set behavioral expectation.

Ken continually infuriated other patients. He was frequently the object of physical assaults, after which he sought out staff for protection and was reluctant to examine his own provocative behavior. He portrayed himself as the helpless, dejected victim. Toward other patients he was sarcastic, teasing, and condescending. He tattled and set up scuffles between them. One handicapped boy bore the particular brunt of his brutal verbal abuse —it seemed as if this boy's very imperfection was an affront to Ken. He also worried that this handicapped boy would receive more staff attention, so Ken subsequently developed an "appendicitis" attack and an "injured" leg.

With the staff, Ken lied fluently and without remorse. He continually sought special treatment—he was "above" cleaning, and had his mother do his laundry. He likened himself to "John-John Kennedy," a rather clear proclamation that he saw himself as the "crown prince" of the unit. He utilized every opportunity to show off. He displayed himself to the best advantage at sports, modeled new outfits of clothing, schemed to have himself declared the champion Ping Pong player, and on a field trip even asked a waitress for her phone number.

He was as unctuous with the staff as he was sarcastic with other patients. In his first week on the unit he told no fewer than six staff members that each was his "favorite." He inquired of another—at best, casually attired—staff member whether his jacket was tailor-made. He was very infrequently "straight" in his discussions with the staff; more frequently he attempted to butter up in a rather obvious fashion. Words for Ken were used to defend, confuse, and charm. The staff noted early:

> He perceives quickly the right way to talk, the correct attitude, and presents these attitudes to whomever wants them. He becomes panicky if someone

doesn't indicate that he is giving the approved line, and will ask if he is doing all right. He expresses undying devotion to the rules.

Summary: Narcissistic Delinquent

Kenneth demonstrated the narcissistic delinquent's resistance to psychotherapy. His defensiveness and tendency to deny problems caused many staff members to feel depressed when they discussed him. He was changed very little by his participation in the hospital program, due primarily to his consistent vigilance against experiences which might have led to lower self-esteem. He was not so disturbed that he would fragment under either painful narcissistic injury or grandiose narcissistic exhilaration and elation. Once he is able to establish a supportive environment, with minimal requirements to participate in intimate relationships, Kenneth should function fairly well. His narcissistic character disorder, however, would continue to be apparent under careful clinical scrutiny.

The Empty-Borderline Delinquent

Precipitants of Hospitalization

Lorraine G., an attractive seventeen-year-old white adolescent from an upper-middle-class family, was admitted to the program after forging several checks against the account of the parents of her best friend. During the five months prior to admission, she had lived with a boyfriend with her mother's consent, and it was during this time that she forged the checks. After the forgery her mother issued the ultimatum that, if Lorraine chose not to involve herself in treatment, she would declare her "ungovernable" and have her sent to the juvenile detention center. Criminal charges were never pressed against Lorraine; she had participated in the forgery with her wealthy girl friend, and the latter's parents were prominent citizens and leery of the publicity that a trial might engender. Lorraine had no previous arrests. Her mother reported that she had run away three times for brief periods of time, but that these incidents were generally discounted as Lorraine's way of "blowing off steam."

Lorraine had no clear notion of why she was admitted to the center. She thought it might be due to her "unstable home situation." She was able to give only the most diffuse account of her history, and focused mainly on the cities in which she had lived. She chronicled in some detail her mother's three marriages and numerous affairs, and felt that she was in some way responsible for her mother's psychiatric hospitalization, which had occurred four years previously and coincided with the onset of Lorraine's adolescence. Her mother had behaved in a maniclike fashion prior to her commitment, engaging in extravagant spending, outlandish schemes, shoplifting, and excessive sexual behavior. Lorraine and her younger sister had resided with their natural father during their mother's two-month hospitalization, and Lorraine remained with him for the year following her mother's institutionalization, when the latter felt that she could no longer handle her daughter. It was at her father's insistence that she later returned to her mother. While with her father, Lorraine was frequently truant and was accused of pushing drugs. On her return to Chicago she spent most of her time outside of the home, drifting from one friend's house to another and spending a few days with each. Her mother corroborated Lorraine's description of this period, stating that her daughter "chronically stayed away."

Developmental and School History

Lorraine was a planned child, and the result of a full-term pregnancy. In the ninth month of that pregnancy Mrs. G. suffered a serious fall, broke her leg, and experienced much discomfort. She described the labor and delivery as "very unpleasant." Lorraine was depicted as a colicky baby who suffered from projectile vomiting throughout early infancy; her mother recalled resenting the baby, and being incensed that she could not satisfy the child's needs. She portrayed Lorraine as crying and fretting constantly; all developmental tasks, however, were reported within normal limits. At age two the child was hospitalized for asthma, and was described during this time as being obstinate and argumentative. Her younger sister was born when she was three. Mrs. G. remembered Lorraine becoming more placid and agreeable after the birth of her sibling. She was again hospitalized at age five, this time to undergo a bilateral inguinal herniorrhaphy.

Lorraine's parents were divorced when she was six, and the memory of that period in her life was singularly unpleasant to her. Her father moved to another city at some distance from Chicago, making visits virtually impossible. Mrs. G. stated that Lorraine was "irritable and unhappy" when she started school, but she did well both behaviorally and academically until the seventh grade. That year her grades began to suffer and she stubbornly refused to do schoolwork. It was, in her mother's words, a "quiet rebellion," with Lorraine feigning compliance but refusing to work. In the eighth grade her disobedience became overt defiance and was seriously upsetting to her mother. She withdrew from family activities, was sarcastic and provocative with her mother, and allegedly began to stay out all night and to lie about her whereabouts. When she was caught smoking marijuana a physical battle ensued, and Mrs. G. reported "knocking Lorraine across the room." At this point, Lorraine was sent to live with her father.

It should be noted that Lorraine's sister, Debbie, was not without her share of psychiatric difficulties. Debbie developed a severe school phobia shortly after her mother's third marriage, was unable to sleep in her own room until she was ten years old, and was extremely frightened of being left alone. She had been in outpatient psychotherapy for years, and was currently functioning adequately, although she experienced great difficulty in making friends and was still extremely anxious about school.

Family History

The history of the extended family documented serious psychopathology. Lorraine's mother was an extremely attractive, educated woman in her early forties. She was described by her social worker as being narcissistic, unstable, self-centered, and so seriously impaired that her own difficulties precluded any kind of consistently positive relationship with her daughter. She herself was the daughter of a mercurial, charming father who was employed in show business, and she saw her own mother as the "sacrificial lamb" in a difficult marital relationship. Family finances in her youth fluctuated between the extremes of having a home and several cars to not having sufficient food to eat. Curiously, Mrs. G.'s mother was also psychiatrically hospitalized when Mrs. G. was an early adolescent, and remained in the hospital for two years, during which time she reportedly was extremely withdrawn and received electroconvulsive therapy. Another parallel between Mrs. G.'s history and that of her mother is that both had had therapeutic abortions.

Mrs. G. was a good student who enjoyed school. She married her first husband shortly after her graduation from college, and Lorraine was conceived almost immediately. Three years later, after several miscarriages, Lorraine's younger sister was born. Throughout this marriage Mrs. G. saw herself predominantly as a housewife, although she had a lucrative part-time career as a fashion model. During the latter half of this eight-year marriage she claims to have become "bored," and to have initiated several extramarital affairs. Her husband could not tolerate this behavior, the couple separated, reconciled at her request, and finally separated for good. Mrs. G. came to Chicago to further her career as a model and a year later, after a divorce from her first husband, she married a politician. That marriage was stormy from the start, and the couple divorced three years later. It was after this divorce that Mrs. G. was psychiatrically hospitalized. She had been in outpatient psychotherapy since her first divorce, and she remained in treatment thereafter. A year after her hospitalization she married a man ten years her junior and separated from him within a year. At the time of Lorraine's hospitalization, however, four years after their separation, Mrs. G. was contemplating a reconciliation with this last husband—in any case, they were dating frequently. She reported hypersexual behavior; it was not unusual for her to meet and have relations with a man when her husband or current lover was out of town for a night. Her self-esteem was elevated by these erotic conquests which "proved to her" that she was desirable and loved. However, she was ambivalent about these multiple partners, seeing them as inappropriate for any sustained relationship. Her active sexual life resulted in numerous abortions.

Lorraine described her relationship with her mother as unloving and distant. She viewed her mother as promiscuous and hateful, while simultaneously feeling that she herself was just like her. On her part, Mrs. G. viewed Lorraine as a peer, and frequently as a rival. She often reminded her daughter that there was nothing that the latter could do or try that her mother had not already sampled. Lorraine was fully cognizant of her mother's abortions, of her sex life, drug usage, and shoplifting arrest. During Lorraine's hospitalization it became clear that she and her mother were frequently merged; as evidence, when signing Lorraine into the hospital for treatment, her mother signed her own name as that of the patient. Mrs. G. was extremely erratic in visiting her daughter. When she did not receive sufficient attention during her visits to the hospital, she would threaten to withdraw monetary support and to cease visiting Lorraine altogether; similarly, she would sometimes visit another patient and spend all her time there. When accompanied by her younger daughter, she seemed unable to involve both girls in her attention; one or the other of them was always excluded.

Test Findings

On the OSIQ, Lorraine answered an unusually large percent of the questions in an extreme fashion, and generally portrayed herself in a deprecatory light. She saw herself as characteristically unhappy in the present and pessimistic about the future; she disparaged her abilities both interpersonally and academically; she was dissatisfied with her physical appearance and the bodily changes that puberty had wrought. She characterized herself as needing others desperately, while simultaneously recognizing that she was generally quite distant and isolated in peer relationships. She depicted her family life as totally disruptive, and as an impediment to adjustment rather than a source of support.

She was described as follows on the psychological testing:

Lorraine is currently functioning in the average range of intelligence. However, her performance showed a good deal of variability from test to test, reflecting disrupted performance due to anxiety. Despite this fluctuating level of concentration, Lorraine appeared quite able to attend to, to recall, and to accurately reproduce information.

She possesses the ability to think abstractly; however, it seems that she is most comfortable with a concrete, "common sense" application of her intelligence. For one so bright, she displays relatively little drive to integrate and organize information. She shows some tendency to be critical or argumentative and may, at times, stubbornly do things her own way in order to assert herself.

Lorraine has apparently experienced both early and severe rejection by mother (or maternal figures), and consequently she experiences intense feelings of deprivation. Her craving for a stable, dependent, affectional relationship pervades all her testing responses. She craves warmth and affection of a basic sort, and fantasizes about the security and closeness of the "truly satisfying" relationship.

She has precariously low self-esteem, and constantly seeks to shore up her faltering self-conception with the approval of others.

Lorraine's capacity for mature object relations is severely limited. She lacks figure and intensity and may appear to others as emotionally flat and unresponsive. She is a passively recipient individual whose self-preoccupations interfere with her relationships with others. In confronting her problems she is impeded by a guarded evasiveness—she cannot or will not self-disclose. She "talks around" pertinent or possibly revealing material.

She shows uncertainty and confusion over sexual identity which undoubtedly stems from the hostility which she feels towards her mother. The combination of resentment with great dependence upon her mother's acceptance, and a deep-seated need for affectional response from mother, produces a highly conflictual relationship which is not particularly conducive to identification.

Lorraine is quite uncertain about close relationships with other people. She seeks the caretaking and security which others can offer her, while fearing they will ultimately desert her, or betray her in some fashion.

Lorraine deals with her environment in varying manners—at times she is passive; as previously discussed, she wishes to be the nurtured child. At other times she confronts the environment by boldly acting out her hostile impulses directly, with minimal or inadequate behavioral controls. In dealing with others, Lorraine is further hampered by an unwillingness to assume responsibility for herself. She tends to blame difficulties on others or on unnamed environmental forces.

Diagnostic Impression: Borderline Character Disorder

Hospital Course

Lorraine was hospitalized for over a year. One week after hospitalization the staff discovered that she was ten weeks pregnant. Lorraine claimed that she had informed her mother of her condition prior to admission, but that her mother chose to ignore it. It was speculated that her mother may have used the hospital as a means to secure her daughter an abortion, since the procedure was illegal at that time unless prescribed for medical reasons. Although initially uncertain, Lorraine decided in favor of an abortion. Her individual therapist felt this to be indicative of Lorraine's pattern of running away, which was documented in her history and was also emerging on the unit. She tended to "hide away" when under stress, or to camouflage her real feelings. She showed no particular affect about the pregnancy, and assumed an overtly passive "I don't care, you decide" attitude about it. Although she tried to wall off depressive feelings, she was extremely upset and depressed after the procedure.

Throughout the initial months of her hospitalization, Lorraine was not readily drawn into the life of the unit. She seemed to be afraid of people, and was repeatedly described as "distant, isolated, unhooked, and blank-looking." She was obviously socially skilled, but showed no tendency to ally with other patients. It was noted, however, that she was overdependent on staff. She needed others so much, and had learned to expect so little, that she preferred isolation to the risk of dealing with a possibly non-gratifying environment. She had an extraordinary need, a real hunger for human contact and for relationships. She frequently used somatic complaints to attract and maintain attention. She was comfortable with asking for and obtaining care in an impersonal situation by stressing her physical needs; that way she never had to acknowledge that it was she who sought tenderness and care.

She had no real and abiding sense of self. She was at a preidentification stage; her identity consisted of reflecting significant sources of gratification. She would imitate her therapist and try to please the staff when they were being particularly nurturant to her, and she attempted to reflect the personality traits of these gratifying individuals as long as her needs were being satisfied. When frustrated, she was subject to temper tantrums and to precipitous, seemingly inexplicable rages. It was not unusual for her to express suicidal ideation after seemingly minor traumas such as a missed visit by her mother or a confrontation by the staff.

Lorraine was not impulsive in the usual sense of the word—she did not give in to every impulse regardless of the consequences. Her deficient sense of self and fragile defensive structure, however, left her at the mercy of her feelings of the moment. If these feelings were bad or depressive, her tendency was to run away, withdraw, or, failing these options, to "blow up." This pattern is aptly illustrated by the response to her therapist's vacation. She initially expressed suicidal urges and then demonstrated her feelings behaviorally by throwing and dropping dishes: next she spoke repeatedly of signing out, and of eloping from the hospital; finally, after her therapist had been gone for a week, Lorraine spoke of having "lost interest" in her. Her ego structure was simply not competent to deal with the anxiety and depression associated with loss, and she needed to act out by some form of destruction or to escape by withdrawal or cynicism.

Her search for self-affirmation through the approval of others is exemplified by her performance in school and in occupational therapy. In school she was initially quite disdainful, but when she achieved some success in her schoolwork, she was able to admit to ignorance and to ask for help. She desperately wanted to achieve, but often her self-confidence was so minimal that she was unable to make an active and constructive effort to attempt solutions. In order to do so, she would have had to risk failure. In occupational therapy she remained extremely reluctant to ask questions, and was generally immobilized by her need to achieve at an unreasonably high level.

Lorraine showed a viable alliance with her therapist in individual therapy, moving from global fear and wariness, to denial of her feelings about the abortion, to making the therapist take the brunt of her rage when she felt her demands for nurture to be unsatisfied. Slowly an exploration of the mother/daughter relationship was begun. Lorraine felt defiance, anger, and hatred toward Mrs. G., but at the same time she was intensely close to her mother. Her aggression stemmed from her fear of loss and abandonment. She was able to explore the same fears in relation to her therapist after the latter's vacation, and also prior to discharge.

As discharge approached Lorraine showed a need to distance herself from the therapist, and accused her of violating confidentiality and of betraying her. She expressed feelings of worthlessness, emptiness, and confusion. She needed to be fulfilled, made whole, gratified. During her final psychotherapy sessions she confused her therapist with her mother. As discharge became imminent, somatic complaints reappeared, and she expressed fears that her mother would abandon her. She became extremely irritated and sarcastic with the staff, and began to refuse to participate in the program.

Summary: Empty-Borderline Delinquent

Lorraine demonstrated the typical emptiness and need for merger, union, or reunion with the maternal self-object that is so characteristic of the borderline delinquent. Because of her emotional depletion, her future was seen in somewhat pessimistic terms; she herself was, for the most part, incapable of planning or orienting herself to the future. She would vacillate between a schizoid withdrawal and an open, clinging need, frequently engaging in delinquent behavior designed to fill herself up emotionally or to support her shaky boundaries. She struggled with problems of separation and individuation, but experienced these primarily as a sense of emptiness and not as a clearly experienced depressive affect. Her orientation was passive, rather than object-seeking.

The Depressed-Borderline Delinquent

Precipitants of Hospitalization

Martha was seventeen years old, a white suburban adolescent, who felt that her hospitalization was the result of "doing too much to get along with the crowd, [but] I am not getting along with my parents." She was transferred from the County Juvenile Detention Center to our program. Four years of sustained turmoil had preceded her hospitalization. Her parents dated her first defiant behavior at the seventh grade, when she began to acquire the "wrong kinds" of friends; she also began to use makeup, to smoke, and to shoplift. Her parents attempted to exert discipline by making her return shoplifted items and by grounding her, but their interventions had little effect. While being punished, she would sneak out of the home to go to the movies with boyfriends, stealing money from her mother's purse to finance these excursions. She was so disruptive at school dances and teenage functions that the chaperones would call her parents at home. She continually stole money from her mother and cigarettes from her father, and would run away from home for one or two days to avoid confrontation about the thefts. On her return she would continue to steal, and her parents were totally unsuccessful in stopping such behavior.

When she entered high school, Martha associated with a much older

73

peer group; the girls were juniors and seniors, and the boys were in general already out of school. She was "tremendously aware" of boys. She pressured her parents insistently to allow her more privileges; as a freshman she wanted to attend the senior prom, and to stay out all night at a beach party. She was refused permission, as both parents felt that such privileges were the prerogative of an older, more mature adolescent. Martha's reaction was to run away for a day or two to stay with friends. At this stage she would return home on her own volition. She was doing extremely poorly in school, was frequently tardy or truant, and responded to all limit-setting by running away.

At the beginning of her sophomore year, she informed her parents that her "real family" were her friends. Her behavior—drinking, smoking, participating in sexual relations—was consonant with the values of her peers, and it openly flouted parental values. Her antisocial behavior acquired an almost stylized quality in which she repeatedly seemed to invite her parents to control her and to establish some limits on her behavior. She now needed to emphasize her pseudo-independence from her family by exaggerated and self-destructive acts. She ran off alone to distant cities, and began to experiment with hallucinogens, financing the venture by forging her father's checks. Her parents, alarmed, responded by having her psychiatrically hospitalized, and by becoming involved in treatment themselves.

Martha returned to school upon her discharge from the hospital, but attempted to foment a rebellion around the high school's dress code and smoking restrictions. Her teachers complained to her parents that she was a nuisance, and that she needed to focus her energy on academics rather than on "politics." She began to cut classes, and was eventually expelled for stealing and truancy.

She got a menial job after her expulsion, and continued in therapy. Shortly thereafter she became pregnant, and overdosed on barbiturates to "get rid of the baby" and to "get out of this family for good." After hospitalization for a therapeutic abortion, she again ran away from her suburban home to the city, where she became heavily involved in the drug subculture and began to prostitute herself—an activity she described as "fascinating" and "exciting." She soon was hospitalized for gonorrheal peritonitis and pneumonia. Following medical hospitalization, she once again was psychiatrically hospitalized, but she left against medical advice.

Again she ran away, and continued to abuse drugs, to forge checks, and to prostitute herself. A "jealous girl friend" informed the police and Martha was arrested. She expressed apparently sincere remorse, and after release from detention once again found a menial job. Before her case came to trial, however, she hitchhiked across the country with a friend. Months later she contacted her parents and asked for their help, claiming that she was frightened by the people with whom she was living. Her father advised her to contact the police. She did so and was returned home to her parents, who brought her to the detention center while they searched for appropriate treatment facilities.

Developmental and School History

As the oldest girl in a family of five children, Martha had a brother one year older, a sister one year younger, and two brothers eleven and twelve years younger than she. Her parents gave a rather unelaborated developmental history, and seemed to have had some difficulty in differentiating Martha's experiences from those of their other children. In general, her early development was described as normal. According to her mother, Martha was somewhat shy as a youngster, and was inhibited at school and in other "public" gatherings. She sought out one close friend at a time, and feared to initiate interactions, expressing concern to her mother that her feelings of friendship were not reciprocated. Both parents felt that she had formed meaningful relationships with other children, that she had been a good child up until puberty, that until then she had excelled in schoolwork and was obedient at home.

Martha's report of her own early history parallels this account, at least partially. She portrayed herself as a well-behaved and talented student in primary school, and remembered herself as being compliant and eager to please until the age of twelve. She recalled that her grades declined in junior high school when she had conflicts with teachers over some poems she had written with graphic sexual references. About this time, Martha reported, her mother became inordinately strict with her, accused her of sexual thoughts, and physically beat her. Allegedly, Mrs. V. would tell her, "Everyone in the family hates you, Bitch." According to Martha, Mrs. V. demanded perfection both in her children and her husband, and tried diligently to uncover faults and to correct them. Martha claimed that her mother intercepted her mail, and would ask her about sexual involvement with boys well before her sexual activity actually began. She reported contemplating suicide after being corrected by her mother; on some of these occasions she put scarves around her neck and pulled them until it hurt. Once, during the eighth grade, after an argument with her mother, she drank drain cleaner in an attempt to kill herself.

Martha saw herself frequently as a pawn in a strained marital relationship. It is a fact that her behavior led the parents to seek marital counseling. She recalled many battles between her parents—which, she noted, were most likely to occur on supposedly happy occasions. Her earliest memory involved coming home to find the Christmas tree and decorations strewn across the floor and her parents at loggerheads.

Family History

Mrs. V. was an attractive woman in her late thirties who tended to complain vociferously about all the hardships she had endured. She was a strict Baptist, college educated, and employed part-time. Coming from a very poor family—her father was an alcoholic and her mother had supported the family—and as the eldest daughter in a sibship of three, she had been expected to care for her younger brother and sister. The brother was described as a wild "ne'er-do-well" who frequently embarrassed Mrs. V. and expected her to rescue him. She reported sudden mood swings, and frequently felt that she was the victim of everyone's wrath. After the death of her mother she became seriously depressed and required psychotherapy.

Mr. V. was a college-educated Catholic in his early forties. He had a highly technical job in which he immersed himself. He, too, was the eldest child in a sibship of three, and remembered a life of hardship and poverty. His mother died when he was five, and he lived with his maternal grandparents until his father remarried two years later.

The V.s' marriage seemed to be filled with conflict. Mrs. V. made many demands, and even physically assaulted her husband; Mr. V. responded by withdrawing to his work in a rather emasculated way, rather than confronting his wife's anger. Mrs. V. externalized her conflicts, while her husband internalized his and suffered from a variety of stress disorders—ulcers, bowel problems, and angina. Both parents were proud of having achieved upper-middle-class status through their own hard work and perseverance. A constant theme in the family was this notion of immense sacrifice, allegedly for the exclusive benefit of the children. Neither parent had ever been physically cared for in a manner comparable to the material care they provided their children, and they were chagrined that their children were not humbly appreciative of all their efforts.

During the course of family therapy, it was revealed that Mrs. V. had had a therapeutic abortion in her early teens, which gave rise to speculation about a possible incestuous relationship. When she revealed this history in the session, her husband wanted to discontinue the treatment immediately, as he felt it might precipitate a nervous breakdown in his wife. Martha dealt with the incident by taking drugs. Her mother's therapeutic abortion is noted as an interesting parallel to Martha's own history.

Both parents reported that Martha was the only one of their children who suffered any personal difficulties. They had experienced some minor concern about their eldest son, feeling that the boy—an Eagle Scout—was excessively passive and overly compliant, but they felt that he would eventually "find" himself. Martha, however, reported that her brother was heavily involved in barbiturates and other drug-taking activities. She also felt that her younger sister was seriously suicidal.

Test Findings

Martha presented herself on the OSIQ in a generally positive manner. Her only extreme responses dealt with parent/child relationships and recognition of guilt. She indicated a strong preference for strict authoritarian parenting, expressed much anxiety about possible wrongdoing, and evidenced general disappointment in herself. She admitted that she had experienced self-destructive impulses at times, and felt that she might be "hypersensitive."

The report of psychological testing follows:

Martha's intellectual capacity is clearly above average, and some of her abilities border on the superior. It is probable that Martha is capable of functioning intellectually on the superior level. Her informational and cultural interests are particularly weak, while her knowledge of conventional behavior is outstanding, although pervaded with a highly moral tone.

Martha's level of aspiration is exceedingly high, so high that the compulsive need to achieve academically may tax the creative capacities of her personality. Her very strong drive to please others with her accomplishments is undoubtedly functioning at the expense of other important satisfactions.

Depression, emotional lability, anxiety, and overwhelming dependency needs are all conspicuous in Martha's current functioning. She appears quite depressed, and much of her fantasy production reflects morbid anxiety. She apparently feels inferior and unworthy, and is beset by guilt and anxiety over the expression of both hostile and sexual impulses. She tries mightily to adhere to conventional ways of behaving. However, she is a highly suggestible person who frequently relies on others to set standards for her. Thus, she may be frequently swayed by the crowd, or by a persuasive individual. However, the strict internalized moral code of her family intrudes, and she frequently feels guilty for real or imagined transgressions.

Her relationships with parental and authority figures are highly dependent. She accedes to their wishes in attempts to curry favor and acceptance. She feels intense guilt when she does not live up to the expectations of her parents and other authorities. Martha is not entirely comfortable with this submissive posture, yet a more independent stance may jeopardize (or so she believes) affection and may subject her to retribution for being "bad."

Martha's passivity and dependence on others often assume an aggressive, demanding quality. She so desperately craves the affection and approbation of others that when it is not forthcoming she becomes resentful and hostile. She has some capacity for mature object relations as she is sensitive to the needs and feelings of other people, and is capable of limited identification with others. She is able to identify, to some extent, with adult female figures.

Martha is generally capable of controlled emotional reaction to her environment. However, under stressful conditions, impulsive, even explosive expression of her feelings is likely.

Diagnostic Impression: Predominantly neurotic makeup, with both hysterical and compulsive features. Strong depressive overlay.

Hospital Course

Martha was significantly overweight, and at times rather slovenly in appearance. Her affect was characteristically tense, bewildered, hostile, and depressed. She set harsh expectations for herself, and she truly struggled to understand why she was not the obedient and virtuous young lady that her mother wished her to be. She tried to cope with the torments of self-contempt by being self-destructive and rebellious. In a way, her acting-out on the unit and her delinquency on the outside might be conceptualized as her compulsive need to provide the fodder for her internalized guilt, to substantiate her "badness."

The overriding pattern of Martha's ten-month hospitalization might be seen as self-incrimination. She expressed the feeling that she "blew the whole world away" when she made an elopement attempt, and was sincerely astonished and elated when other patients did not reject her for trying to elope. She continually termed her need for closeness as "evil," and referred to herself as a "bitch" and an "animal." She was constantly confessing misdeeds—she turned in drugs, a knife mistakenly left in her room by her parents, and she informed the staff of several planned elopement attempts.

At times the internalized conflicts overwhelmed her, and she would plead with the staff not to expect so much of her. One such episode occurred on a camping trip; she begged not to be included, but the staff felt that with substantial support she would be able to go. She became extremely disorganized on the trip, burned down her tent, and huddled traumatized under a car. She frequently sobbed that she didn't know what to do with herself, but that she felt "awful" about herself. A similar incident occurred after she falsely accused herself of stealing someone else's food in the community meeting. (She left the meeting, went to her room, stuffed bedsheets under her door, and ignited them. Fire engulfed the room and, as one male staff member fought it with an extinguisher, other members of the staff screamed at Martha to get out. She stared blankly, was completely immobilized, and made no attempt to help herself.)

Throughout her hospitalization Martha repeatedly challenged the external unit structure, and "tested the limits" on all rules. This seemed to be both a test of whether she could be controlled, and a need to project her confusion, fear, and hostility upon the environment. Such a projection allowed her to legitimize her rebelliousness. She might construe her experience as anger toward a punitive staff rather than as her need to discharge the anxiety stimulated by her own internal struggles. The attempt to externalize her internal stress was shown in her many thwarted efforts to elope from the hospital. She ran away several times, and tried to walk off the unit, although she was careful to take an obvious route or to ascertain beforehand that the staff was watching her. She "confessed" to elopement thoughts with other patients on three other occasions.

Martha's disorganization under stress and her tendency to externalize were also shown in her school behavior. She missed enormous amounts of school because she was unable, despite superior intellectual ability, to separate her own needs and issues from what was needed for the class and pertinent to the class discussion.

It was difficult for her to deal with warmth and tenderness without sexual involvement or its implications. She tended to eroticize any message of concern from the staff or the patient group. Nursing notes were replete with notations that she feared she was a lesbian (after a positive interaction with female staff), or that she feared she was sterile (after a seductive request for special attention from male staff). As she became engaged with the staff and felt warmly about them, she began to wonder "whether she was a boy or a girl." She simply could not distinguish between sex and nurturance, and was therefore fearful of closeness and resistant to it.

Martha slowly began to take responsibility for her behavior and attempted to short-circuit her acting-out. Ten months into her hospitalization she turned eighteen and was in a position to decide for herself whether to continue hospitalization. After much struggle, she decided to sign herself in. She became extremely withdrawn and depressed, and three days later had her first session with her new therapist—a staff member with whom she had already established a firm alliance. She expressed despair over starting all over again. She left the session and struck a staff member, stating that she knew this ensured discharge. She was subsequently discharged.

Summary: Depressed-Borderline Delinquent

Martha demonstrated overt clinical depression and strongly internalized values, along with the need to achieve academically and artistically. She also showed clinging behavior and object hunger, with great sensitivity to separation and a chronic struggle to individuate. Her involvement with her family and her acting-out behavior were also quite characteristic; utilization of physical punishment even to the point of brutality had resulted in the internalization of a severely punitive superego structure. Her delinquent behavior, including heavy drug usage, represented an attempt to relieve herself of a severe depression, which at other times manifested itself in suicidal and self-destructive behavior. Psychological testing confirmed both aspects of this patient's difficulties—namely, the severe superego guilt, and the clinging need for objects.

There might appear to be a contradiction between the neurotic and structural conflict aspects of Martha's personality and the symbiotic clinging aspects. Someone with a clear-cut neurotic depression would not require hospitalization, and would undoubtedly show little or no delinquent behavior. Yet Martha showed not only initiative, guilt, and strong internalized values, but also a need for object contact.

Normal and Delinquent Adolescents

A General Comparison

Before understanding the disturbed or deviant, we need to know more about normative baseline behavior and development among adolescents. One of the authors (DO) spent the 1960s studying a group of normal, well-adjusted, nonpatient adolescents from the beginning of high school until five years post-high school, seeking to ascertain how these subjects coped with the period of adolescence (Offer, 1969; Offer and Offer, 1975). After the data on normal subjects were obtained, we decided to undertake the current study of disturbed and delinquent adolescents in order to: 1. explore some variables which distinguish delinquents from their normal peers; and 2. begin to discover the psychological etiology of the juvenile delinquent. When comparative data were available, we used that data to enrich our understanding of delinquents by contrasting their adaptation to that of normal adolescents.

In the course of this study, we compared our normal subjects with their delinquent peers along three specific lines: 1. the Offer Self-Image Questionnaire for adolescents (OSIQ); 2. teacher ratings of the adolescents; and 3. interviewer ratings—by a psychiatrist in the case of the normal teenager and by a psychotherapist in the case of the juvenile delinquent. The reliability and validity of these psychological instruments and how they were constructed can be found in the following publications: the

Offer Self-Image Questionnaire in the monograph entitled *The Self-Image of Adolescents* (Offer, Ostrov, and Howard 1977), and the two rating scales in *The Psychological World of the Teenager* (Offer 1969).

Instruments and Their Method of Application

1. The Offer Self-Image Questionnaire was given to the normal subjects at age fourteen, and to the juvenile delinquents when they were screened for admission to the hospital at an average age of fifteen.

2. The teacher's rating scale was given to teachers of the normal subjects at the end of junior high and in high school. The scale was a slightly modified version of that used in both suburban high schools where the study was undertaken. Teachers of juvenile delinquents were given the same scale at the end of thirteen weeks of hospitalization. For comparison purposes we are using only the males.

3. The interviewer/therapist rating scale for normal adolescents was filled out during the junior year of high school when the normal subjects were sixteen to seventeen years old; by that time each teenager had been interviewed approximately six times. For the juvenile delinquent, the therapist filled out the scale at the end of the patient's first thirteen weeks of therapy in the hospital. Obviously a different type of alliance existed between the interviewer and the psychotherapist and their two populations of adolescents. We believe, however, that a comparison was of interest because the basic nature of the alliance showed the capacity of the individual teenager to develop trusting relationships with these adults, so that the data should represent a valuable perspective on the respective groups of adolescents.

The Offer Self-Image Questionnaire

The OSIQ is a self-descriptive personality test that can be used to measure the self-system of teenage boys and girls between the ages of thirteen and nineteen. Self-concept is a particularly crucial personality dimension for adolescents (Masterson 1967; Erikson 1950; Blos 1962; Block 1971) and, empirically, has been directly correlated with the mental health and adjustment of adolescents in a number of studies (Rosenberg 1965; Offer and Howard 1972; Offer, Ostrov, and Howard, 1977). Self-concept, in addition, has been shown to be a relatively stable personality trait from adolescence onward (Engel 1959; Vailliant and McArthur 1972). The

OSIQ was originally developed to provide a reliable means of selecting a representative group of modal or "normal" adolescents from a larger group of high school students (Offer and Sabshin 1963; Offer 1969) and eight years of follow-up research confirmed the efficacy of that selection process (Offer and Offer, 1975). The questionnaire has since been used in many studies, and has been administered to over 15,000 teenagers in the United States, Australia, Ireland, Israel, India, and Brazil. The population sampled in some forty different metropolitan centers includes males and females, younger and older teenagers, and rural, urban, and suburban adolescents who are normal, disturbed, and delinquent. The samples cover the range of the middle class, but more recently have included rural, ghetto, and other groupings of teenagers.

Our particular operational approach rests on two major assumptions: First, it is necessary to evaluate the adolescent's functioning in multiple areas, since he can master one aspect of his world while failing to adjust in another. Second, the psychological sensitivity of the adolescent is sufficiently acute to allow us to utilize his self-description as a basis for reliable selection of subgroups (Offer, Ostrov, and Howard 1977).

As can be seen in Table 4.1, the OSIQ differentiated significantly

TABLE 4.1

Comparison of Offer Self-Image Questionnaire and Total Score Means:
Normal vs. Delinquent and Disturbed Subjects (Americans only)

Offer Self-Image Questionnaire Scale[a]	Normal[b]	Delinquent[b] and Disturbed	Probability Levels[c]
Scale 1: Impulse Control	2.34	2.76	.01
Scale 2: Emotional Tone	2.33	2.90	.0001
Scale 3: Body and Self-Image	2.42	2.86	.001
Scale 4: Social Relationships	2.19	2.54	.05
Scale 5: Morals	2.24	2.67	.0001
Scale 7: Family Relationships	2.31	3.02	.0001
Scale 8: Mastery of the External World	2.30	2.68	.001
Scale 9: Vocational/Educational Goals	1.87	2.25	.01
Scale 10: Psychopathology	2.32	2.81	.001
Scale 11: Superior Adjustment	2.37	2.80	.0001
Scale 6: Sexual Attitudes	2.71	2.68	NS
Total Score	2.27	2.73	.0001

[a]The higher the score, the less well adjusted.

[b]240 subjects were used in each of three analyses; the 240 subjects were drawn in each analysis from a grand pool of 1,522 subjects; means shown are for the total sample.

[c]The least significant of the three probability levels derived from three independent analyses is shown.

TABLE 4.2

*Comparison of Offer Self-Image Questionnaire Scale and Total Score Means:
Delinquent vs. Disturbed Subjects (Americans only)*

Offer Self-Image Questionnaire Scale[a]		Delinquent[b]	Disturbed[b]	Probability Levels[c]
Scale 1:	Impulse Control	2.65	2.87	NS
Scale 2:	Emotional Tone	2.75	3.04	NS
Scale 3:	Body and Self-Image	2.64	3.08	.01
Scale 4:	Social Relationships	2.44	2.65	NS
Scale 5:	Morals	2.65	2.71	NS
Scale 7:	Family Relationships	2.84	3.20	.05
Scale 8:	Mastery of the External World	2.51	2.85	.05
Scale 9:	Vocational/Educational Goals	2.07	2.42	.01
Scale 10:	Psychopathology	2.69	2.93	NS
Scale 11:	Superior Adjustment	2.66	2.94	.01
Scale 6:	Sexual Attitudes	2.54	2.83	NS
Total Score		2.59	2.87	.01

[a]The higher the score, the less well adjusted.
[b]160 subjects were used in each of three analyses; the 160 subjects were drawn in each analysis from a grand pool of 561 subjects; means shown are for the total sample.
[c]The least significant of the three probability levels derived from three independent analyses is shown.

between a random sample of normal adolescents, male and female, young and old, and the contrasted sample of delinquents and emotionally disturbed adolescents. This was true for all scales and for the total score, with the exception of Scale 6 (Sexual Attitudes). In the comparison between the delinquent and the emotionally disturbed teenagers (see Table 4.2), the delinquents had healthier self-image on five scales and on the total score. The remaining six scales showed the same trend (i.e., delinquents having a healthier self-image).

With the exception of the scale for sexual attitudes and behavior (Scale 6), we have demonstrated that the OSIQ can differentiate significantly between normal, delinquent, and emotionally disturbed adolescents. As expected, normals show the healthiest self-concept, and delinquents had a more positive self-image than did emotionally disturbed adolescents. We are currently gathering data to determine the extent to which these differences hold up in other countries, such as Ireland.

The Teacher Rating Scale

As expected, the majority of the ratings (leadership, social sensitivity, responsibility, industry) showed highly significant differences between the teachers of the normal subjects and the teachers of the delinquents.

This presumably reflects differences between the two groups of teachers, and between the two populations as perceived by the teachers (see Table 4.3). However, a surprise result showed in the second variable, Initiative/Creativity, where no significant differences were found between the teachers' ratings of the two populations. The multivariate analysis had showed a significant race effect among the juvenile delinquents, so it was appropriate to compare the normal subjects to the racial group among juvenile delinquents to whom they corresponded, i.e., the white male juvenile delinquents. However, it is unlikely that the finding is an artifact.

This finding—and the observed trend—that delinquents were rated as having more initiative and creativity than normals—accords with what is described in chapter 6 regarding cognitive styles: that the delinquents tended to be more field independent than their relatively healthier siblings and a group of controls. Since we have no cognitive studies on our normal populations, it would be hard to compare the two. Nonetheless it raises some interesting questions which future research might attempt to answer: are the deviant—and often brilliant—individuals those who are responding more to internal cues, hence responding less to what is socially desirable in a particular culture? What if any is the similarity between those deviant/brilliant individuals and antisocial people (adolescents or adults)?

Interviewer/Therapist Rating Scale

The comparison between ratings made by psychiatrists who interview normal adolescents and those who work with their patients is fraught with methodological difficulties (see Table 4.4). Ratings of the first two variables—depth of emotional experience and emotional expressiveness—show what would be expected: the normal adolescents are rated healthier.[1] The third rating—relationship with the interviewer or psychotherapist—shows no difference. Since we assume that disturbed delinquents would have a harder time than their normal peers in relating to any adult, psychotherapist included, we wonder whether this finding is not more a reflection of the interviewer/therapist than of the adolescent. Isn't the psychiatrist more comfortable in relating to mentally sick youngsters? Isn't there a greater degree of motivation on both sides to either help and understand (that of the psychiatrist), or to get help and be understood (that of the patient)? Or did we obtain more complex and meaningful data from our normal subjects because we were able to develop with them a better research alliance, a difference not reflected in the ratings?

We cannot answer these questions, but it has been our impression that the normal subjects did cooperate more with the purely research aspect of the project, while the delinquents were more likely to do so if they

TABLE 4.3

Comparison of Teacher Rating Scale Distributions
Normal vs. Delinquent Males

Variable	Normal $(N = 68)$[a]		Delinquent $(N = 30)$	
	n	%	n	%
Leadership				
1. Active	1	(2)	1	(3)
2. Occasional/accepted	8	(12)	2	(7)
3. Sometimes/not accepted	39	(57)	5	(17)
4. Cooperative	15	(22)	15	(50)
5. Negative	5	(7)	7	(23)
	68	(100)	30	(100)

chi-square = 15.70, 4d.f.; $p < .005$
Average normal rating = 3.22
Average delinquent rating = 3.82

Variable				
Initiative/Creativity[b]				
1. Creative/contributes	5	(7)	2	(11)
2. Some originality/self-reliant	15	(22)	7	(37)
3. Routine assignments	35	(52)	5	(26)
4. Conforms only	13	(19)	5	(26)
	68	(100)	19	(100)

chi-square = 3.89, 3d.f., *not significant*
    comparing white delinquents and normals
Average normal rating = 2.82
Average white delinquent rating = 2.68

Variable				
Social Sensitivity				
1. Deeply concerned/sensitive	5	(7)	0	(0)
2. Generally concerned/sensitive	29	(43)	1	(3)
3. Somewhat concerned/varied	27	(40)	8	(27)
4. Usually self-centered	7	(10)	14	(47)
5. Seems indifferent to others	0	(0)	7	(23)
	68	(100)	30	(100)

chi-square = 42.43, 4d.f.; $p < .001$
Average normal rating = 2.53
Average delinquent rating = 3.90

Variable				
Responsibility				
1. Thoroughly dependable	10	(15)	1	(3)
2. Conscientious, but not for others	27	(40)	3	(10)
3. Not consistently dependable	28	(41)	5	(17)
4. Somewhat dependable	1	(1)	14	(47)
5. Unreliable	2	(3)	7	(23)
	68	(100)	30	(100)

chi-square = 49.31, 4d.f.; $p < .001$
Average normal rating = 2.38
Average delinquent rating = 3.77

TABLE 4.3 *(continued)*

Variable	Normal (N = 68)[a]		Delinquent (N = 30)	
	n	%	n	%
Industry				
1. Eager and interested	8	(12)	2	(7)
2. Regular preparation	21	(31)	4	(13)
3. Needs occasional prodding	26	(38)	5	(16)
4. Frequently does not complete	13	(19)	17	(57)
5. Seldom works	0	(0)	2	(7)
	68	(100)	30	(100)

chi-square = 20.26, 4d.f.; $p < .001$
Average normal rating = 2.65
Average delinquent rating = 3.48

[a]Five normal subjects were not rated by teachers on this scale.

[b]Only male delinquents' data are presented because all the normal subjects studied were male; multivariate comparisons among delinquents by demographic category showed significant differences between white and black delinquents with respect to the initiative/creativity variable; therefore, percentages for the nineteen white male delinquents only are shown for this variable.

felt that our treatment program was helping them. It is also possible that we have what Rosenthal (1966) calls the experimenter effect in behavioral science research.

Therefore, it is possible that the normal teenagers have tried to impress us by appearing "normal" while the delinquents may have tried to confirm their status as delinquents.

Communication Patterns in the Families *
of Delinquents and Nondelinquents

Despite the important role played by family structure and relationships in sociologic and psychologic interpretations of personality development, not enough has been done to explore these variables in delinquency research. Most of the family issues have been inferred, probably due to methodological difficulties in studying family relationships. Family struc-

* This section was written by T. Garrick, M.D.

TABLE 4.4

Comparison of Therapist/Interviewer Rating Scale Distributions
Normal vs. Delinquent Males

Variable	Normal (N = 73)		Delinquent (N = 28)[a,b]	
	n	%	n	%
Emotional Experience[c]				
1. Excellent	7	(9)	1	(4)
2. Good	38	(52)	8	(28)
3. Fair	26	(36)	16	(57)
4. Poor	2	(3)	3	(11)
	73	(100)	28	(100)

chi-square = 8.22, 3d.f.; $p < .05$
Average normal rating = 2.32
Average delinquent rating = 2.75

Variable	Normal		Delinquent	
Emotional Expressiveness[c]				
1. Excellent	21	(29)	3	(17)
2. Good	19	(26)	5	(28)
3. Fair	31	(42)	8	(44)
4. Poor	2	(3)	2	(11)
	73	(100)	18	(100)

chi-square = 3.14, 3d.f., *not significant*
   comparing white delinquents and normals
Average normal rating = 2.19
Average white delinquent rating = 2.50

Variable	Normal		Delinquent	
Relationship with Interviewer[c]				
1. Excellent	26	(36)	9	(32)
2. Good	30	(41)	14	(50)
3. Fair	16	(22)	5	(18)
4. Poor	1	(1)	0	(0)
	73	(100)	28	(100)

chi-square = .99, 3d.f.; *not significant*
Average normal rating = 1.89
Average delinquent rating = 1.86

[a]Only male delinquents' data are presented because all the normal subjects studied were male; two male delinquent subjects were not rated by a therapist.

[b]Multivariate comparison among delinquents by demographic category showed significant differences between white and black delinquents with respect to Emotional Expressiveness; therefore, percentages for eighteen white male delinquents only are shown for this variable.

[c]Ratings on the Therapist/Interviewer Rating Scale were available for normals for these variables only.

ture and communication inferences have been drawn primarily from data gathered about the outward structure of the family; e.g., communication patterns among family members; psychiatric data about family dynamics; and parental values as revealed by psychotherapy of the children.

Several quantitative measures and structural variables have been linked to delinquency rates. In correlating the incidence of broken homes with rates of delinquent behavior, Shaw and McKay (1969), using court-reported cases, found only slightly more broken homes in the delinquent population than in the normal. Weeks and Smith (1939) reported significantly higher numbers of delinquents from broken homes, however, and studies by Glueck and Glueck (1950) revealed that 60 percent of the delinquent subjects came from broken homes and 34 percent did not. Browning's (1960) findings showed significantly higher numbers of delinquents coming from "disorganized" homes, while Monahan (1957) found more delinquency recidivism in broken homes, and Slocum and Stone (1963), using Nye short self-reports of delinquency, showed positive correlations between delinquency and broken homes. Many reports have dealt with broken homes and general delinquent behavior, but the relationship between types of delinquent behavior and the timing and type of family disorganization has not been carefully delimited.

Relatively subjective reports on the family structure and its connection to delinquency have been culled from psychiatric case and self-reports. McCord et al. (1959) correlated quarrelsome and negligent homes with delinquency, and found a greater degree of association than that between delinquency and broken homes. Browning (1960) successfully correlated marital adjustment and family solidarity with truancy and auto theft. Nye (1958), using his self-report delinquency scale to measure marital happiness, showed a relationship between parental discord and delinquency, and the Gluecks (1950) found more delinquents than nondelinquents in families where the parents had poor conjugal relations. Using self-reports by school children and scales of self-report delinquency, Slocum and Stone (1963) established that uncooperative families tended to produce the worst delinquency; using self-reports of discipline and delinquency, they correlated reports of "fair" parental discipline with conforming children, and "unfair" parental discipline with "most delinquent." Lax and erratic discipline was correlated with higher rates of juvenile delinquency by the Gluecks (1950), while McCord et al. (1959) reported that consistent discipline, whether oriented toward punishment or love, was associated with lower rates of delinquency. According to Nye (1958), higher numbers of children in the "most delinquent" categories reported that parents did not carry through with threatened punishment. There are conflicting reports on the relationships between delinquency, physical punishment, and love-withdrawal punishment. Generally, however, with the exception of McCord et al. (1959) all of these studies depend on the reports of the children, are after the fact (retrospective), and are, therefore, certainly highly subject to bias.

Affection/acceptance by parents—particularly the father—has been directly related to delinquency (André 1957; Slocum and Stone 1963; Nye 1958). According to Bandura and Walters (1959), aggressive delinquents complained of parents who had not allowed them opportunities to express dependency feelings. These studies are difficult to interpret, since parents may have shown rejection when the child's delinquency became a family issue.

Positive relationships between parents and children have been implicated by psychoanalysts in the effective internalization of parental values, and more particularly in the internalization of positive self-esteem. Johnson (1949) and Johnson and Szurek (1952) studied "superego lacunae," gaps in conscience presumably arising because of inconsistent discipline or messages, while Bowlby (1966) related early internal deprivation to the development of affectionless children. Though these factors do seem to lead to mental illness (Goldfarb 1945), separation alone does not appear to relate to delinquency.

In the past ten years, there has been added to these data-gathering reports an increased number of direct observation studies in which interactional patterns are directly assessed and coded. These methods, too, are plagued by major methodologic weakness in that they assess current and not developmentally prior interactions. Thus they are subject to the bias of any laboratory situation (Fontana 1966; Hatfield et al. 1967; Moustaken et al. 1965; Jacob 1975) in its possible lack of generalizability to a wider field of application, as well as to bias due to the interview method.

Some of these weaknesses in methods of investigation may be lessened in the long run by using multiple approaches in the application and analysis of data, as in Hetherington et al. (1971). The present pilot study uses a kind of self-report technique, and compares different reports by members of the families of juvenile delinquents with those obtained from the families of normal adolescents.

As part of the continuing project which compared juvenile delinquents hospitalized in a psychiatric unit and their families (Offer, Marohn, and Ostrov, 1975; Marohn, Offer, and Ostrov, 1971) with groups of normal adolescents and their families studied previously (Offer 1969), this study attempts to verify three hypotheses: (1) that parents of delinquents see their children as having more difficulties than do parents of normal adolescents; (2) that parents of delinquents are less in touch with their children's feelings about themselves—self-perceptions—than are parents of normal adolescents; and (3) that there is greater disagreement between the parents of delinquents concerning the child's self-image (less communication) than between parents of normal adolescents. Due to the relatively small number of delinquents on whom we have data from parental questionnaires, no distinction was made between types of delinquents in this particular phase of the study. Further nosologic separation and analysis, with respect to the variables studied below, will depend on future investigations. All the delinquents in this study who had two-parent families capable of completing the questionnaires were included in the study. There were forty-six such families (see Table 4.5). Only forty-two were used in this study because two sets of parents were incapable of following the Revealed Differences Procedure described later, while missing OSIQ data precluded the use of two others. The Offer Self-Image Questionnaire (OSIQ) was administered to the delinquents at the time of their admission to the hospital while the Offer Parent-Child Questionnaire (OPCQ) was administered about seven weeks thereafter.

TABLE 4.5

Composition of Hospitalized Delinquent Study Population
Subjects from Two-Parent Families
Used in the Study of Family Communication

Sex	N	Race	N	Age	N
Male	22	White	34	Younger (< 5)	18
Female	20	Black	8	Older	24
Total:	42		42		42

The normal (modal) population with which these delinquents were compared has been studied extensively. Its members were selected from two suburban, largely white, midwest high schools during their sophomore year to be part of a longitudinal study of normal adolescence (Offer 1969). The selection was based on performance on the OSIQ, supplemented by teacher ratings. The OSIQ was given to the children in their sophomore year (i.e., when they were fifteen years old), and the Offer Parent-Child Questionnaire (OPCQ) was given to their parents at the same time. These two questionnaires were also used in the present research with delinquent subjects and their families.

Instruments Used

The OSIQ, previously described in detail, is a self-descriptive test consisting of 130 items which are rated by the child as being more or less true of him on a scale that runs from 1 to 6. Its use in several studies indicates that the findings based on this test correlate with those made by interview and by teacher evaluations.

Using the OPCQ, parents separately rated their child's self-image on a scale from 1 to 6. The OPCQ consists of forty items, each of which also appears in the OSIQ. Items selected were felt from clinical experience to be the items through which parents could best express their understanding of their children. An example of an OPCQ item reads: "My son/daughter thinks he/she will be a source of pride for me in the future"; on the OSIQ this item is phrased: "I think I will be a source of pride for my parents in the future." Items were chosen from eight scales of the OSIQ: impulsivity, external mastery, emotional tone, family relationships, sexual relationships, social attitudes, superior adjustment, and vocational goals.

Statistical Procedure

Multivariate analyses[2] of variance were performed on scale scores from questionnaires, and univariate (t-test) analyses were performed on total questionnaire scores to search for group effects. The demographic factors—age, race, sex, socioeconomic status—were studied with respect to all individual OSIQ and OPCQ scales as well as to total scores. When examined in this fashion, only two group or interaction effects were noted: (1) males and females differed significantly in the OSIQ total scores, with males claiming to be better adjusted than females, and (2) on the total mother's OPCQ scale score, there were major differences between the sexes, with mothers of delinquent girls seeing their daughters as healthier than the mothers of delinquent boys saw their sons ($p < .04$). Because of these differences, and because we had no normal female population to use as a control group, the following comparisons were performed between delinquent and normal boys, with the female delinquent group eliminated.

Past studies with the complete OSIQ have shown highly significant differences between delinquent and normal children. The shorter version of the questionnaire also yields significant differences, with the delinquent boys reporting poorer self-adjustment than normal boys. Moreover, when parental assessment of their children is studied, equally significant differences are found between the parents of normal and delinquent children; the delinquents are seen as having more difficulty in coping, and as having less well-adjusted self-images (see Table 4.6)

TABLE 4.6

Sources Derived from Offer Parent/Child
Questionnaire and Offer Self-Image Questionnaire:[a]
A Comparison of Delinquent and Normal

Questionnaire	Delinquent Boys (N = 22)	Normal Boys (N = 57)	P[b]
Offer Self-Image Questionnaire: Total Score[c]	10.33	8.32	< .001
Offer Parent/Child Questionnaire: Total score:[c] mother	12.94	9.29	< .001
father	13.48	8.87	< .001

[a]Total score is computed so that the lower the score, the healthier the adjustment.
[b]Student t-test: 77 degrees of freedom, two-tailed.
[c]Score is total of component scale scores, and is based on the 40 items used in the OPCQ.

TABLE 4.7

Difference between Parents and Their Individual Children
on the Child's Self-Image as Measured by the
Offer Parent-Child Questionnaire (OPCQ)
and the Offer Self-Image Questionnaire (OSIQ)

	Delinquent Boy's Family	Normal Boy's Family	P[a]
Father: (OPCQ − OSIQ)[b]	31.46	4.56	< .001
Mother: (OPCQ − OSIQ)[b]	26.09	8.72	< .001
Father/Mother: Total Scored Differences question by question[c]	53.77	40.61	< .001

[a]Student's t-test: 77 degrees of freedom, two-tailed.
[b]Total OPCQ score minus total OSIQ score. Each parent-child unit was evaluated and mean result is reported.
[c]Sum of absolute value of differences between father's and mother's responses to each OPCQ item.

The groups were also compared to see how well the parents understood, or communicated with, their children (see Table 4.7). Results indicate that among the families of delinquents differences were greater between parents' view of their child's self-image and that of the child himself than was true among families of modal adolescents. This result was obtained despite the fact that both delinquents and their parents agreed that the delinquents are less well-adjusted than are the normals. Moreover, despite the agreement between parents of delinquents that their child is less well-adjusted, there is more disagreement between them on an item by item basis than there is among parents of normals.

Discussion

This report confirms the three hypotheses noted above: parents see their delinquent children as less well-adjusted than do parents of normal children; parents of delinquents appear to be less in touch with their child's self-image than are parents of modal adolescents; and there is greater lack of understanding about their children between the parents of delinquents than between parents of modal adolescents.

There are three major sources of bias in this study. The first and most important is the mismatch between the experimental and control groups. The controls are a relatively homogeneous group of fifteen-year-old suburban, middle-class whites, while the experimental groups are urban, biracial, and of various ages and classes. Despite this nonuniformity, however, there were no demonstrable effects of age, socioeconomic status, or race noted within the delinquent group on the family variables studied. A sex effect was noted, and for this reason the comparison was limited to boys.

The second major source of bias concerns the generalization of the results: the delinquents were all inpatients in a psychiatric hospital and were referred by law enforcement and social welfare agencies. Since they were sent for psychiatric treatment, this delinquent population might be expected to have a greater number of children with emotional problems than are found in the delinquent population as a whole. Therefore generalizations about communication among delinquents' families in general must be guarded.

Still another source of bias stems from the questionnaire method. Self-report is susceptible to conscious and unconscious distortion (Cronbach and Glaser 1965). One might expect self-flattery to lead self-reports to be more favorable than reports by others, and, in fact, both delinquent and normal groups saw themselves as healthier than their parents saw them. These differences, however, could also result from differing norms between the two generations. In any case, despite any self-flattery, the delinquents typically saw themselves as significantly less well-adjusted than did their normal counterparts. Another perspective on these data is that of the labeling theory (Erikson 1962). The process of arrest leads to identification as a delinquent and admission to a hospital is certain to have an effect on both the delinquents' self-image and on their parents' image of them. This phenomenon could explain the poorer images held by the delinquents themselves and their families but not the poor communication within the delinquents' families.

The Offer questionnaires tap aspects of an adolescent's self-image and of his personal sense of emotional and social adjustment which have been found to correlate with delinquent behavior.

It is possible that the poor affective ties (communication) between parents and children and between the parents themselves as reflected in our OPCQ and OSIQ difference measurements predispose the teenager to seek sources of normative values, self-esteem, affirmation, and reinforcement outside the family—in particular at a time when identity resolution is a prime concern. Relatively close parent/child relationships (Erikson 1950) are important for stable ego development. When these relationships are weak or missing, and are replaced by relationships with deviant peers, deviant and/or poor development can be reflected in delinquent acts, low self-esteem, and instability.

This research illustrates a major difficulty in the study of juvenile delinquency. Delinquency is a legal and social category; it is not a psychiatric diagnostic category. Yet measures of an important area of psychological functioning can yield significant results when applied to delinquent behavior as if it were reflective of a specific pattern of ego development—like a diagnostic category—rather than a set of behaviors reflective of many developmental patterns and personality types.

NOTES

1. The race effect among the delinquents was significant with respect to the rating of emotional expressiveness. Comparing white male delinquents with normal white male adolescents, we find that the X^2 is no longer significant, but the trend in the same: the normal adolescents are rated as more emotionally expressive.

2. The user of MULTIVARIANCE constructs a hypothetical statistical model for examining the effects of independent variables (like race or sex) on the jointly considered dependent variables. The user may also include a covariate in the model, and

examine the effects of the independent variables with the covariate effects statistically eliminated. In this study, for example, we hypothesized that the sex and race of the subjects, when age is controlled, are significantly associated with ratings made by an observer of their behavior. Interactions between the independent variables (race and sex) may also be considered in the model. In order to have sufficient numbers of subjects in each cell, socioeconomic status, also hypothesized to be an important independent variable, was studied separately.

The Prediction of Antisocial Behavior Using the Impulsivity Index

A long tradition of empirical and theoretical work relates impulsivity to delinquent behavior, using the Porteus Maze Test (Porteus 1945), the Matching Familiar Figures Test (Kagan et al. 1954), and reactivity to color on the Rorschach as criterion measures. Our research replicates some of that literature and amplifies it by applying a measure of impulsivity to antisocial behavior as measured repeatedly and objectively through the Adolescent Behavior Check List (ABCL), which also differentiates antisocial behavior into violent and nonviolent categories. In this way we are able to test the relationship between impulsivity and antisocial behavior in a more rigorous, objective fashion than has hitherto been done. At the same time we can make a more rigorous discrimination regarding that relationship by testing the correlation between impulsivity and violent behavior on the one hand, and nonviolent behavior on the other. According to our measures, impulsivity relates more to violent behavior than to nonviolent behavior.

In the present study, impulsivity is conceptualized as a tendency not to delay in a situation calling for a choice among almost equally prepotent alternatives, or as a tendency to act without foresight or long-range planning. A good deal of research evidence indicates that impulsivity is a trait which can be reliably and validly measured, and that it is an important factor in the etiology of delinquent behavior. In this chapter we attempt to predict the extent of observed antisocial behavior among a group of hospitalized delinquents by the use of Rorschach indices and an IQ measure of impulsivity. The following specific hypotheses were tested:

1.   There are no differences by race, sex, social class, or age among the juvenile delinquents in extent of impulsivity as measured by Rorschach and IQ indices, or in the extent of antisocial behavior quantified through use of the ABCL.

2.   There are positive correlations between several separate measures of impulsivity, i.e., the sum color percent, affective ratio, chromatic vs. achromatic time for first response scores on the Rorschach, and the performance minus verbal IQ scores on the Wechsler IQ test (Wechsler 1949, 1955).

3.   There are positive correlations between measures of impulsivity and ABCL measures of antisocial behavior. It was predicted that these correlations would not significantly differ across the various sex by race and social class cells.

Review of the Literature

Freud (1911) viewed impulsivity in terms of the domination of mental functioning by the pleasure principle; impulsive behavior was seen as a failure to postpone immediate gratification despite potentially adverse long-term consequences. Later theorists have written about impulsivity as an aspect of cognitive style (Shapiro 1965; Kagan et al. 1964), viewing impulsivity on a continuum of ways of adaptation to inner and outer reality and, in Shapiro's case, connecting impulsivity with life-style characteristics such as unwillingness to engage in long-range planning and failure to assimilate desires to stable and continuous aims and interests. Another, not very different, tradition has described impulsivity in terms of a proclivity toward choosing smaller, short-term rewards as against larger, long-term rewards in hypothetical situations (e.g., Mischel 1961a; Ainslie 1975).

Impulsivity has been operationally defined on the Rorschach test as a tendency to react more swiftly and intensely to color than to form (Rorschach 1942; Shapiro 1960; Schachtel 1966), while on the Porteus Maze Test it has been defined in terms of carelessness and hastiness (Porteus 1945). It has also been operationalized as a tendency to respond swiftly and inaccurately on the Matching Familiar Figure Test (MFFT; Kagan et al. 1964); to view events with a short-time perspective on a structured test (Stein et al. 1968) or in the course of an unstructured interview (Siegman 1961); and to draw a line or write relatively swiftly when asked to perform these acts as slowly as possible (Siegman 1961; Singer, Wilensky, and McCraven 1956). IQ and specific patterns of intelligence-test functioning are less clearly related to impulsivity, and we will later deal with them more systematically.

Various studies indicate that impulsivity as a character trait is stable over time, and that it generalizes across different testing and nontesting situations. Using Fels Institute longitudinal data, Kagan et al. (1964) reported that vigor of motor activity and degree of sustained attention to visual stimuli were inversely proportional to one another, and were moderately stable from ages eight weeks to fifty-six weeks. The data also indicated that hyperactivity, defined in terms of lack of inhibition or motor discharge, was highly stable for both sexes from ages three to fourteen (Kagan and Moss 1962). The same study reported that boys who were hyperkinetic through ages six to fourteen were found to be "competitive, sexually active and not highly involved in intellectual pursuits" as adults; this correlation, however, was not true of girls. Surveying various longitudinal studies, Schaefer (1964) concluded that the stability from infancy to adulthood of a personality dimension representing degree of extroversion and intensity of affective response was more impressive than the stability of any other personality dimension considered.

Other evidence indicates that the time used by subjects to choose among several almost equally prepotent alternatives is moderately consistent across tasks and modalities and moderately stable for periods of at least a year (Kagan et al. 1964; Kagan 1965). Important cases in point are data which indicate that reaction time for defining vague stimuli presented in a tachistoscope and time for first response on the MFFT are moderately correlated (Kagan 1965), and evidence that the degree of reactivity to color on the Rorschach is relatively stable over an eight-year period (Buben 1975). However, there is also evidence that the extent of impulsivity may be as much a function of reward contingencies, experimenter effects, and other situation variables as it is a function of stable and generalizable characteristics of individual subjects (Mischel and

Metzner 1962; Mischel and Gilligan 1964; Walls and Smith 1970; Shybut 1968). Significant experimenter effects on Rorschach performance have also been demonstrated (Sanders and Cleveland 1953).

Evidence exists pertaining to the concurrent validity of the various indices of impulsivity. Thus it was learned that long response times on several different tasks corresponded to relatively careful and systematic performance on the same tasks (Kagan et al. 1964; Kagan, Pearson, and Welch 1966; Drake 1970), as well as to an analytic attitude on a test of conceptual style (Kagan et al. 1964). Defining reflectives as subjects with above-average reaction times and a below-average propensity toward giving erroneous responses, and defining impulsives as subjects with opposite response characteristics, researchers using direct behavior observation have concluded that impulsive boys are more restless and distractible, have more momentary lapses of attention during involvement with school tasks, and spend more time engaging in gross motor activity than do reflective subjects (Kagan et al. 1964). Campbell (1973) confirmed some of these conclusions when she found that hyperactive second and third graders tended to be impulsive in their cognitive styles as measured by the MFFT, though she also found that another group of equally impulsive children were not hyperactive. Evidence of the validity of one measure of impulsivity was also adduced by Kagan (1965) who, utilizing a developmental perspective, concluded that children tend to manifest fewer errors and increased response latencies on the MFFT as they grow older.

Using the Rorschach, several studies have demonstrated that normal subjects who were rated as showing delay, or who directly exhibited high use of delay in their overt behavior, tended to be low in their reactivity to color as opposed to form (Holtzman 1950; Gardner 1951; Verrill 1958; Gill 1966). Romanella (1967) described more reactivity to color on the Rorschach among subjects rating themselves high in emotionality than among those rating themselves low in emotionality. In a different type of study, Siipola and Taylor (1952) found that subjects under pressure to respond quickly gave more vague, color-dominated responses than did subjects not under such pressure. However, in contrast to studies which tended to confirm Rorschach hypotheses concerning reactivity to color and delay or inhibition, Wolfensberger (1962) reported more use of color among hypokinetic adolescents than among the hyperkinetic when activity level was measured directly in an experimental situation.

There are fewer studies directly linking the other indices of impulsivity with observations of extent of delay among normal subjects. In 1945 Porteus asked foremen in a factory to select twenty-five workers whose work performance was satisfactory and twenty-five whose work was not. Despite the fact that the groups were not different in education or social status, he found significant differences in the predicted direction in the quality of the groups' Porteus Maze Test performance. Mischel (1961b) successfully predicted relationships among cultural and familial factors and impulsive behavior, defined as preference for immediate reward as opposed to that in the long term. In another study, older children evinced a greater tendency to choose delayed rewards than did young children, confirming the expectation that impulsivity tends to decrease with age (Mischel and Metzner 1962).

Concerning relationships among the various indices of impulsivity, when given a choice between matching on the basis of either form or color, subjects classified as reflectives by their MFFT performances were more likely to use form to match a standard (Katz 1971). In solving the Porteus Maze Test, MFFT-defined reflectives tended to perform more successfully than did impulsives (Shipe 1971; Weintraub 1973). La Barba (1965), however, found no correlation between careless performance on the Porteus and reactivity to color on the Rorschach. With respect to feelings about the future, one study indicated that subjects who are reflective on the MFFT are more inclined to tell stories on projectives which involve expectations of success than are impulsives, while the latter are prone to accept frustration as inevitable (Campbell and Douglas 1972). Evidence also exists that impulsives are less able to inhibit action than are reflectives (Harrison and Nadleman 1972) and that subjects who commit many errors on a paper and pencil test have relatively poor ability to prolong drawing a line when requested to do so (Kagan et al. 1964). Moderate correlations also have been obtained between various indices of impulsivity and IQ (Porteus 1945; Mischel and Metzner 1962; Kagan et al. 1964), and more specifically between one measure of reactivity to color on the Rorschach and discrepancies in performance-verbal IQ (Ostrov et al. 1972).

In contrast to studies which show positive interrelationships between impulsivity measures, results have been more mixed concerning relationships between preference for short- or long-term reward and impulsivity/ reflection as measured by performance on the MFFT (Shipe 1971; Mann 1973). However, defining delayers as subjects who chose a pack of cigarettes nine days later instead of one cigarette right away, Roberts and Erikson (1968) published evidence tending to confirm the hypothesis that delayers would perform more carelessly on the Porteus. The authors of that study obtained similar results by defining the subjects' propensity toward a long- or short-term future perspective by using subjects' answers to a question about how they would spend a given sum of money. With the possible exception of the ability or inability to prolong motor tasks, all the various indices of impulsivity cited above have been linked repeatedly with extent of delinquency and, in particular, with violent behavior.

Studies using the Rorschach Test have frequently shown that patients or criminals with histories of assaultive behavior tend to give more color-dominated responses than do less assaultive patients or criminals (Storment and Finney 1953; Misch 1954; Finney 1955; Townsend 1967; Ostrov et al. 1972). Similarly, in 1954 Singer and Spohn found that high color reactivity on the Rorschach characterized the more active among schizophrenic subjects whose behavior in a waiting room was under covert observation. Cerney and Shevrin (1974) demonstrated a significant association between assaultive or acting-out behavior on an inpatient ward and responsiveness to color on the Rorschach. Studies contrasting delinquents and nondelinquents have not been as successful. Robbertse (1955) did find that one hundred children who manifested conduct disorders were more reactive to color than were matched, nondelinquent controls. But no significant differences along this dimension were found between delinquents and control subjects by Boynton and Walsworth (1943) or Schachtel (1950), though the latter claimed to have used labile or impulsive reactivity to color as one factor in his successful blind differentiation of delinquent Rorschach protocols from those of matched nondelinquents.

Attempts to link impulsivity with extent of delinquent behavior, using measures of impulsivity based on tests other than the Rorschach, have also met with some success. Studies using the Porteus Maze Test have consistently shown delinquents to be less careful and more impulsive in executing the mazes than are nondelinquents, though they are not necessarily less effective (Porteus 1942, 1945; Wright 1944; Foulds 1951; Docter and Winder 1954; Fooks and Thomas 1957). Moreover, significant Porteus Q-score differences have been found among delinquents differing in quality of adjustment in a training school (Erikson and Roberts 1966, 1971), and extent of recidivism after discharge from the training school (Roberts, Erikson, Riddle, and Bacon 1974).

Other studies indicate that stories told by delinquents cover shorter time periods than those of matched control subjects (Barndt and Johnson 1955). Shorter future time perspective among delinquents has also been reported by Siegman (1961), Davids, Kidder, and Reich (1962), Stein, Sarbin, and Kulik (1968), Erikson and Roberts (1971), and Roberts, Erikson, Riddle, and Bacon (1974).

Defining impulsivity in terms of preference for immediate smaller rewards as opposed to larger delayed rewards, Mischel (1961a) showed that a significantly larger proportion of delinquents as opposed to nondelinquents were impulsive, and that within each group those subjects who preferred delay tended to rate themselves higher in social responsibility; Mischel and Gilligan (1964) demonstrated that children who prefer delayed larger rewards are less apt to cheat than are children who prefer immediate smaller rewards; if they do cheat, they resist doing so longer. More recently, using measures of impulsivity analogous to those used by Mischel, Shybut (1968) reported findings which indicate that psychotic patients are more impulsive than patients characterized as having neuroses or character disorders, while the latter, in turn, give evidence of being more impulsive than normal subjects.

As mentioned earlier, impulsivity, defined by performance on the MFFT by preschool and grade school children, has been connected with restlessness and distractibility, a tendency to engage in gross motor activity, lack of persistence in solving tasks, and an inclination toward physically dangerous activities. Consistent with these results, Keogh and Donlon (1972) adduced evidence that children with severe learning disorders are more impulsive in their performance on the Matching Familiar Figures Test than are children with moderate learning disorders. In a study by Zern, Kenney, and Kvaraceus (1974), moreover, adolescent patients who presented symptoms involving assault or other delinquent behaviors performed more impulsively on the MFFT than did adolescent patients characterized by withdrawal, fear, or depression.

Several authors have noted a link between a specific IQ-score pattern (higher performance IQ than verbal) and psychopathy (Wechsler 1944; Schafer 1948). Schafer's description of the psychopath's IQ test performance could be linked with impulsive behavior; the psychopath was described as a "bland, unreflective, action-oriented person whose judgment is poor, whose conceptual development is weak, but whose grasp of social situations may be quick and accurate." The psychopath's chief psychological feature was qualitatively described as "blazing recklessness in guessing at answers." Empirical findings that compared delinquents and nondelinquents have been mixed (Glueck and Glueck 1950; Vane and Eisen 1954; Blank 1958; Wiens, Matarazzo, and Garver 1959; Field 1960; Kingsley 1960; Fisher 1961; Manne, Kandel, and Rosenthal 1962), a situation complicated by the fact that many studies fail to control for social class when comparing groups. The best-controlled and largest study, however, that of the Gluecks (1950), did find differences between delinquents and nondelinquents which tended to confirm observations by Wechsler and Schafer.

PART II / RESULTS

Method and Instruments

The sample under study consisted of the subjects admitted to the Adolescent Unit (as described in chapter 2) who gave at least ten responses on the Rorschach. Only one of the fifty-five subjects studied did not give as many as ten Rorschach responses so that data from fifty-four subjects were available for analysis.

Rorschach Measures

During the first week of hospitalization, the Rorschach and Wechsler intelligence tests were routinely administered to all patients admitted to the unit. The Rorschach was administered and scored according to Beck et al. (1961). Following Ostrov et al. (1972), three indices of reactivity to color were chosen; the subjects were ranked on: (1) Sum color divided by the total number of responses (sum color percent); (2) The affective ratio—that is, the number of responses to the last three all-color cards on the Rorschach divided by the number of responses to the first eight black and white or part-color/part-black and white cards; and (3) The average time for first response for color cards, subtracted from the average time for first response for noncolor cards, divided by the average time for first response for all cards taken together (called the "time for first response measure" in this chapter). Ranks were used, and not absolute values, to ensure that extreme scores on any of the measures would not unduly affect the results.

Wechsler Measures

The Wechsler was scored in the standard way (Wechsler 1949, 1955), and performance/verbal IQ discrepancies were expressed as a percentage of total score to allow for the possibility that, say, a 10-point discrepancy meant more with a total IQ of 80 than with a total IQ of 120.

Impulsivity Index

When the ranks on the above measures were added, the subject's rank on the sum of ranks comprised his impulsivity index score. In the statistical procedures, the identity of the components of the impulsivity index were also retained in separate multivariate analyses to obtain more information about the contribution to any significant results made by individual impulsivity index components.

104

Adolescent Behavior Check List (ABCL)

The behavior of each of the fifty-four disturbed adolescent delinquents was rated during the initial thirteen weeks of hospitalization by use of the ABCL, a coded list (see chapter 2) containing about 350 items, each describing a discrete act of antisocial behavior and weighted for severity according to ratings made by a panel of judges prior to utilization of the ABCL. At the end of every shift, school day, or activity, each patient's antisocial behavior, if any, was assessed and coded by the staff onto IBM coding sheets, using the listed numbers. Behavior ratings for each patient were converted into weighted scores and summed by computer across shifts and activities into categories of violence toward property, violence toward others, violence toward self, and nonviolent antisocial behavior. The ABCL scores served as dependent variables for the study.

Statistical Analyses

The hypotheses were tested by use of a preprogrammed multivariate analysis of variance program called MULTIVARIANCE (Finn 1972) (See note 2 in chapter 4). In this study, the impulsivity index scores were intercorrelated and then regressed onto the ABCL scores, with age, sex, social class, and race effects statistically removed. Demographic effects on the ABCL scores and the impulsivity index were weighed, using multivariate analysis of variance techniques. Parallelism of regression planes across various demographic cells was tested with respect to the association between the impulsivity index, on the one hand, and the ABCL scores on the other. Furthermore, the components of the impulsivity index (the Rorschach and IQ measures separately) were run against ranked ABCL scores in a canonical correlation analysis to assess the contribution of each component to predictions of ABCL variance. ABCL ranks were used to eliminate the possibility that outlyers were accounting for any significant associations found between impulsivity and ABCL scores.

Results

1. The impulsivity index components did not, for the most part, significantly correlate with one another. The only significant correlation was that between the Wechsler measure and the time for first response measure (see Table 5.1).

TABLE 5.1

*Intercorrelation of the Wechsler and Rorschach Measures that Comprise
the Impulsivity Index with the Effects of Race and Sex Eliminated
(N = 54)*

		1	2	3	4
1.	Performance minus verbal IQ divided by total IQ	–	–	–	–
2.	Average time for first response for achromatic Rorschach cards minus average time for first response for chromatic Rorschach cards divided by average time for first response on all Rorschach cards	.26[a]	–	–	–
3.	Affective ratio	−.10	.14	–	–
4.	Sum color percent	−.04	.03	.13	–

[a]Significant at the .05 level in a one-tailed test.

2.   There were no significant effects on the impulsivity index of social class, age, sex, race, or sex by race. There was only one significant demographic effect on the four ABCL measures taken together: that of sex. Girls showed less antisocial behavior than boys in every dimension except violence toward self. With respect to the latter variable, girls were more antisocial.

3.   Adding the impulsivity index to the regression equation predicting ABCL scores, with age and social class as the other two predictors and sex and race as independent ways of classification, it was found that the impulsivity index contribution was significant at less than the .01 level (see Table 5.2). Examination of the contribution of impulsivity index scores to the variance of each of the ABCL scores individually shows that the main association is between the impulsivity index and the three measures of violent behavior; the association of the impulsivity index and nonviolent antisocial behavior was not significant. A test of parallelism of regression hyperplanes between impulsivity index and ABCL scores across status by sex by age cells shows a significant effect of status (upper-white, lower-white, black), sex, and age on the degree of association between the impulsivity index and ABCL scores. A canonical correlation relating the impulsivity index to ABCL scores also shows the relationship between impulsivity and violent as opposed to nonviolent antisocial behavior (see Table 5.3).

4.   In a canonical correlation analysis comparing components of the impulsivity index with ABCL-score ranks, with age, sex, and status as

TABLE 5.2

*Multiple Regression of the Impulsivity
Index onto Adolescent Behavior
Check List (ABCL) Scores*
(N = 54)

Items from the ABCL[a]	Standardized Regression Coefficients[b] for the Impulsivity Index[c]
Violence toward property	.44
Violence toward others	.36
Violence toward self	.25
Nonviolent behavior	−.02

Adding the impulsivity index to the regression equation predicting all four ABCL scores, $F = 4.5035$ with 4 and 44 degrees of freedom, $p < .0039$.

[a]The higher the score, the more antisocial behavior.
[b]A test of parallelism of regression hyperplanes across sex, age, and status (upper-white, lower-white, and black) cells produced an F-statistic = 2.3524 with 40 and 108 degrees of freedom, $p < .0003$, for the association of ABCL scores and the impulsivity index.
[c]The higher the score, the more impulsive.

independent ways of classification, it was found that the impulsivity index components accounted for 12 percent of the ABCL score variance, and that the two variable clusters were associated at the .05 level (see Table 5.4). In addition, detailed examination of the canonical coefficients showed that violence was associated with a relatively large number of responses on the Rorschach, high affective ratio score, low IQ, and low time of first response for color as opposed to black and white (see Table 5.4).

Discussion

This study obtained some success in predicting the extent of observed antisocial behavior through the use of selected measures of impulsivity. The results therefore support the theories which link impulsivity and delinquent behavior. The data here presented link a measure of impulsivity

PART II / RESULTS

TABLE 5.3
Canonical Correlation Relating the Impulsivity Index to
Adolescent Behavior Check List (ABCL) Scores with Age and
Social Class as the Other Predictors and Race and Sex
as Independent Ways of Classification
(N = 54)

Variables	Correlations with First Canonical Variate[a]
Dependent:[b]	
1. Violence toward property	.85
2. Violence toward others	.75
3. Violence toward self	.50
4. Nonviolent antisocial behavior	.09
Independent:	
1. Social class[c]	.36
2. Age[d]	−.23
3. Impulsivity index[e]	.91

[a]The first canonical correlation accounts for 8.05 percent of the variation in the dependent variables.
[b]The higher the score, the more antisocial behavior.
[c]The higher the score, the lower the social class; score is derived from Hollingshead (1965).
[d]The higher the score +2, the older; the age was measured in months.
[e]The higher the score +2, the more impulsive.

to systematically recorded, direct observations of violent and nonviolent antisocial behavior. This method of quantifying the extent of delinquent behavior contrasts with the use of self-report or official records. By using the ABCL, we avoided the retrospective exaggeration or minimization to which self-reported attestation of delinquency is susceptible (McCandless, Persons, and Roberts 1972; Fabianic 1972). By conducting comparisons within a delinquent group instead of contrasting "delinquents" and "non-delinquents," and by using observed behavior as a data source, we avoided the systematic biases that tend to operate on decisions about whether to arrest or convict (Arnold 1971; Williams and Gold 1972; McCord, McCord, and Zola 1959) and, on the personality level, on who gets caught for misdeeds and who does not. On the negative side, the findings presented herein may be limited in their general application, since it is possible that within-hospital delinquency is not connected with the extent or type of delinquency in a less-structured setting.

Another consideration is the validity of the unitary concept of "impul-

TABLE 5.4

Canonical Correlation Relating Components of the Impulsivity
Index to Adolescent Behavior Check List (ABCL) Rank Scores
with Age, Sex, and Status (Upper White, Lower White, and Black)
as Independent Ways of Classification
(N = 54)

Variables	Correlation with First Canonical Variate
Dependent:[a]	
1. Violence toward property	.69
2. Violence toward others	.67
3. Violence toward self	.57
4. Nonviolent antisocial behavior	.07
Independent:	
1. Total number of responses, Rorschach[b]	.59
2. Affective ratio[c]	.54
3. Overall time for first response, Rorschach[d]	−.25
4. Performance minus verbal IQ[e]	−.08
5. Total IQ[f]	−.38
6. Average time for first response for chromatic Rorschach cards minus average time for first response for achromatic Rorschach cards[g]	−.70
7. Sum color[h]	.14

In the regression analysis linking the dependent and independent variables, the F-value for the test of the hypothesis of no association between these sets of variables − 1.7751 with 28 and 117 d.f., $p < .0184$.

The first canonical correlation accounts for 12 percent of the variation in the dependent variables.

[a] The higher the score, the more antisocial behavior.
[b] The higher the score, the more Rorschach responses.
[c] The higher the score, the more affective ratio.
[d] The higher the score, the longer time for first response.
[e] The higher the score, the higher the performance IQ relative to verbal IQ.
[f] The higher the score, the higher the total IQ.
[g] The higher the score, the longer the chromatic time for first response on the Rorschach relative to achromatic time for first response.
[h] The higher the score, the higher the total color score on the Rorschach.

sivity." Pertinent to this issue are the nonsignificant correlations found among the various Rorschach indices of impulsivity. The fact that the time for first response measure and the affective ratio did not significantly correlate with one another, but that each did associate in the predicted direction with ABCL violence scores, implies that these measures either tap into more than one kind of impulsivity, or that associations between violence and constructs other than impulsivity are being measured. Similarly, the separate association with violence of both overall time for first response to the Rorschach and time for first response to chromatic as opposed to achromatic cards suggests that at least two possible kinds of impulsivity, a lack of delay in the face of multiple choices (Kagan et al. 1964) and a proclivity to being swept away by emotion (Schachtel 1966), may be separately and effectively operative. Studies cited earlier, which indicate that impulsivity as defined by Kagan does not significantly intercorrelate with impulsivity as defined by Mischel, would also suggest that impulsivity may not represent a unitary psychological concept. The fact that associations between impulsivity and antisocial behavior were not consistent across demographic cells further complicates the picture by suggesting that the psychological constructs may not operate the same way in each cell. However, the importance of this result is mitigated by the fact that there were small numbers in each cell, a fact which increases the possibility that sampling artifact was the controlling factor.

Further research is generally needed to elucidate relationships between various indices of impulsivity and various kinds of overt behavior. The contribution of situational factors, motivational states, and previous training or life experiences all need to be considered and systematically weighed. The relationship between impulsivity and violence particularly needs clarification with respect to the role of ego deficit (cf. Friedlander 1945), hostility (cf. Ostrov et al. 1972), and expectations of reward and punishment.

Another area calling for clarification is the relationship between impulsivity/reflection and other cognitive style dimensions. Data from Kagan et al. (1964) seem to suggest that verbal IQ, impulsivity/reflection, and field independence/dependence are orthogonal psychological constructs. In this paper the failure of performance/verbal IQ differences to predict violent behavior probably reflects the muddling of separable factors such as motivation, impulsivity/reflection, and field independence/dependence (cf. Cohen 1957) in as gross a concept as performance IQ.

In sum, an attempt was made to use reliable, valid, relevant measures of personality functioning to compare delinquents to one another, thus avoiding either differences attributable to having been labeled as delinquent or treated as such, or differences corresponding to traits which led the subject to get caught or labeled as opposed to those which led to the delinquent act. This chapter also endeavored to assess and to statistically control for a variety of demographic effects and to measure delinquent behavior through quantified observations of violent and nonviolent delinquent behavior, thereby making it unnecessary to rely on unsystematic or biased reports of behavior. A measure of success was obtained in predicting, not explaining post-hoc, the extent of violent behavior. Future research is needed to clarify relationships among various indices of impulsivity and factors such as motivation, situational variables, and specific learning experiences which may modify the relationship between an impulsive style and overt behavior.

6

Patterns of Cognitive Control Functioning Among Delinquents

There is a large body of evidence that connects cognitive style functioning with behavioral manifestations (Klein 1954; Gardner et al. 1959; Gardner, Jackson, and Messick 1960; Witkin et al. 1954, 1962). Witkin (1964, 1969) for example, found that field-independent people tend to be self-assertive, self-reliant, and cold and distant toward others. Field-dependent people tend to be impulsive and to have poor body image, as well as to be conforming, warm, and gregarious. Sharpeners tend to confront anxiety-provoking situations directly (Israel 1969) while levelers are likely to use repression as a defense (Holzman and Gardner 1959).

Another body of psychological literature describes delinquents as having particular kinds of characterological functioning—as being cold and distant, self-reliant, nonconformist, and impulsive (e.g., Healy and Bronner 1936; Aichorn 1935; Glueck and Glueck 1950; Conger 1966). Despite the evidence of particular kinds of delinquent psychological functioning, and evidence described above which connects cognitive style functioning with certain behavioral and psychological manifestations, few studies of delinquents' cognitive styles have ever been conducted.

In this project our studies of biopsychosocial aspects of hospitalized juvenile delinquents included an analysis of cognitive control functioning, using two control groups to help elaborate the meaning of our findings.

This chapter will report on the hypotheses and the methods used in the study of delinquents' cognitive control functioning and will describe main findings. A discussion of the significance of the results and an attempt to integrate them with other findings will be found in Part Three.

Studies comparing the functioning of delinquents and nondelinquents were surveyed in 1950 by Schuessler and Cressey, who concluded that such research generally suffers from (1) use of inadequate control groups, (2) reliance on unreliable or invalid measures of psychological functioning, and (3) failure to recognize situational and demographic influences on the psychological measures used. By using measures of cognitive controls, measures which have been shown to be reliable, valid, and stable (references cited below), and by using carefully matched nondelinquents as control groups, this study sought to avoid some of the pitfalls Schuessler and Cressey described.

Cognitive controls refer to observations of relatively enduring intrapersonal consistencies in cognitive and perceptual behaviors by which individuals encounter their environments, interact with them, and shape them. Klein (1954), Holzman (1954), Gardner et al. (1959), and others have used the concept of cognitive controls to indicate relatively autonomous structural arrangements that help to shape drive expression, that mediate between drives or intentions, and that manifest themselves as individual consistencies in cognitive behavior. As distinguished from defenses, cognitive controls are apparent as typical modes of adaptive functioning across situations, whether or not the situations evoke intrapsychic conflict. Cognitive controls, in fact, are usually measured through the use of non-threatening, anxiety-free psychophysical tasks (Klein 1958).

Cognitive controls have been shown to be reliable and stable over time (e.g., Gardner and Long 1960; Witkin et al. 1962). Evidence of the stability of field articulation is particularly notable. Infants who were later to become relatively field independent, for instance, showed more vigorous and smoother sucking, a slower rate of falling asleep, and a milder response to body contact than did infants who were to become more field dependent (Witkin 1969). Children whose test results implied that they were field independent at age six were rated at age two-and-a-half as having a higher degree of sustained directed activity in play than did field-dependent children, and as having a lower proclivity toward physical contact and less frequent attention-seeking behavior (Wender, Pedersen, and Waldrop 1967).

As noted before, despite evidence that cognitive control functioning is relevant to psychological aspects of delinquent behavior, a survey of the literature revealed only a small number of studies pertinent to delinquents' cognitive styles. Eskin (1960) found that the group of convicts he studied was somewhat more field dependent than was a control group; his control group, however, was not matched with the experimental group for social class or race. Other indirect evidence, in fact, indicates that delinquents by and large may be more field independent than are control subjects. Shulman (1929) reported that delinquents were less intelligent than same-sex nondelinquent siblings on the Stanford-Binet test, which is largely verbal, but were superior on a test of mechanical ability, an ability often associated with spatial ability or field independence. Delinquents, moreover, are reported to do particularly well on the Object Assembly and Block Design subtests of the WISC or WAIS (Wechsler 1949; Glueck and Glueck 1950; Blank 1958). Of the various Wechsler subtests, Cohen (1957) and Witkin (1964) found that Block Design and Object Assembly are among the best measures of "perceptual organization" or field independence-dependence. Other studies (Kissel, 1966; Levy, 1972) have described delinquent subgroups according to differences in cognitive style; but as far as could be determined there has never been a systematic comparison of the functioning of delinquents and nondelinquents on several cognitive control dimensions other than the research herein presented.

The validity of designating the target group as "delinquent" and the control groups as "nondelinquent" was tested by including a self-report measure of the extent of previous delinquent behavior in the test battery. The need for validation of these designations is illustrated by the numerous studies mentioned in the previous chapter (Short and Nye 1957; McCord, McCord, and Zola 1959; Arnold 1971; Williams and Gold 1972) which have found evidence of bias in the judicial process whether at the police or court level, a bias which tends to cast doubt on official designations as adequate indicators of the extent of actual delinquency.

Three specific hypotheses were tested in the present study:

1.   Adolescents designated as "delinquent" by various authorities claim to have committed significantly more delinquent acts than control groups who, as indicated by various authorities, are less delinquent.[1]

2.   Delinquents show patterns of cognitive control functioning which differ from the patterns shown by a group of nondelinquent siblings. Differences between these two groups do not reflect the effects of sex, race, social class, and IQ.

3.   Differences in cognitive controls between delinquents and nondelinquent but psychiatrically disturbed control subjects parallel the differences in cognitive control functioning found between delinquents and their nondelinquent siblings.

Method and Measures

The delinquent subjects who made up the sample used herein were consecutive referrals to the adolescent delinquency treatment and research program used in the larger research project described in this book. Overlap between subjects used in this study and those used in the main project while extensive is not identical for three reasons. First, this study began about a year after the main project as additional research. Second, subjects were used in this study whether or not they were admitted to the inpatient ward—referral for delinquency was sufficient. Third, to ensure a control group matched for sex, race, social class, neighborhood, and family of origin, a subject was used only if he or she had a sibling who was within three years of his or her age, and who was identified by the referral source

TABLE 6.1

Number of Subjects in the Delinquent Target Group, the Nondelinquent Sibling Control Group, and the Nondelinquent Institutionalized Psychiatrically Disturbed Control Group, and the Number of Sibling Pairs

| Subjects | Delinquent Target Group | Nondelinquent Siblings | | | Nondelinquent Institutionalized Adolescents |
		Pairs	Higher Class[a]	Lower Class[a]	
Male	17	17			11
Female	20	20			19
Male/female pairs		11			
Female/male pairs		5			
Same-sex pairs[b]					
Male: 17					
black			2	6	
white			2	7	
mean age (in months)	175.6	175.5			
Female: 20					
black			1	6	
white			9	4	
mean age (in months)	191.7	183.4			

[a]The division of social class into "higher" and "lower" is based on Hollingshead's (1965) rating of father's occupation; classes 1-3 were considered "higher" and classes 4-7 were considered "lower."

[b]In each demographic cell.

as being relatively nondelinquent.[2] The completed experimental and control groups consisted of thirty-seven same-sex sibling pairs.[3] On the average, the delinquent girls were eight months older than their same-sex siblings, while the delinquent boys and their male siblings had almost exactly the same mean age (see Table 6.1).

Another control group was selected from adolescents institutionalized in the state hospital in programs other than that concerning delinquency, and from the psychiatric wards of a private hospital. Thirty adolescents whose charts indicated that delinquency was not a major aspect of their symptomatology were chosen for this group.

Cognitive Control Measures

The standard battery of tests for measuring cognitive controls has been extensively described by Gardner et al. (1959), Gardner and Moriarty (1968) Holzman and Rousey (1971), and Otteson and Holzman (1976); their reliability has been documented by Witkin et al. (1962), and Gardner and Long (1960). Briefly, the tests given to all subjects in this research substudy were:

Rod and Frame Test. This measure was included because of its reliably high loadings on a field articulation factor (Gardner et al. 1959; Gardner and Moriarty 1968; Holzman and Rousey 1971; Witkin et al. 1954, 1962). Field articulation is assumed to reflect the degree to which subjects are able to differentiate aspects of a stimulus field.

The apparatus used in the present study, a portable variation of Witkin's original test,[4] consisted of a chamber into which the subject looked so that all he could see was a rod contained in a frame both of which were tilted at various angles with respect to the vertical. The rod and frame rotated separately with respect to a common axis. After the instructions (Oltman 1968) were read to the subject, he or she was given eight trials to adjust the rod to the vertical position, each trial beginning with both the rod and frame tilted 28° in the same or opposite directions. The score was the sum of the absolute value of the deviations of the rod from true vertical across eight trials. The larger the score the more the subject's judgments were influenced by the position of the frame and the more field dependent that subject was considered to be.

Concealed Figures Test. This pencil-and-paper test, used by Thurstone (1944) as an indicator for "flexibility of closure," has also been found to be a reliable measure of field articulation (Gardner and Long 1960; Gardner and Moriarty 1968; Holzman and Rousey 1971). The subject was presented with rows of test items in which a simple figure was located at the left, followed by a row of four complex designs. Each subject was then asked to locate the figure in as many of the designs as possible within a five-minute time period. The score was the total number of figures correctly checked minus the total number of incorrect checks.

Size Estimation Test. In this test the subject sits before a screen on which a circle of light is projected. He can change the size of the circle by turning a crank and his task is to make the circle appear to be the same size as a disc he holds in his left hand. Measures include the sum of size errors across trials, time per trial to complete the task and the number of times per trial the subject looked from the disc to the circle of light as he performed the task. Size estimation was included as a measure of the extensiveness of scanning. Originating with the work of Schlesinger (1954), scanning is currently thought to reflect style of attention deployment, especially in tasks that require precise comparisons of sizes (Holzman and Rousey 1971). Although earlier studies relied on constant error scores in size estimation tasks as the primary measure of this cognitive control, recent studies (Gardner 1970; Holzman and Rousey 1971) have suggested that meticulousness as reflected in the number of looks at the standard may be a more appropriate measure of scanning.

Stroop Color-Word Interference Test. Thurstone's (1944) modification of Stroop's original test was used as a measure of constricted/flexible control. This cognitive control was first formulated by Klein (1954) in a study of the differential effects of needs on perception as mediated by the individual's cognitive control preference. The task consists of three parts: first the subject reads the names of various colors "red," "blue" etc. printed on a page; next the subject reads off the colors of asterisks printed on a second page; the asterisks are printed in colors corresponding to the color names printed on the previous page. Finally, the subject reads color names printed in ink of a different color than that designated by the name. To perform this last task successfully, the subject must inhibit irrelevant over-learned, and highly compelling responses in order to read words rather than to name competing visible colors. The expected performance is based on a regression equation computed from the subject's reading scores when naming the colors. The interference score is the difference between the subject's actual time for reading color names printed in the wrong colors and his expected performance. Subjects were penalized for mistakes by multiplying the total number of errors by one-hundredth of the total time on a particular page and adding that to the total score.

Another score reflected differences in the time subjects took to read the colored asterisks and the time they took to read the names of the colors printed in black ink. Stroop (1935) used this score to measure subjects' development throughout grade school with respect to cathexis of words as opposed to the colors designated by the words.

Schematizing Test. This test is used to quantify the leveling/sharpening cognitive control, a cognitive control that reflects the extent to which subjects are influenced by previous and similar stimuli in making size judgments. The Schematizing Test involves judging the size of ninety squares presented sequentially on a screen in such a way that the mean size of the squares projected increases subtly across series of five, while, within each series of five, the squares are presented in a fixed, not necessarily increasing-size order. A detailed description of the apparatus and instructions was provided by Gardner et al. (1959). The test measures (a) the degree to which subjects are capable of making accurate size discriminations between the successively appearing squares (as reflected in an accuracy score), and (b) the degree to which subjects lag behind the progressive increase in the size of the squares throughout the total test sequence (as reflected in a mean increment error score and a lag score). These two scores are thought to reflect assimilation effects; for example, new squares of a larger size may tend to be assimilated into the trace aggregate of the previous squares, thereby resulting in underestimation of the increase in series means across time. Levelers show extreme underestimation (i.e., high assimilation effects), and are therefore assumed to form relatively undifferentiated memory schemata; sharpeners, however, seem to form relatively discrete memories of successive stimuli which remain relatively unaltered and recoverable. The scores used are the (a)) mean increment error, (b) accuracy, and (c) lag scores (Gardner and Moriarty 1968).

Cognitive Abilities

Estimates of general intellectual and visual-motor abilities were obtained by administering five subtests of the Wechsler Adult Intelligence Scale (WAIS) for subjects over sixteen years old (Wechsler 1955), or the Wechsler Intelligence Scale for Children (WISC) for subjects under sixteen (Wechsler 1949). Specifically, all subjects took the Information and Vocabulary subtests as measures of verbal facility, and those of Block Design and Object Assembly as additional measures of field articulation. A fifth subscale, Digit Symbol, was also included because it was thought to measure a simple perceptual-motor skill as opposed to the inhibitory restructuring task presented by a test like the Rod and Frame (Broverman, Klaiber, Kobayashi, and Vogel 1968). Finally, the Spatial Relations Test (Thurstone and Thurstone 1963), a subtest of the Thurstone Primary Abilities Test, was administered; this could be expected in a factor analysis of ability scores to load on a field articulation factor as well.

Delinquent Behavior

All subjects completed the Delinquency Check List (DCL) (Kulik, Stein, and Sarbin 1958)—a self-report of various delinquent acts committed by the subject (see chapter 2). Four subscores and the total score were the measures of extent and type of delinquency.[5]

The dependent variables used in this study were:
1. Information subtest score (WISC or WAIS)
2. Vocabulary subtest score (WISC or WAIS)
3. Object Assembly subtest score (WISC or WAIS)
4. Block Design subtest score (WISC or WAIS)

5. Digit Symbol (or Coding) subtest score (WISC or WAIS) [6]
6. The raw score (number right minus number wrong) on the Spatial Relations subtest (Primary Mental Abilities)
7. The lag score (Schematizing Test)
8. The mean percent increment error score (Schematizing Test)
9. The ranking accuracy score (Schematizing Test)
10. Mean number of looks to the standard per trial (Size Estimation Test)
11. Time per trial (Size Estimation Test)
12. Average error per trial (Size Estimation Test)
13. Regressed time to read colors (Color/Word Test)
14. Color-word interference score (Color/Word Test)
15. Sum of absolute value of degrees of deviation from vertical (Rod and Frame Test)
16. Number correct minus number incorrect answers (Concealed Figures Test)
17. Total score (DCL)
18. Delinquent role score (DCL)
19. Drug usage score (DCL)
20. Parental defiance score (DCL)
21. Assaultiveness score (DCL)

Statistical Analysis

Multivariate analyses of variance were performed using a program called MULTIVARIANCE (Finn 1972) based on algorithms developed by Bock (1963). Specifically, differences between scores of delinquents and the less-delinquent, same-sex siblings, with respect to nineteen dependent variables without Vocabulary or Information, were subjected to multivariate analysis of variance.[7] Race and social class were independent variables, while age and the Vocabulary subtest score were treated as covariates. Since there were only seventeen pairs of males and twenty pairs of females, degrees of freedom were not sufficient to consider the fourteen cognitive control variables simultaneously in one multivariate analysis. These variables therefore were clustered in groups based on information in the cognitive style literature. The DCL variables were considered together in separate multivariate analyses. To increase the number of degrees of freedom in the denominator of the F ratio, the error term for these analyses was obtained by pooling within cell variance across male/male and female/female sibling pairs. This pooling technique seemed justifiable, since standard deviations for the difference scores for male and female sibling pairs respectively were reasonably close to one another in value.

In another analysis, the psychiatrically disturbed groups—delinquent and nondelinquent—were contrasted through multivariate analyses with respect to fourteen cognitive control variables [8] and five DCL variables; race, social class, and sex were other independent effects, and age and Vocabulary were covariates.

Results

Sibling Pair Contrasts

Tables 6.2, 6.3, and 6.4 show the results of comparisons between the male sibling pairs. With age and Vocabulary partialed out, the delinquent group reported significantly more overall delinquent behavior for all social class and race categories. Differences between male delinquents and their siblings were greatest with respect to assaultive behavior; according to the observed means, the delinquents reported almost four times as much assaultive behavior as their siblings.

Multivariate analysis of the cluster of tests tapping field articulation

TABLE 6.2

Delinquency Check List Score Differences between Male Delinquents and Their Nondelinquent Siblings
(N = 17 pairs)

| | Raw Data | | Covariate Analysis | |
| | Observed Means | | Estimated Mean Difference Scores[a] | Univariate p Less than:[b,c] |
Score	Delinquents	Nondelinquents		
Delinquency checklist:				
Total score	53.59	30.59	24.20	.01
Parental defiance	7.76	5.12	2.56	.05
Delinquent role	14.41	9.29	5.08	.05
Drug use	3.0	1.82	0.97	NS
Assaultive behavior	2.35	0.65	1.73	.005

[a]Main effects model with age and Vocabulary as covariates.
[b]Univariate probability levels with age and Vocabulary as covariates. Multivariate probability level for grand mean effect for all delinquency checklist variables taken together less than .05; F = 2.2656 with 5/27 d.f.; social class, race, and interaction effects were not significant.
[c]One-tailed test.

TABLE 6.3

Verbal IQ, Spatial Ability, and
Field Articulation Score Differences between
Male Delinquents and Their Nondelinquent Siblings
(N = 17 pairs)

Score	Observed Means		Univariate p Less than:[a]
	Delinquents	Nondelinquents	
Information[b]	9.06	9.35	—
Vocabulary[b]	9.53	9.53	—
Rod and frame[c]	59.76	99.00	.10
Concealed figures[d]	17.65	16.35	NS
Object assembly[b]	10.18	8.71	.10
Block design[b]	10.18	9.88	NS
PMA: Space[e]	30.47	24.29	NS

[a]Univariate probability with age and Vocabulary as covariates; multivariate probability level for grand mean effect for all field articulation variables together; $F = 1.283$ with $5/27$ d.f. (error term based on 37 sibling pairs); NS. Social class, race, and interaction effects also were NS.
[b]Age-adjusted WISC or WAIS scale scores.
[c]Total, absolute values of deviation from true vertical over eight trials.
[d]Number right minus number wrong checked as correct in 5 minutes.
[e]Number right minus number wrong responses.

TABLE 6.4

Schematizing Test Score Differences between
Male Delinquents and Their Nondelinquent Siblings
(N = 17 pairs)

Score	Observed Means		Univariate p Less than:[a]
	Delinquents	Nondelinquents	
Schematizing test:			
Lag score	.0235	.0390	.10
Percent increment	149.44	240.03	.05
Percent accuracy	53.82	54.00	NS

[a]Univariate probability levels with age and Vocabulary as covariates; grand mean effect for three schematizing test variables taken together. $F = 2.9183$ with $3/29$ d.f. (error term based on 37 sibling pairs), $p < .06$; social class, race, and interaction effects NS.

(Block Design, Object Assembly, Spatial Relations, Concealed Figures, and the Rod and Frame) did not substantiate the hypothesis that there would be significant differences between delinquents and their nondelinquent siblings along this dimension (see Table 6.3). Closer inspection of these results, however, shows that the delinquents and, although not shown, especially the white delinquents, tended to score in a more field-articulated way than did their nondelinquent siblings, although delinquent/sibling differences with respect to verbal IQ were nil or reversed. These results are weak, however, and do not reach the .05 level with respect to any subtest, while they reach the .10 level with respect to only two subtests.

The male delinquent/sibling contrast for all the Schematizing Test variables taken together, with age and verbal IQ partialed out, showed a trend toward significance at the .06 level, while multivariate race, social class, and interaction effects were not significant (see Table 6.4). Male delinquents showed more sharpening on the schematizing test than did their siblings. Lag score differences were significant at the .10 level, while percent increment differences were significant at the .05 level. These results were stronger and more consistent among the white sibling pairs than among the black sibling pairs. Male delinquent/nondelinquent sibling

TABLE 6.5

Delinquency Check List Score Differences between
Female Delinquents and Their Nondelinquent Siblings
(N = 20 pairs)

| | Raw Data | | Covariate Analysis | |
| | Observed Means | | Estimated Mean Difference Scores[a] | Univariate p Less than:[b,c] |
Score	Delinquents	Nondelinquents		
Delinquency checklist:				
Total score	59.80	23.20	37.11	.0001
Parental defiance	10.60	4.50	5.77	.0001
Delinquent role	17.30	7.30	10.34	.0001
Drug use	5.85	2.35	3.23	.01
Assaultive behavior	1.30	0.20	1.05	.05

[a]Main effects model with age and Vocabulary as covariates.
[b]Univariate probability levels with age and Vocabulary as covariates; multivariate probability level for grand mean effect for all Delinquency Check List variables together less than .01. F = 6.0731 with 5/27 d.f.; social class, race, and interaction effects NS.
[c]One-tailed test.

differences were not significant with respect to the Size Estimation Test variables or the Color/Word Test variables. Black but not white delinquents obtained lower scores than their siblings on the Digit Symbol subtest; this race effect approached but did not reach significance. In addition, the black delinquents showed somewhat less verbal ability relative to their siblings than did the white delinquents.

In sum, there was evidence that, according to the subjects' own self-report, the male delinquents in this sample were more delinquent in behavior than were their nominally less-delinquent siblings; this conclusion seemed valid for both levels of social class and race. The data also suggested that male delinquents had a weak tendency to be somewhat more field independent or to have more spatial ability than had their less-delinquent siblings; in addition, they were sharpeners to a greater degree than were their siblings. Delinquent/nondelinquent differences with respect to field articulation and leveling/sharpening were greater among whites than they were among blacks.

Tables 6.5, 6.6, and 6.7 present results of analysis of female/female

TABLE 6.6

Age, Verbal IQ, Spatial Ability, and Field Articulation
Score Differences between Female Delinquents
and Their Nondelinquent Siblings
(N = 20 pairs)

Score	Observed Means		Univariate p Less than:[a]
	Delinquents	Nondelinquents	
Information[b]	8.45	8.85	—
Vocabulary[b]	9.00	8.55	—
Rod and frame[c]	83.75	111.40	NS
Concealed figures[d]	21.17	17.73	NS
Object assembly[b]	10.25	9.10	.10
Block design[b]	10.45	9.55	NS
PMA: Space[e]	29.67	25.47	NS

[a]Univariate probability levels with age and Vocabulary as covariates; multivariate probability levels for grand mean effect for all field articulation variables taken together. F = .7803 with 5/27 d.f. (error term based on 37 sibling pairs); NS. Social class, race, and interaction effects also were NS.

[b]Age-adjusted, WISC, WAIS scale scores.

[c]Total absolute values of deviation from true vertical over eight trials.

[d]Number right minus number wrong checked as correct in 5 minutes.

[e]Number right minus number wrong responses.

sibling pair differences. Self-reported delinquency scores of the nominal delinquents in the female group were significantly higher than those of their siblings (see Table 6.5). Unlike contrasts among boys, where differences in self-reported delinquency were greatest with respect to assaultive behavior, those among girls were not especially large with respect to any one subscore; the differences in total score seemed to best distinguish the delinquents from their siblings. Contrasts between the two races and between the two levels of socioeconomic status were not significant in the variable difference scores of the DCL.

As with males, female/female sibling differences, according to Table 6.6, showed some tendency for the delinquents to be more field articulated or to have greater spatial ability when age and verbal IQ were used as covariates, although the multivariate F was not significant. Differences appeared to be concentrated among the white sibling pairs as opposed to the black. In contrast to males, however, only one univariate field articulation variable contrast even approached significance among females; Rod and Frame Test differences were not significant, as might be expected, but were in the same direction as differences in the male sibling pairs.

Considering the Schematizing Test scores in one multivariate analysis, the effect of the social class by race interaction approached significance. Observed scores indicated that the effect was due to the fact that the higher-class white and lower-class black delinquent girls tended to show more leveling than did their siblings, while the opposite was true among the lower-class white and higher-class black sibling pairs. This finding was based on too few numbers to warrant detailed interpretation, since only five sibling pairs were in the two latter cells. It is clear, however, that female delinquents, unlike males, showed no consistent tendency to exhibit a more sharpening style than did their siblings.

Contrasts with respect to the Size Estimation Test scores were significant in the female sample (see Table 6.7). For the three test variables taken together, the grand mean effect for delinquent/sibling differences was significant at less than the .05 level, and test scores indicated that the female delinquents tended to look at the standard less frequently and took a shorter time to complete the task than did their siblings.

Among the females, there were no apparent racial variations with respect to verbal IQ score differences or Digit Symbol Test results. A significant effect of race by social class interaction on the Vocabulary and Information scores in the female group was probably due to sampling artifact. As was true among the males, the female delinquents were not

TABLE 6.7

Size Estimation Test Differences between
Female Delinquents and Their Nondelinquent Siblings
(N = 20 pairs)

	Observed Means		Univariate p Less than:[a]
Score	Delinquents	Nondelinquents	
Size estimation test:			
Number looks/trial	5.84	7.89	.005
Time/trial[b]	14.70	18.47	.05
Average size/trial[c]	43.91	44.17	NS

[a]Univariate probability levels with age and Vocabulary as covariates; grand mean effect for three size estimation test variables taken together. $F = 3.682$ with 3/29 d.f. (error term based on 37 sibling pairs); $p < .05$; social class, race, and interaction effects NS.
[b]Time in seconds.
[c]Size in cm.; true size = 40 cm.

significantly different from their less-delinquent siblings in their functioning on the Color/Word Test.

In summary, the female delinquents admitted to considerably more delinquent behavior than did their siblings. As to the cognitive control variables, female delinquents manifested less care and less delay in taking the Size Estimation Test than did their siblings. At the same time, they showed a trend toward being somewhat more field articulated than their nondelinquent siblings, a trend which paralleled that found among the males. Females did not show evidence of delinquent/nondelinquent differences in leveling/sharpening obtained by contrasts among the male/male sibling pairs. Racial differences in contrasts with respect to field articulation scores seemed to hold for females as well as for males. On the verbal IQ and Digit Symbol tests, however, the racial variations in delinquent/ sibling differences among the male sibling pairs did not obtain among the female sibling pairs.

Delinquent/Disturbed Contrasts

With other effects eliminated, the contrast shown in DCL variables between fifty-three delinquents [9] and thirty nondelinquent disturbed subjects was significant and all interaction effects were nonsignificant. With respect to both the total score and the various subscores, group means indicated that the nominal delinquents reported more delinquency than did the control group. The discriminant analysis showed that the best differentiator between these groups was the total score; the score on which the groups differed least was that reflecting parental defiance.

Analyses of the cognitive control and cognitive ability variables proceeded in three stages. First was an examination of the effects of the demographic variables, the delinquent/disturbed contrast, and the various interactions on the verbal IQ scores individually with age as a covariate. Second, a study was made of demographic, delinquent/disturbed, and interaction effects on all the other cognitive control or ability variables except spatial relations. For this multivariate analysis, age and Vocabulary were used as covariates. The last analysis was performed in a parallel manner, with the spatial relations score as the single dependent variable.

The three-way interactions regarding the Information subtest scores approached significance. The interaction effect was largely due to an extreme score recorded on this variable for a single subject who was black, disturbed, and of higher socioeconomic status. In any case, in both social classes and both races the delinquents tended to score lower on the Information subtest than did the disturbed subjects. The delinquent/disturbed contrast regarding Vocabulary tended to be significant with race, sex, and social class eliminated and age as a covariate. Interaction effects did not approach significance. Observed means indicated that the delinquents had lower average Vocabulary scores than did the nondelinquent disturbed subjects.

In the multivariate analysis of thirteen cognitive control variables, a trend toward significance was found for all the three-way interactions taken together. Examination of the estimates in adjusted standard deviation units shows that, in general, the largest three-way interaction effect was the social class by race by delinquent/disturbed interaction. The greatest effect was shown in the various measures of field articulation and scanning. To learn more about the details of this interaction effect, delinquent/disturbed estimated means were plotted separately for each race and each social class level on each of the dependent variables in question. These plots showed that, with Vocabulary and age as covariates, the delinquent whites were more field articulated than were corresponding nondelinquent disturbed subjects, while differences among blacks were either reversed or less consistent. All the delinquents tended to be less accurate on the Size Estimation Test than were comparable disturbed subjects. Other results were less significant and seemed confounded by chance factors, due to the small numbers in each demographic cell, with the exception of a tendency for delinquent males to show more sharpening than disturbed males.

Discussion

Results obtained by administering the Delinquency Check List to the various groups confirmed that the delinquents in this study were indeed more delinquent than were their siblings or the nondelinquent, psychiatrically disturbed group according to their own testimony, although these results do not indicate that delinquent acts were performed only by the delinquent group. In actuality, according to their own report, all the subjects in this study engaged in a number of acts that could be labeled as delinquent. Differences, in other words, were only relative, although significantly so.[10]

In this study delinquents tended to show greater field articulation than did nondelinquents; in addition, male delinquents were more likely to be sharpeners, while female delinquents showed carelessness on a size estimation task as compared to their respective control groups. Generally, all of these findings were more characteristic of white subjects than of black subjects. While far from definitive, the differences noted in this research between delinquents and nondelinquents in tests of cognitive control functioning do seem consistent with other studies in the literature on intellectual and personality functioning among delinquents, in the light of the theoretical implications of various kinds of cognitive control functions.

The finding that delinquents tend to be more field articulated than control subjects is compatible with reports cited earlier, which showed that delinquents tend to do relatively well on IQ subtests thought to measure field articulation; studies showing that delinquents are proficient at Object Assembly are especially relevant.

Studies which report that delinquents are defiant, unfriendly, and self-assertive are consistent with the idea that delinquents are relatively field independent when evidence of the active directedness over their own lives, the self-assurance, and the ambition of field-independent subjects is considered. Similarly, data indicating that field-independent persons are more oriented to the physical than to the social environment, that their relations with others are sometimes cold and distant, and that they show a relative disinclination to look toward authority figures for approval and direction suggest that a finding that a group of delinquents is relatively field independent should not be surprising. The greater sharpening ability of male delinquents would conform to the portrayal of delinquents as self-assertive and defiant if sharpening is associated with a tendency to confront anxiety-provoking situations without resorting to repression.

These findings permit speculation about the etiology of certain male delinquent behavior. Some male delinquents who may rely on a field-independent, sharpening style that ordinarily should be consistent with independent action, self-directedness, and a tendency to directly confront disturbing situations may express this style by inconsiderateness, hostility, and rebelliousness. Thus some forms of delinquency may take their manner of expression from a field-independent, sharpening style. Such delinquents may be predisposed or led to be less empathic with others, may need less approval and affection from others, and therefore may be less subject to ordinary social sanctions based on withdrawal of approval and affection.[11]

An apparent inconsistency between the results reported here and descriptions of delinquents in psychological literature stems from describing delinquents as uncontrolled and impulsive. The evidence that the female delinquents studied were more careless than control subjects on the Size Estimation Test does suggest that at least this group of delinquents was relatively impulsive. However, the male delinquents were not more careless than their siblings on the same test, and their relative field independence theoretically should correspond to purposeful and directed expression of impulses—the reverse of impulsivity.[12] One possibility is that male delinquents may have differed from the females in that impulsivity may characterize the males' behavior only when they are under emotional stress; under neutral conditions or when external controls are provided, the male delinquent may exhibit a capacity to delay and plan which is not seen when he is driven to act precipitously or when he is acting in an unstructured situation. On a task like the Rod and Frame Test, where stimuli are neutral and task demands are clearly delineated, some male delinquents may function quite efficiently; on the Size Estimation Test, in contrast, where task performance is timed, they may be less effective, though still trying to be careful; on the Rorschach, where choice is maximal, stimuli is least neutral, and a stopwatch is used, some field-independent male delinquents may well appear quite impulsive (cf. chapter 5). Female delinquents, on the other hand, may act impulsively under a greater range of conditions, since the kind of overtly passive-yielding style that leads to impulsivity (Shapiro 1965) may be more consistent with the traditional female role than with that of the male in our culture (cf. Kagan and Moss 1962), a role expectation that may still be affecting our subjects.

Differences along racial lines were also suggested by the data. Regarding field articulation and leveling/sharpening, delinquent/control group differences among black sibling pairs for the most part were either smaller or less consistent than among whites. With respect to delinquent/disturbed contrasts in field articulation alone, racial variations in intergroup comparisons analogous to those found among the sibling pairs were obtained. It is possible that these results reflect differences in reasons for referring delinquent subjects to the treatment center. Referral personnel such as probation officers may use varying criteria in determining whether delinquents of different races should be sent to a mental hospital. To the middle-class probation officer, a black delinquent may seem to be emotionally disturbed only if his delinquency is accompanied by gross signs of psychopathology such as a thinking disorder, since the probation officer may feel delinquent behavior to be normative in some black areas. But white delinquents may seem disturbed to that officer or another referral source simply because they committed extensive delinquent acts, since such behavior may seem abnormal for a white youth, especially one who is white and middle class. The black hospitalized delinquent thus may be more psychiatrically disturbed than delinquent, while his white counterpart may be more delinquent than psychiatrically disturbed.[13] If so, black delinquent/nondelinquent differences might be attenuated in measures related to delinquency but not to psychiatric disturbance. These speculations indicate directions for future research.

In a broader perspective, results obtained in this study can be contrasted with those described by Otteson and Holzman (1976), who found no differences in patterns of cognitive style functioning between psychotic subjects and a normal control group; the divergences between those groups seemed to reflect general disorganization on the part of the disturbed subjects rather than differences with respect to cognitive controls per se. One reason for discrepancies between Otteson and Holzman's results and the findings presented here may have to do with differences among the target subjects under study. Psychosis is a state variable which takes many forms, while delinquency may represent a trait, in the sense of a relatively enduring type of adaptation. Among psychotics, therefore, cognitive control functioning may primarily represent individual consistencies which antedate and shape schizophrenic disorganization, while not reflecting primarily the psychotic condition itself. As Holzman (1969) wrote, cognitive style "may determine the *nature* of the psychopathological disorganization—not *whether* disorganization will occur." Delinquency, on the other hand, may represent the final common pathway for individuals subject to a variety of conditions, both emotional and sociologic. In a sense, delinquency *is* the nature of the disorganization—or organization. Thus, no matter what the cause, delinquency may often represent a certain style of coping with the environment which could reasonably be related to enduring cognitive control functioning. The finding that delinquents but not psychotics are characterized by a particular kind of cognitive style functioning therefore seems tenable on a theoretical level, though this finding is in need of future confirmation.

Another area of research with which this study could be compared is the work of scientists such as Hare (1970) and Mednick and Christiansen (1977) who have explored the psychophysiological functioning of delinquents or, in Hare's case, psychopaths in particular. Some contrasts between our findings and theirs will be explored in the discussion section of this book.

Implications for Future Research

This research provided some very tentative answers to questions about the cognitive styles of delinquent adolescents and some guide to further research. It demonstrated the feasibility of isolating a delinquent group and a less-delinquent group matched for sex, race, ethnic group, social class, neighborhood, and family of origin by using siblings of the delinquents. Furthermore, the work supported the usefulness of self-reported delinquency as information supplementary to official designations of who is delinquent and who is not.

The attempt to learn more about the cognitive control functioning of delinquents is part of a larger interest in learning about the roots of different kinds of adaptation to the adolescent process. One limitation of this study is that the samples were so small and the populations studied were so heterogeneous along demographic lines that the numbers of subjects available in each cell were inadequate to allow for a detailed analysis of the dependent psychological variables, especially when delinquent/nondelinquent demographic variable interaction effects were present. Another consequence of the small numbers was that finer distinctions among delinquents, such as "psychopathic" vs. "neurotic" subtypes (Peterson, Quay, and Cameron 1959), could not be tested. On the other hand, the small numbers in each sample should be considered when weighing the significance levels of findings obtained in this study, since small samples increase the chance of Type II error and consequently enhance the potential relevance of trends in the data. Consistent with this reasoning, trends in the results presented here were liberally interpreted, but can only provide indications for future research. The results of this study seem consistent with the idea that delinquency may often reflect stable adaptive styles which are affected by various other psychological and various demographic variables. Additional research is needed to amplify these findings, to identify whether there are subtypes of delinquency characterized by particular kinds of cognitive styles, and to learn about the behavior of delinquents with various cognitive styles in the "real" world outside the laboratory.

NOTES

1. Assuming hypothesis 1 to be true, we will from this point on refer to designated delinquents as "delinquents," and to designated nondelinquents as "nondelinquents," keeping in mind that these terms require empirical backing and are only relative terms. In this and the two following hypotheses it will be assumed that sex, race, social class, and age effects are controlled or weighed, even if that fact is not specifically stated. We are aware that the term "delinquents" can embrace various subgroups whose individual identity would ideally be preserved. However, small sample size precluded looking at the delinquent group in a more differentiated way, a weakness only future research with larger sample sizes can correct.

2. The use of siblings as a control group is explained in text.

3. An additional sixteen male and female delinquent adolescents and their opposite-sex siblings were also tested, though data on these sixteen siblings were not used.

4. Manufactured by the Polymetric Corporation.

5. Reliability and validity data for the DCL were mentioned in chapter 2. Other data were also collected during the testing sessions with these subjects, and have been described in Ostrov (1974).

6. Age-adjusted scaled scores were used in the statistical analysis of the five WISC/WAIS subtest findings.

7. One pair of female siblings did not take the spatial relations test; the mean spatial relations difference score for the appropriate female race-by-social-class cell was used instead.

8. The spatial relations variable was run separately from other cognitive variables because of problems of missing data among the nondelinquent, psychiatrically disturbed group.

9. Thirty-seven same-sex paired delinquents plus the sixteen opposite-sex paired delinquents were pooled to form the delinquent cognitive control experimental group.

10. Intergroup differences in extent of delinquency are possibly less than is usual when delinquent–nondelinquent comparisons are made. On the average, siblings of delinquents are more delinquent than are other equivalent populations (Robins 1966; Glueck and Glueck 1950). In this sample, the delinquency scores by self-report of nondelinquent disturbed groups were about equal to the delinquency scores reported by the siblings. It is possible that, given that delinquency is related to cognitive style, differences in cognitive control test scores between delinquents and the control groups studied here may have been less than if, say, nondelinquent school children had been used as control subjects.

11. Personal communication from D. Bock, Ph.D.

12. According to Witkin et al. (1954). Kagan et al. (1964), however, adduced evidence that impulsivity, field independence, and verbal IQ are all orthogonal attributes.

13. Other data, not reported here, tended to confirm this assessment (Ostrov 1974). Comparing the responses to a word-association test made by delinquent and nondelinquent disturbed subjects, it was found that white delinquents gave more "common answers" and fewer "unique answers," based on Palermo and Jenkins' (1964) norms, than did white disturbed subjects. Differences between black delinquent and disturbed subjects were much smaller. This racial effect in the delinquent/disturbed comparison was highly significant. It should be noted that Johnston (1973), using a similar word association test, found that disturbed children more frequently gave unique answers and gave significantly fewer common answers than did normal children.

PART III

DISCUSSION

The Individual Juvenile Delinquent

Psychodynamics

This book describes in detail an intensive and in-depth study of a select group of fifty-five juvenile delinquents. The project was set up to examine the psychological factors which contribute to the outbreak of juvenile delinquency. It was not a study of gang delinquency; it was also not a study of biological factors which, it has been asserted, contribute to juvenile delinquency. The subjects were not random referrals, nor was the choice controlled. Patients came from throughout the metropolitan Chicago area, and the majority were referred by the Juvenile Justice System. They came from all walks of life—from different socioeconomic levels, different races, and different sexes. We consistently eliminated those who exhibited organic brain syndromes, epilepsy, mental retardation, psychotic or schizophrenic states. We looked for adolescents who were seriously acting out against the social system in which they were living, and yet were at neither emotional extreme: they were not functioning as relatively healthy gang members, nor were they individuals who—because of idiosyncratic mental functioning or "the call of God"—acted out violently to relieve some bizarre fantasy.

The fifty-five subjects of the study varied in severity of psychopathology and had different psychodynamic constellations. They could be placed roughly along four psychological dimensions, each represented by a sub-group, namely (1) the impulsive delinquent, (2) the narcissistic delinquent, (3) the empty-borderline delinquent, and (4) the depressed-borderline delinquent. The statistical and clinical sense of these subgroups was demonstrated in chapter 2. It is important to stress again that we are dealing with people, and that although in theory the subgroups are easy to distinguish, in practice we do not find "pure" syndromes. Our juvenile delinquent subjects only approximate the four subtypes or their combinations. Usually, the most that can be said is that they have mixed scores with leanings toward a particular subgroup.

Another limitation is that we only studied those adolescents who were referred to us. Our ability to generalize from the data is limited because of the selective nature of the sample. We feel, however, that the conclusions can be extended in fairness to psychiatrically disturbed juvenile delinquents in other settings. We also believe that a significant number of juvenile delinquents have psychological problems which approximate those described above. What discrepancies are found between delinquents in general and those we studied may relate to degree of disturbance rather than to differences in basic psychodynamics. Our results are presented to the social and behavioral scientists in the hope that more such studies will be undertaken in order to better understand the psychological underpinnings of the individual juvenile delinquent.

Before discussing our psychodynamic formulations of the four types of juvenile delinquents, it seems in order to briefly summarize the individual studies by Peterson and Quay, whose methodology is similar to our own. Together with their coworkers, they explored dimensions of delinquent behavior building on the work of Jenkins and Glickman (1947) while bringing new methodological sophistication to that exploration. They also demonstrated that there are no readily identifiable delinquent types; instead, there may be three or four independent dimensions which covary at random.

Quay and Peterson's work can be traced back to a questionnaire developed by Gough and Peterson (1952) which was designed to differentiate between delinquents and nondelinquents with respect to delinquent behavior and role-taking ability; in 1958 Quay and Peterson constructed a short scale also designed to measure this differentiation by emphasizing attitudes and feelings. In both cases, the instruments were able to successfully distinguish between various delinquent and nondelinquent groups. Peterson, Quay, and Cameron (1959) factor-analyzed both questionnaires, using 116 white delinquents and 115 white nondelinquents, both groups matched for age and place of residence. Their results showed

(1) a "psychopathy" factor in which rough, rebellious qualities were endorsed; (2) a "neuroticism" factor in which remorse, tension, and guilt were acknowledged; (3) a factor indicative of family dissension and conflict with school authorities; and (4) a factor labeled "inadequacy," summarized as an "inability to cope with the problems of a complex world" (e.g., "I hardly ever get excited or thrilled"; "When something goes wrong I usually blame myself rather than the other guy").

The next article (Peterson, Quay, and Tiffany 1961) replicated the previous work, using 406 white male delinquents and nondelinquents and several new item pools, including MMPI * items and the Kvaraceus KD Proneness Scale. The results were strong psychopathy and neuroticism factors in the various item pools. "Inadequacy" did not appear in this study; instead, various factors reflecting response sets, such as social desirability or delinquent subcultural attitudes, emerged. Similarly, Peterson (1961) factor-analyzed teacher ratings of problem behavior among grade-school children and found two factors: conduct problems (corresponding to unsocialized or psychopathic), and personality problems (corresponding to "overinhibited behavior" or neuroticism). Quay (1965) extended this study to the seventh and eighth grades and found the same two factors—plus, in the eighth grade, a third they identified as "immaturity" or regression (preoccupation, short attention span, lack of interest, inattentiveness, laziness, irresponsibility, daydreaming). In 1964, Quay obtained comparable results using Jenkins's variables as rated by five parole officers from male delinquents' case history data. Factors were labeled socialized delinquent, unsocialized-psychopathic, overinhibited-disturbed-neurotic, and inadequacy-immaturity. Factor scores were reasonably independent.

A study by Tiffany, Peterson, and Quay (1961) is very important to our thinking. In this research, the authors gave items which loaded on the factors obtained in their 1961 work to 103 delinquent males, and asked each subject to describe himself by Q-sorting those items. They then factor-analyzed the ratings, treating each subject in a way analogous to the treatment usually given to a series of variables. The result was four subject dimensions, but to quote the authors: "Subjects did not coalesce into types. They distributed themselves diffusely and normally over the four-dimensional space defined by the vectors." In other words, there was no clear tendency for subjects to load highly on one factor and not on the others. The authors concluded:

> These delinquents did not "naturally" group themselves into distinct types
> . . . trait analyses seem to offer more promise, but it must be recognized

* Minnesota Multiphasic Personality Inventory.

that these define dimensions of behavior rather than types of people, and that the actual existence of distinct, unitary groups within the delinquent population has not yet been demonstrated.

It seems hard to dispute the recurrent nature of the factors previously described. They do not all appear each time, but variants of each recur often across different authors, methodologies, and data. Our research may have added a narcissism factor, though one could argue that this is similar to the socialized delinquency factor described by Hewitt and Jenkins (1946). In this work we do not claim to have discovered a new typology of delinquency. We are impressed with the way in which our work, using so few and such a heterogeneous group of delinquents, was able to replicate the work of Hewitt and Jenkins (1946) and Quay (1966). What we do feel is that we have added clinical and psychological depth to the findings presented in other case studies. This addition, we feel, is in keeping with the Offer and Offer (1975) approach used in the study of normal adolescents which combined intensive case study and statistical analysis.

The variables which make up the dimensions and the separate subgroups were discussed in chapter 2. These psychodynamic formulations enrich our understanding of delinquency. They enable us to utilize more exact psychotherapeutic interventions, and may lead to better preventive measures in the future.

To enlarge on the subject, the *impulsive* delinquent is a patient whose problems are primarily caused by a poorly differentiated ego. He has few if any internalized controls; since he has little tendency to exercise delay, therefore, any impulse he experiences leads to immediate action. Constructive fantasy or planning, so important in the lives of most human beings, are almost eliminated in the impulsive delinquent. In psychoanalytic terms, drive leads to immediate discharge. Another perspective is provided by Shapiro (1965), who stated that the impulsive person is oriented to short-term goals toward which he can act precipitously without having to deal with long-term consequences. Social learning theory stresses the environmental aspects of impulsivity, and investigates the correlation between the subject's training and his impulsive or nonimpulsive response to different kinds of environmental situations. The emphasis here is on specific situations which differentially stimulate impulsive behavior, and it requires that we specify the environment as well as the person.

The early psychoanalytic formulations about impulsivity dealt with the drives that were mastered or tamed by countercathexis or defenses. Eventually a structural model of ego, id, and superego evolved, and the concept of control of impulses was found to be the function of that aspect

of the personality called the ego. The ego mediates the relationship between inner drive and outer reality, hopefully achieving some kind of
compromise in which gratification of the person's needs and wishes is
consistent with the demands of the outside world.

More recent work on narcissism (Kohut 1971) talks about this control
mechanism in terms of the neutralizing matrix of the personality; in this
sense, the early maternal soothing of the child eventually becomes part
of the child's own psychological functioning, largely through minute and
tolerable frustrations when the child turns to the mother and wishes omni-
potently that control and gratification be provided. The mother, in an
appropriate manner, frustrates the child, and eventually the latter is able
to perform these functions for himself. It is conceivable that the child who
grows into an impulsive delinquent has had serious disruptions in the
mother/child relationship, and that the mother did not appropriately or
tolerably frustrate the child, thus prolonging the child's dependency. Or
shifts from appropriate to inappropriate performance by the mother may
have been erratic and inconsistent, and may have left the child with a
hunger for an outside object who would provide structure and control. As
mentioned earlier, it seems that impulsivity may not always be a pan-
impulsivity, but may occur only in unique situations. This can also be
viewed from the context of transference: there are specific psychogenetic
issues that stimulate certain children to be impulsive, and there may be
considerable variability within any given child as to which context will
stimulate his impulsivity.

The *narcissistic* adolescent's main problem is one of esteem regulation.
The juvenile delinquent attempts to maintain his self-esteem by acting-
out. Because he perceives himself as having been hurt, he compensates
by doing a variety of things which are called antisocial by his peers and
by the social system. This person wants to get back at people who hurt
him. He may have developed a superego, but it is primitive and very
personal. Of our four types, he may be the closest to the classical psychopath (or sociopath) so often described in psychiatric literature. With his
disregard for the needs of other people, his inability to ascribe to commonly
shared and commonly held ideals, he is an intensively self-oriented person. His vulnerability to personal injury and narcissistic hurt, and his
tendency to act out in order to distance himself and to relieve himself
from the pains of interpersonal interaction, are reminiscent of Cleckley's
(1964) description in *The Mask of Sanity*.

As described by Marohn (1977), a number of narcissistic motivations
lead to delinquent behavior. The delinquent's grandiosity causes his need

to control the world around him, including other people, and much of his delinquency results from his attempt to achieve such control or to compensate for lack of control in his personal relationships. Some delinquency represents the acting-out of revenge motives, and of the adolescent's own narcissistic rage in the face of hurt feelings. The delinquent also searches for an idealized parenting figure who will nurture him, and he is disillusioned in many of his searches. Some delinquency is an attempt to deal with the pain of such disappointment; it may also represent the acting-out of frustrated rage, displacing it at times onto seemingly innocent victims. In other cases, delinquency seeks the idealized parent in a search for money, in the drug scene, in alcoholic bliss, and in life itself. Running away, particularly to sunny climates, is a concrete acting-out of the search for the nurturing parent.

The *borderline* juvenile delinquent described earlier is divided into two main clusters: the *empty-borderline* who is close to the Grinker and Werble (1977) fourth group of borderline classifications, and the *depressed-borderline* who is suffering from an anaclitic depression in addition to borderline problems. Central psychological difficulties in both groups include a lack of object constancy and problems in interpersonal relationships. The *depressed-borderline* juvenile delinquent acts out mainly to relieve his depression. Because of that, he theoretically should also be relatively easier to treat in individual psychotherapy. Once the acting-out avenue has stopped, depression comes to the foreground and the motivation for psychotherapy increases. These subjects are most likely to be introspective, and hence would respond to insight-oriented psychotherapy. They can use the psychotherapist as an external object, which relieves the lack of object constancy. Interpretation and use of verbal communication is most helpful.

The *empty-borderline* juvenile delinquents act out to relieve their emotional emptiness and are, therefore, much harder to treat as patients. They are quite passive, which makes them almost as difficult to treat as a person who has a strong underlying masochistic element (e.g. Masterson 1972). This type of delinquent is apt to have transient psychotic episodes which occur when emptiness becomes most frightening. Such episodes occur when the acting-out avenue is prevented or made impossible for him, and he feels that he is standing on top of a void.

In the *depressed-borderline* adolescent there is some internal structure and conflict, indicated by the experiencing of painful affect, even though there remains a serious problem in the quality of object-relating. On the other hand, the *empty-borderline* appears somewhat sicker, primarily because he seems to be devoid of affect—even painful affect—and therefore of internalized structure and conflict. He has serious problems in object-relating. Masterson (1972) sees various clinical pictures shown by Grinker and Werble (1977) borderline types I, II, III, and IV as they utilize various defensive operations against the abandonment depression he describes. It seems that our two kinds of borderline have different states of feeling, both, perhaps, related to abandonment, depression and emptiness, the empty borderline being sicker, more impoverished, and with less structure.

We know that our characterization of four delinquent "subtypes" does not imply that we expect that all delinquents will neatly fit into these four categories and these four only. On the contrary, we expect that there are delinquents who do not exhibit any one dimension to a marked degree or who exhibit several at once. It is true that certain combinations may be unlikely (empty and narcissistic, for instance), but in general we describe subtypes to dramatize certain dimensions of delinquents' psychological functioning.

Cognitive and Physiological Perspectives

As an illustration of the ways in which factor dimensions can interact, we may say a word about the interaction of narcissism and impulsivity. In the previous section we noted that of our four subtypes the narcissistic delinquent group may be the closest to the classical psychopath. Points of convergence between psychopaths and our narcissistic group are egocentrism, vulnerability to narcissistic injury, and lack of remorse or shame. The psychopath has also been described as often being extremely impulsive (Cleckley 1964), though Arieti (1967) has described a "complex" psychopath who can plan complicated crimes. The statistical independence of our impulsiveness and narcissism factors implies that our sample included nonimpulsive psychopaths (or narcissists) and impulsive delinquents relatively low in narcissism.

The implication is that some grandiose delinquents can exercise delay even under stress, perhaps by maintaining narcissistic equilibrium through the pursuit of egocentric goals. In contrast, whatever the quality of their self-esteem, impulsive delinquents tend to react quickly when under stress, focussing on short-term goals to the exclusion of long-term interests. Generally, it is the impulsive delinquent who tends to be violent according to both our factor analysis and multiple regression analysis and this is true no matter what the associated state of self-esteem regulation or affect. Impulsivity, in other words, is a style which crosscuts other ways of characterizing delinquents. From this point of view, it is not surprising that both impulsive and nonimpulsive psychopaths have been described in the literature.

Our work contrasting delinquents' and nondelinquents' cognitive styles is not directly comparable to our study of adaptation *among* delinquents. The fact that delinquents may be more or less impulsive, or may become delinquent in order to combat depression or a sense of emptiness despite a relative lack of impulsiveness, says nothing definite about how impulsive delinquents are when compared to nondelinquents. No direct data on the relative impulsiveness of delinquents and nondelinquents were available in this study though the usual belief is that delinquents are generally more impulsive than are nondelinquents (see chapter 5 for a review of studies relevant to this point). Our data did indicate that male delinquents show a more sharpening, field-independent style than do nondelinquents while female delinquents tend to be more field independent as well as more impulsive than their nondelinquent counterparts. These results reflect tendencies common to all the male or female delinquents in our sample—not individual differences among delinquents. Our inference is that these styles correspond to characteristics of the delinquent adaptation itself, not to differences within the delinquent group. Thus, as pointed out in chapter 6, our delinquents may share a general tendency to be defiant and aloof which corresponds to their relatively field-independent style. Similarly, a tendency to confront anxiety-provoking stimuli may have been reflected among our sample's male delinquents by a relatively sharpening style.

In brief, we have two separable issues: among delinquents, we can differentiate cognitive functioning which is independent of other aspects of their psychological functioning but could not be thought of as contributing to their becoming delinquent per se; between delinquents and nondelinquents we can identify cognitive style factors which may make more likely the choice of a delinquent form of adaptation, in combination with other, psychodynamic and/or sociologic factors. Both kinds of studies are necessary because presumably we are as interested in learning about traits or circumstances that make *any* kind of delinquency more likely as we are in learning about differences among delinquents.

One investigator who focused largely on intradelinquents differences, is Hare (1970). At this point it might be instructive to consider briefly Hare's findings regarding the physiological functioning of one group of delinquents. Using Cleckley's criteria, Hare selected psychopaths from among the delinquents he studied and compared their physiological responses to those of nonpsychopaths under a variety of laboratory conditions. Given Cleckley's criteria (e.g. absence of "nervousness," "failure to follow any life plan"), we would expect relative lack of anxiety and perhaps relatively greater impulsivity among those chosen. That Hare's psychopaths tend to be impulsive is indicated by two other studies presented by him. Hare (1965) found that psychopaths show little physiological arousal in anticipation of shock as compared to nonpsychopaths. Hare (1966) showed that psychopathic criminals chose delayed shock as opposed to immediate shock in a forced-choice situation much more often than did nonpsychopathic criminals. Low arousal in anticipation of shock could stem from an impulsive focus on the present to the exclusion of future concerns. A preference for delayed pain seems directly analogous to the preference for immediate gratification equated with impulsivity by Mischel and Gilligan (1964). At any rate, Hare's (1970) key findings involve lower levels of physiological arousal, less habituation to repetitive stimuli and less response to a new stimulus after repetition of a previous stimulus among psychopaths as compared to nonpsychopaths. Looked at psychologically, that delinquents low in anxiety tend to be less aroused physiologically than are delinquents high in anxiety may be less than surprising. Moreover, low habituation rates may reflect impulsivity or even a sharpening style. Israel (1969) found that sharpeners tend to keep paying attention even in the face of repetition of stimuli or after anxiety-producing stimulation. Repetition of a stimulus like a tone may not cumulatively bore an impulsive subject to the same degree that it bores a nonimpulsive subject since the impulsive subject is more focused on the here and now and therefore may be less oriented to the cumulative nature of the repetition. It is also possible that the exaggerated need to relieve boredom and seek stimulation noted by Quay (1965b) and Hare (1970) can be related to an impulsive style. Impulsive delinquents may lack goals around which to organize their lives and from which to derive a sense of competence and mastery. As a result these delinquents may try to fill the void with stimulation in the here and now, deriving a sense of well-being and accomplishment from immediate, not future, gratification. Generally, it is possible that Hare's psychopaths were at an extreme among delinquents with respect to impulsivity as well as psychopathy and that his physiological measures reflect and do not antedate the type of psychological functioning his subjects were exhibiting.

Mednick and his coworkers (Mednick and Christiansen, 1977; Siddle et al. 1976) have also presented data regarding the physiological functioning of delinquents. According to these investigators, delinquents, and especially severe delinquents, tend to remain aroused longer when stimulated under laboratory conditions than do nondelinquents (Siddle et al. 1976). The implication the investigators draw is that delinquents have a lower capacity to learn passive-avoidance responses than do nondelinquents and therefore fail to learn to avoid committing antisocial acts. These conclusions are based on the theory that people are reinforced for passive-avoidance responses when the act of avoidance relieves anxiety generated by the wish to do something forbidden. When delinquents avoid performing acts for which they have previously been punished that avoidance does not in itself relieve anxiety since their anxiety tends to persist despite their restraint. An illustration of the process would be the anxiety a child might feel when thinking about crossing the street after having been punished for doing so. Not crossing the street would ordinarily relieve this child's anxiety and refraining from crossing would consequently be reinforced. In a delinquent's case, the rewards consequent upon doing the forbidden act might outweigh the rewards to be obtained by exercising restraint since his not crossing the street would not be associated with relief of anxiety and therefore not be felt as rewarding. The data upon which this theory is based seems hard to reconcile with data adduced by Lippet and Senter (1966) which showed that after stress spontaneous GSR activity of psychopaths dropped much more than did that of non-psychopaths. However, Mednick's data may be compatible with ours in the light of data presented by Israel (1969), which showed that after stress sharpeners tend to keep paying attention at a rate greater than do levelers. But clearly, more investigation is needed comparing and elaborating data concerning physiological and cognitive data comparing subgroups of juvenile delinquents to one another and comparing delinquents to nondelinquents. Studies comparing subgroups must be careful not to confuse etiology with an elaboration of the criteria used to differentiate the groups in the first place. Similarly, studies contrasting delinquents and nondelinquents must, as we saw in chapter 2, allow for the influence of being caught and labeled—must, in short, take into account the psychology of the identified delinquent. These caveats apply to investigators at all levels of human functioning—physiological, psychological, and sociological.

8

Delinquency, Psychopathology, and Learning Disabilities

There has been much discussion recently about the role of learning disabilities in the etiology of delinquency. Lewis and Balla (1976) present evidence of widespread organically caused learning disability and psychosis among juvenile delinquents. We found little evidence of either form of pathology among the delinquents we studied. There is, of course, no real conflict, since we screened our subjects ahead of time in order to eliminate brain damage and psychosis. The issue of prevalence of brain damage and psychoses among delinquents is clearly valuable to raise. For this reason, Lewis and Balla's evidence concerning the prevalence of organic and psychotic pathology among delinquents bears close scrutiny. Lewis and Balla base their assertions about the generalizability of their work on epidemiological studies which they performed. We would, therefore, like to examine those studies in some detail.

The subgroup studies by Lewis and Balla comprised 150 out of 2,800 or 5 percent of referrals to a juvenile court in which they worked. The authors' epidemiological work mainly compares other court referrals with the clinic children whom they studied, and court-referred delinquents with the population-at-large. The thrust of their argument is that the clinic children were not much more disturbed than other court-referred children, while the court-referred children as a group were much more disturbed than were people in the larger population. The main weakness of Lewis and Balla's evidence for the generalizability of their findings is that they have no *direct* evidence of the relative degree of psychiatric impairment of clinic vs. other court-referred children since, with the exception of two nonclinic referrals, they studied no court-referred children other than those referred to the psychiatric clinic.

What Lewis and Balla did find is that parents of both sets of children referred to the court—clinic and nonclinic—had similar records of psychiatric treatment at state facilities. The extensiveness of the parents' criminal records in the two different groups of court-referred children was also found to be not significantly different. Looking at the court-referred delinquents as a whole, however, the authors learned that the severity or frequency of a child's offenses was not related to the hospitalization or psychiatric treatment of the parents. The only relationship found between parental "pathology" and child delinquency was that children of hospitalized and treated fathers committed their first offenses at significantly earlier ages. The severity and number of parents' offenses also tended to be associated with the younger age at the time of their child's first offense.

Surveying these results, it does not seem to have been conclusively established that the two groups in question are comparable with respect to degree of disturbance. The most impressive finding is that parents of both clinic-referred and nonclinic-referred delinquents are equally liable to have been institutionalized. But an inference concerning the degree of their children's pathology is highly speculative, since the degree of parental pathology was not related to extent or severity of their children's offenses.

The other type of epidemiological evidence presented by Lewis and Balla pertains to noncourt-connected populations. One aspect of this evidence is that parents of court-referred children had higher treatment rates at state facilities than did a group of adults from the general population, similarly situated socioeconomically, who were surveyed elsewhere. Parents of court-referred children also manifested more "pathology"—suicide, psychosis, hospitalization, and neglect—as rated on a three-point scale, than did general-population adults of comparable social status.

In a related type of comparison, the authors examined the records of state psychiatric facilities decades later to determine the rate at which former court-referred delinquents had received treatment. They found that 23 of the 255 boys checked had received inpatient or outpatient treatment at a state facility; 16 of those 23 had been hospitalized. Another group traced from an earlier period showed similar results. This hospitalization rate, according to the authors, is much higher than the comparable rate shown by a population from a similar demographic area. The authors conclude from this evidence that the delinquents are psychiatrically an especially vulnerable population. Confirming this conclusion, in Lewis and Balla's opinion, was the fact that former delinquents were found to have had a very high subsequent arrest rate (34 percent), while those among them who were "disturbed psychiatrically" had an even higher arrest rate (50 percent).

What are we to make of the epidemiological evidence just discussed? It is clear that delinquents referred to juvenile court tend to come from disorganized homes. But that disorganization may not necessarily be correlated with the delinquents' psychopathology. Instead disorganization may be related to a lack of supervision which leads to early delinquency, early detection, or early institutionalization.

Similarly, the fact that many former delinquents subsequently became criminals and/or received psychiatric treatment, also can generate alternative etiological speculations. As the authors suggest, there is the possibility that severe mental illness and delinquency are positively associated, and that—even more speculatively—the former leads to the latter. But another possibility is that these populations include some persons with institutional careers. In other words follow-up associations between arrest rates and rates of psychiatric hospitalization may be due to a tendency for a certain subgroup to be especially liable to institutionalization and disability of whatever kind. It should be recalled that only 23 of the 255 boys retrospectively surveyed in the first follow-up study had been hospitalized psychiatrically and, of those 23, only 16 had both psychiatric and criminal records.

Overall, Lewis and Balla's results seem compatible with the idea that many children referred to the courts come from families in a severe state of breakdown, manifesting neglect or parental institutionalization. The greater the breakdown, the earlier the child reaches an extreme, such as being referred to a court. But among the children referred to court, it is not clear what proportion are emotionally disturbed. Actually it is possible that among court-referred children there may be many children who are rebelling as a healthy adaptation to a pathological situation. Lewis and Balla's model—that parental pathology leads to abuse, which leads to biological and psychodynamic trauma in interaction, with possible special vulnerability to stress on a genetic basis—is only one possibility. Like us, they studied disturbed delinquents—in their case delinquents particularly likely to be psychotic or brain-damaged. But like us they are left with the problem of the generalizability of their findings. Their data is valuable but must be interpreted cautiously when applied to the delinquent population as a whole.

Lewis and Balla's anecdotal evidence is even more susceptible to the possible lack of generalizability argument. Given the highly selected nature of the sample, there is no proof that the pathology described is uniquely associated with delinquency. The authors tell us that every one of the children they studied was found to have had a history of some sort of serious insult to the central nervous system. But this observation was not made blindly, and we cannot tell whether the authors might not have reached similar conclusions about any group of children whom they had reason to believe were severely delinquent. After all, "some sort of serious insult" takes in a host of behavioral observations—peculiar gait, narcolepsy, history of dizziness, fainting, headaches, *deja vu,* temper outbursts, impaired perceptive functioning, and abnormal EEG. The authors did not use independent assessments of "neurological damage" by the psychiatrist, the neurologist, and the psychologist who were making the investigations. Nor were they troubled if one professional saw damage to the central nervous system and the others did not; the authors admit that after all these evaluations, in fact, they usually obtained a series of contradictory findings. Actually, it is quite conceivable that some of the delinquent children were psychotic and some were neurologically damaged but that this occurs among delinquents to a greater degree than among any other group of identified children was not proven by these data.

Another perspective on the issue of links between learning disabilities and delinquency is provided by Murray (1976). With his coworkers, Murray surveyed all the literature published in this field up to 1975, using computer search packages, abstracts, and other sources. He summarized, that

> repeatedly, articles and speeches about learning disability and delinquency presented it as a relationship which has been more than adequately documented and still is denied the attention it deserves. A survey of the evidence argues against this view. As of the end of 1975, the existence of a causal relationship between learning disabilities and delinquency has not been established; the evidence for a causal link is feeble.

It is true that Murray feels more research in this field is essential, especially given the extensive qualitative data that have been presented by clinicians working with juvenile delinquents and learning-disabled children. More rigorous studies, however, have certainly not demonstrated a causal link between learning disabilities and juvenile delinquency. Murray found only one published study, in fact, which compared delinquent and nondelinquent children with respect to perceptual and integration deficits:

an article by Hurwitz et al. (1972). According to Murray, not only do other studies suffer from lack of control groups, but they also suffer from a lack of rigor concerning the definition of learning disability, and sometimes from a failure to exercise adequate statistical analysis.

Turning to the original Hurwitz et al. study, we find a well-done—albeit small sample—research which indicates, according to the authors, that the delinquents they examined do indeed suffer from deficits in cognitive-sensory motor functioning. There were two separate studies within this research. The first compared three groups of fifteen boys each—one a group of institutionalized delinquents, one a group of normal youths from a junior high school, and the third a group of learning-disabled boys. The authors say that these samples did not differ in their mean or median IQ scores. Closer reading, however, shows that different IQ tests were used to test each of these groups. Be that as it may, the authors then compared the groups on performance using the Lincoln-Oseretsky test of motor development and obtained a rather dramatic result: while only one of the normal boys obtained a score below the 70th percentile, all but one subject with learning disabilities and all the delinquent subjects scored below the 50th percentile. More refined analysis demonstrated that the delinquent boys showed deficits particularly on items which called for rhythmical repetition.

A separate study compared a different sample of juvenile offenders with a sample of normal boys. These samples differed in IQ, as we might expect, the normal boys having significantly higher IQ scores. In this study Hurwitz et al. used measures of sequencing skills, automatization measures such as repeating the name of objects, and measures of spatial ability. As before, the delinquent subjects were significantly poorer on tests involving rhythm and automatization, while there was no difference on the tests involving spatial ability. The authors conclude from these results that "juvenile delinquent boys from lower socioeconomic backgrounds and poor learners from middle-class environments were significantly retarded on a broad spectrum test of motor development when compared with normal age mates of similar intelligence." The findings suggest to the authors that the neuropsychological deficits of delinquent boys and of boys with learning disabilities are manifested more clearly in tasks of temporal sequencing than in tasks of perceptual restructuring.

Our analysis of these results suggests somewhat different conclusions. In the first study, a group of lower-class delinquents and a group of learning-disabled boys, the latter two years behind their age mates in reading level, have IQs equal to those of normal boys from a suburban junior high school. To make this result plausible, we can speculate that in fact the performance IQ of the delinquent boys and the learning-disabled boys was much higher than the performance IQ of the normal boys. The logic of this is that since lower-class boys—and especially delinquent lower-class boys—typically have lower verbal IQs than performance IQs, and since we know that the learning-disabled boys were retarded in reading level and therefore in verbal skills, these two groups can be expected to reach a normal IQ by means of an especially superior performance IQ.

Given this result, we are not surprised to find that the delinquents do less well on tests of rhythmical repetition since, as Hurwitz and his co-authors themselves point out, Broverman (1960b) has shown that automatization skills are negatively or inversely related to skills involving spatial relations. We would thus expect that people who are good in spatial relations would be particularly poor in skills that call for automatization. The authors' second set of findings, in fact, seem to confirm this line of speculation. The delinquent boys in the second study were significantly lower in IQ than were the normal boys—in fact, they were twenty-two points lower. Despite this great difference (more than one standard deviation) in IQ, it is notable that the delinquents were as good on the spatial relations tests as were the normal subjects. The surprising result is not that the delinquents were poor on the tests of temporal and automatization measures, since low-IQ subjects would be expected to be poor on various tests involving cognitive functioning. What is impressive is that the delinquent subjects were as high as the normal subjects on the spatial relations tests used, which included the Graham-Kendall Memory for Designs and the Children's Embedded Figures Test. The tests are used, respectively, to diagnose brain damage and to give an assessment of field articulation ability. Hurwitz et al.'s results in fact conform to those cited in chapter 6, which tended to show that delinquents are superior in spatial ability to their nondelinquent siblings. Therefore, what Hurwitz et al. (1972) used as a basis for saying that delinquent boys are more learning-disabled than are normal subjects, we reconstrue as showing a conclusion quite different; namely, that delinquent subjects are in fact superior in certain forms of cognitive functioning.

Other sources question the concept of learning disability more generally. Routh and Roberts (1972) employed factor analysis to show that various measures often used to indicate minimum brain dysfunction do not associate with one another in ways that might be expected. Studying eighty-nine children referred to a childhood development clinic because of poor school performance, the authors obtained measures of difficulty in concentration (according to teachers' ratings), and scores on a digit span task, wide-range achievement tests, neurological tests, and hearing scores. Interestingly, they found that items correlated in the factors only with other items which came from the same modality. Thus, items which reflected ratings by pediatricians clustered with other items that were rated by pediatricians; items that were rated by teachers clustered with other items rated by teachers, and so forth. On that basis the authors questioned the idea that minimal brain dysfunction is descriptive of a unitary syndrome. Similar results were presented by Paine, Werry, and Quay (1968), who found few correlations among various measurements of minimal cerebral dysfunction. For example, a history of abnormal prenatal experiences was associated with few items from neurological or psychological examinations. As in the Routh and Roberts (1972) study, factor analysis revealed few interrelations among the various measures of "brain dysfunction."

Another line of evidence is found in various follow-up studies, including that by Werner et al. (1968) which related severity of prenatal stress to future learning disability. These authors found that intellectual functioning, behavioral functioning, language and perceptual problems, were all more related to socioeconomic status than to degree of prenatal stress. It should be pointed out that this was a longitudinal, ten-year follow-up study of every child on a small island in the Hawaiian archipelago. These findings contrast with those presented by Kawi and Pasamanick (1958), who compared the birth histories of children referred to a reading clinic with those of children whose names appeared next to target subjects who were from the same census tract, were of the same race and sex, and who had mothers of the same age. Kawi and Pasamanick found more birth complications in a reading-retarded group than in the control group. It should be pointed out, however, that selecting subjects from the same census tract does not insure an adequate control for socioeconomic status, since subjects from the same census tract may be from very different socioeconomic groups. The fact that children referred to a reading clinic are more likely to be from the poorer families living in that tract tends to ensure that reading-clinic children will in general be less advantaged economically than their randomly selected same census-tract counterparts.

Other studies have compared, for example, the EEGs of children referred to a clinic because of behavior disorders and those of normal children. Gross and Wilson (1974) found a very high incidence of abnormal EEGs among children referred to a psychiatric clinic and a very low incidence of such abnormalities among normal children. Close inspection of their work, however, shows that the control group was not matched for age or sex with the target population. Furthermore, since the authors themselves defined minimal brain damage in terms of EEG impairment, their findings of a significant relationship between EEG impairment and minimum brain damage is rather suspect. Also questioning this line of research was Lombroso and his associates (1966), who administered EEGs to a group of normal boys in Phillips Exeter Academy and reported that over half of the subjects showed abnormal 14–6 spikes. While other studies have shown much lower incidence of 14 and 16 spiking and other EEG abnormalities among normal subjects, the conflicting figures cast doubt on the value of any of these statistics.

Another line of investigation is in longitudinal studies of hyperactive children. One by Weiss et al. (1971) found that after five years the hyperactive group was significantly lower in hyperactivity in adolescence; although in school they showed more behavior unrelated to the classroom than did twenty-four matched normal subjects, they were not extremely deviant or delinquent. Another follow-up study (Borland and Heckman, 1976) found that a group of males, referred to a clinic twenty-five years earlier because of hyperactivity, were functioning normally in the community, although they had obtained a lower economic status than their brothers who had not been so referred.

We conclude that there is scant evidence for an association between learning disabilities and juvenile delinquency, and that the whole concept of minimal brain syndrome is highly questionable. Much more extensive research needs to be done in this field before definitive conclusions can be drawn.

Society, the Family, and the Delinquent

Many investigators have emphasized that adolescence is a period of *Sturm und Drang*—turmoil, rebellion, and conflicts between the generations (Blos 1962; A. Freud 1958; Erikson 1959; Fountain 1961; Friedenberg 1959; Hall 1916; Keniston 1968; Kiell 1964; Nixon 1962; Deutsch 1967; Feuer 1969). What was a theory or hypothesis has become a self-fulfilling prophecy (Anthony 1969). It is expected—in many social settings it has become the norm—that adolescents rebel against their parents, or should do so if they are to grow into mature and mentally healthy adults. Recent longitudinal research into the developmental psychology of adolescents, however, has thrown doubt on the validity of generalizing the *Sturm und Drang* hypothesis. Studies such as those of Masterson (1967), Douvan and Adelson (1966), Cox (1970), Block (1971), Vaillant and McArthur (1972), Offer (1969), and Offer and Offer (1975) raised a number of questions which have not been satisfactorily answered.

The studies over time of relatively healthy adolescents have shown the *lack* of universal crisis, turmoil, and rebellion in this population. Some investigators found, as we did (Offer and Offer 1975), that there is a significant subgroup of young people who sail through the adolescent process with *relatively* few problems. We described them as moving through adolescence with a smoothness of purpose, with strong support from those who are close to them, and with an ability to cope with internal as well as external trauma. Because their progression from childhood to adulthood is free of unusual problems or conflicts, we called them a continuous growth group. They are similar to the adolescents Block (1971) referred to as having ego resiliency. Other authors simply call them mentally healthy. We and others have documented the existence of this group, stating that it is important that we be able to recognize its members, and avoid being overly suspicious when we find them. There are families where the relationship between the generations has always been good, and where there is stability rather than change. In most families there is great psychological similarity between the parents and their offspring. The sharing of psychopathology is just as frequent and noticeable as the sharing of mental health.

These comments are designed to stress some of the difficulties inherent in understanding adolescence proper. Parents often forget that they too were adolescents, that they engaged in various behaviors and activities which they would rather not share with their children. Therefore, they either come down too hard on their teenagers (being afraid of the worst), or are much too lenient because, after all, they—the parents—outgrew their adolescence, so it is only natural that their children will also outgrow theirs. In talking to parents of our normal subjects about this period in their own lives (Offer 1969), we found that, in general, those whose children did best were those who remembered most about their adolescence. These were the parents who believed that teenagers today are *not* dramatically different from teenagers of a generation or two back. They saw more similarities than differences between themselves as adolescents and their own teenage children.

The parents of juvenile delinquents had a different impression. Even if they themselves had a history of delinquent activities during adolescence, they strongly believed that children had become less obedient, more difficult, more rebellious, less understanding, and definitely more delinquent than the adolescents of their own high school years (Baittle and Offer 1971). Delinquents' parents agreed that *their* children in particular were disobedient and rebellious but, nevertheless disagreed about how their children felt about themselves. This observation contrasts with parents' attitudes and communication in normals' families which were both positive and clear. We can speculate that the communication difficulties in families of delinquents is causal in some way to the delinquency of the child; yet the delinquency of the child may in itself cause the poor communication within the family. What is interesting is that it could also be argued that delinquency should produce good communication, since everyone agrees that the child is delinquent. It is equally possible, however, that the delinquency of the child produces poor communication between the mother and the father—which also is shown in the results. It thus seems likely that the poor communication in the families of delinquents is a long-standing problem. If that is true, we can speculate about the relationship between poor communication in a family and the delinquency of the child.

In addition to everything that has been stated concerning parents vis-à-vis their children, it is important to remind ourselves that, as adults, we have considerably more options available to us when we are tense than do adolescents. Certain options pertain to adults only, whether it is the use of sex, travel, creative undertakings, or—at least in fantasy—the possibility of changing jobs. It is not true of the young. A child cannot transfer schools at will if the social environment is not conducive to his or her growth. He has to "grin and bear it." He or she has not resolved sexual identity in an adult sense, and even if active, sex usually includes considerable anxiety. Sports is the one conflict-free area which is available to adolescents. But here, too, no doubt not coincidentally, the normal teenager is considerably more active in sports than is the delinquent (Offer 1969).

Society and Juvenile Aggression

Is juvenile delinquency a modern invention? Is juvenile delinquency an inevitable consequence of an industrialized and/or a civilized society? Is juvenile delinquency part of prolonged adolescence? Is juvenile delinquency caused by the excess of divorces and broken homes? Is juvenile delinquency caused by a biological-genetic deficit the genes corresponding to which have increased in recent years because we are able to save so many "retarded and physically maladaptive" children? Is juvenile delinquency caused by the separation, or by the mingling of races, religions, and different social classes in the twentieth century? Is juvenile delinquency a result of the destruction of religious values? Is juvenile delinquency a result of the breakdown of the economy? Is juvenile delinquency a result of the tremendous increase in modern communication, be it newspapers, ratio, or television? Is juvenile delinquency a psychological disease?

All the above may be true to some extent, but no theory has been able to satisfactorily explain the phenomenon of crime.

Historically, it has been stated (see Morris and Hawkins 1970, or Spiegel 1971) that juvenile delinquency has not increased in percentage, in frequency, in severity, or in its manifestations during the past century. If anything, delinquency was worse at the turn of the twentieth century than it is in 1970 and 1980. It is as much a part of the human condition as sexuality and emotions. It is expressed differently in different societies; it exists in some social settings more than in others; it has variability across time and space, but it has always existed to some degree. The psychosocial impulses which force certain youths to take part in delinquent activities are omnipresent.

As an example, we found in our eight-year longitudinal study (Offer and Offer 1975) that 27 percent of the well-adjusted suburban, middle-class, mostly white, Protestant, thirteen-year-olds had taken part in relatively serious delinquent activities. What separated them from the delinquents whom we studied in the current project is that the healthy teenagers learned from their experiences and were not repeaters; they therefore did not become chronic delinquents. Only two out of seventy-three of our normal subjects showed chronic delinquency. Another and more comprehensive study, the Illinois Youth Survey (Simon 1975), showed that the majority of young people had been at one point or another involved in some form of delinquency. Is aggression, then, a basic instinct? Is it part and parcel of the human condition?

Morris and Hawkins (1970) attempted to put to rest the question of rates and prevalence of current juvenile delinquency compared to that of past generations.

A hundred years ago whole areas of New York were held in the grip of street gangs like the Hudson Dusters, the Forty Thieves, the Dead Rabbits, the Pug Uglies, the Swamp Angels and the Slaughter Houses. These gangs fought savage battles in the streets. A death toll of 15 or 20 was not uncommon. Even the police feared to enter some neighborhoods.

Yet today "a death toll" of one or two provokes nationwide alarm and prolonged and agonized debate. It is pertinent to ask whether there is any solid basis of fact for the widespread agreement that in the years since World War II there has been considerable increase in juvenile delinquency. (Morris and Hawkins 1970:149; see also Wolfgang 1967, who makes the identical point.)

There is no question but that it is difficult, if not impossible, to compare the incidence of serious delinquent crime across time. It is of interest to note that Taintor et al. (1978) found that the percentage of patients admitted to over three hundred psychiatric hospitals because of violence has remained constant over the past eight years. Granted that there are many reasons why patients are admitted to hospitals, why other individuals end up in prison, or why still others obtain ambulatory care. It seems to us that if there really had been an increase in the outbreak of violence, psychiatric hospitals would have been likely to observe it. Psychiatry is accepted more today than it was a decade earlier. Individuals who might have been jailed then are just as likely to be hospitalized today. But even if our reasoning is incorrect, the fact remains that the percentage of violent patients has remained constant during the past eight years. Currently, we have little data available to us but, in the future, we hope to have more studies like that of Taintor, so that we can truly compare incidence and prevalence of symptoms across time.

Suffice it to say here that we do not have adequate incidence reports with which to compare one social setting against another, whether in our own culture or across cultures and across time. Therefore, let us continue to examine the phenomenon of aggression among youth in general, as well as one of its specific manifestations among youth; namely, juvenile delinquency. We are especially interested in learning whether the mass media (television, specifically) has increased the occurrence of juvenile crimes.

Lorenz (1966) defines aggression as that "fighting instinct in beast and man which is directed against members of the same species." Its universal presence in man also was described by S. Freud (1920), who believed that the destructive (or death) instinct is "at work in every living being and is striving to bring it to ruin and to reduce life to its original condition of inanimate matter." Similarly, Tinbergen (1968) states that "the elimination through education of the internal urge to fight will turn out to be very difficult, if not impossible to achieve."

The question that must concern us, therefore, is not whether we can eliminate aggression and even violence, but rather how we as humans can learn to cope with our aggressive impulses.[1] The learning process must begin early in childhood, when the child is taught how to tolerate frustration and to accept delay of gratification. This "goal-directed behavior" (Herrick 1956) is learned first in the home, and then in the school.

The child who has not been taught to tolerate frustration in the home environment will find it exceedingly difficult to curb his aggression once he reaches adolescence, when his increased strength will make him potentially more dangerous to society. During puberty these aggressive feelings become more intense as he grows in physical stature, experiences intense sexual feelings, and begins to separate from his parents.

The two main pathogenic methods of upbringing—overstrictness and overindulgence—have been well described by Hartmann (1953). To Hartmann, the "unduly lenient and indulgent father" causes his children to form an overly strict superego, because their impression to paternal love leaves them no outlet for their aggressiveness other than to turn it inward. In delinquent children, who have been brought up without love, the tension between ego and superego is lacking, and the whole of their aggressiveness can be directed outwards.

Normal Adolescents

Our normal subjects coped with aggression in several ways. During the formative years—up to high school—they were taught to channel their aggression in ways acceptable to society or to the family. They learned to tolerate frustration, and to internalize their parents' standards and values. They felt very much part of the smaller (familial) and larger (societal) environments. It was not only a matter of obeying an external authority out of fear, therefore, but a true internalization of standards.

In early adolescence the normal subjects had some difficulty controlling their aggressive feelings and impulses. There were some violent outbursts and delinquent behavior. In high school the aggressive impulse was sublimated most often into competitive sports, a sublimation that was supported by the students' total milieu, from teachers and parents to peers. Open aggression in athletics was fostered in the high school setting. The students used sports more than intellectual pursuits as their route for aggressive discharge.

Yet these normal adolescents participated in our project, which demanded a kind of behavior that was passive by nature—i.e., talking, as contrasted with doing. The gratification which they received was twofold: they had the opportunity to talk with an "objective" adult, and they obtained intellectual satisfaction from such participation. They expanded their knowledge about themselves and learned more about other teenagers.

After high school most of the subjects learned to channel their aggression into study, work, or sexual activities. We saw mild depressive feelings at that time, because the method of handling aggression was not yet completely effective. On these occasions the aggression was turned inward—hence the depression. The controlled utilization of anger and hostility was yet another way they sublimated their aggressive feelings and impulses. It might include participation in the college debating team or, in a more mundane way, a "good fight" with a sibling, who almost always served as a handy target.

Humor was frequently used by our subjects as a way of expressing hostility. Tension was released once the joke was told, and the underlying hostility was understood and expressed; no overt harm was done. Our adolescents' use of humor as an expression of hostility was not always as obvious as in the oft-told story of Heine (1887), who said:

Mine is a most peaceful disposition. My wishes are: a humble cottage with a thatched roof, but a good bed, good food, the freshest milk and butter, flowers before my window, and a few fine trees before my door; and if God wants to make my happiness complete, he will grant me the joy of seeing some six or seven of my enemies hanging from these trees.

Obviously there are many factors which enter into an individual's ability to curb his aggression. It seems appropriate to quote the following statement of Sigmund Freud: "The postponement of gratification [is] an important element in the process of sublimation and thereby essential to [normal] development" (Freud, as quoted by Deutsch 1967).

The question has often been raised whether juvenile delinquency could not best be seen as a manifestation of youth rebelling against its elders (see, for example, Feuer 1969, and Bettelheim 1966). Others have discussed the intrinsic conflict between older and younger people on such grounds as the natural aspiration of young people to take control from their elders, which leads inevitably to friction between the generations. The Piagetian point of view would stress the newfound ability of many teenagers to question everything in terms of abstract principles, an ability that dovetails with the limited amount of experience possessed by adolescents. Erikson's point of view on the psychosocial moratorium and experimentation with different life-styles might suggest that some delinquent behavior can be a function of growth, maturity, and finding one's own identity.

The Media and Violence

We are stating the obvious when we say that communication systems are currently by far the most immediate, and the best developed that have ever existed in the history of mankind. A young girl is murdered anywhere in the United States and within minutes—if not seconds—word is flashed as a news bulletin from city desks, television studios, and radio stations across the country if not around the world. Does that kind of informational flood concerning violence, delinquency, and crime have a stultifying effect; i.e., do people react with "Well, I've already seen that" or "If you've seen one you've seen them all"? Possibly, they see it as some sort of science fiction with no application to their daily lives. Another possibility is that it sets an example that makes it much more dangerous for them to deal with their own impulses and feelings; when they get angry, their initial reaction is to emulate what they have seen on television. These issues have not been resolved. The need is to learn what kind of awareness exists in teenagers, and how it impinges upon their psychological functioning. Their eventual behavior is something that requires much more careful research than has ever been done in the past.

People—whether they are mental-health professionals, educators, parents, politicians, law-enforcement officers, or journalists—often seek to blame an external force for internal human failings. When something goes wrong in the raising of children, in marital relationships, in our own handling of our internal feelings, is it not easier to look for an external cause for our problem? Supposedly causal statements like "times have changed," "too much exposure too soon to adult sexuality," "increase in violence," or "people are just less moral and concerned with each other," are used to explain a child's acting-out, a marriage that falls apart, or an occurrence of reactive depression in an individual. There is nothing particularly new about this psychological technique. It is easier to look without than within. It always has been and always will be. Searching one's self for causal links, for explanations, for understanding, requires courage and time. There are no known shortcuts, no special techniques—just hard work. The social environment, the culture, and the family are obviously part of the system, and as such they contribute to what we see in the final product. Sometimes the external variables are more important, sometimes less, but they always play a part. The same is true for our internal feelings.

Our present study stresses the psychology and psychodynamics of fifty-five juvenile delinquents. When discussing the possible etiology of delinquency, it is often easier to blame cultural shifts, or biological deficits, than to study individual psychological constellations. It is because of this that we have decided to use the oft-quoted relationship between violence in television shows and its effect on adolescent behavior. To share with the reader an overview of this problem will illustrate the complex relationship between a social phenomenon (television) and individual behavior (violence).

Much has been written recently about violence and the mass media. Some studies claim to see a relationship between exposure to TV—particularly to the violent programs—and later delinquent and violent acts by the observers (e.g. Bandura 1973). Gerbner (1978) has recently dramatized the view that television has tremendous impact on the lives of our children and adolescents by stating that: "Television becomes a ritual, a repetition as part of the style of life. It is highly institutionalized; it is a total experience: Children are born into it, and it involves the total community. Television is the only common social experience since tribal religion. It is the only thing the penthouse and the ghetto share." And he goes on to state that "television is another religion. It occupies the same relationships with the state as the church does. The only proper historical comparison with the myth-making power of television, a vital process to conduct an image outside of reality, is a form of tribal religion." Gerbner does not seem to recognize the importance of the internal world of the child. It is part of a current emphasis on the power of external stimuli on the human psyche. It seems to be saying that if you want to change a person's behavior, all you have to do is change his or her external environment. Gerbner refers to a study he conducted which found that frequent watchers of television, "heavy" viewers, fear that more violence will happen than do "light" viewers who are from comparable backgrounds (Gerbner 1976). He also found that heavy viewers are more likely to act on their perceptions: "They buy more guns, install more locks on their windows and doors, and buy more watchdogs than do light viewers. The other side of the coin of aggression, it seems, is a sense of fear." (Gerbner 1978). Gerbner is especially impressed by the fact that heavy TV viewers are more likely to express the "television answer" (for instance, express more fear of violence) within almost every grouping he examines: males, females, those over thirty and those under thirty, the college-educated and the noncollege-educated. However, our own examination of his results reveals a curious fact: apparently TV has more influence on the college-educated, those who read newspapers a good deal and those over thirty than it does on their noncollege-educated, less well-read and younger counterparts! The most dramatic example occurs among his data showing answers to the question "can most people be trusted?" (Gerbner 1976). The "television answer" is "can't be too careful." Heavy television viewers among both the college- and noncollege-educated groups give the "television answer" more often. But the percent difference within the college-educated group is more than four times greater than the percent difference within the noncollege-educated group. If television watching were the only causal factor leading to attitude differences within groups, we would, it would seem, have to conclude that TV has a greater influence on the college-educated than the noncollege-educated. Similar differences pertain to almost all of Gerbner's within-group findings. With respect to a question about "own chances of being involved in violence" the over-thirty group shows a larger "television effect" than does the under-thirty group; a startling result in the light of Gerbner's assertion that TV has had a much more extensive impact on younger people than it has had on older people. In fact, a hypothesis different from Gerbner's is as plausible as the causal one he suggests: it is possible that persons who watch TV a great deal do so because it tends to confirm the world view they already hold and this relationship holds true among young and old viewers, college- and noncollege-educated and so forth. Attitudinal differences between light and heavy TV viewers may be greater among the college-educated and older people because frequent watching of television may be more exceptional in those groups. In other words, heavy watchers of television in those groups may hold what are for those groups relatively exceptional attitudes. Among noncollege-educated and younger people on the other hand, compatible views may be common even among light watchers of television. Television, we may suggest, did not invent the array of human affects. They are, for better or for worse, a reflection of what is in us all.

After Goethe's *The Sorrows of Young Werther* was published in 1774 there were over seven hundred suicides throughout Western Europe. To this day one occasionally finds an adolescent committing suicide after reading Goethe's book. Granted, few artists have Goethe's talents but is it not reasonable to speculate that if television really had the kind of power that Gerbner and others think it has, we would have seen more imitative behavior among all people? It is our contention that the vast majority of people compare television to fairy tales. They are (if well executed) enjoyable. They represent part of ourselves. But they should not be taken literally. Human beings have a vast fantasy world available to each and everyone of them. Television is the latest visitor. It is our belief that, despite television, there is a lower propensity for tolerance for violence today than there was a century ago. Perhaps the experience with two terrifying world wars and their aftermath had something to do with it. Richardson (1960) documented the evolution of wars through hundreds of years. In a careful study based on the best historical information, he found that the number of deaths, by percentage, which result from war has decreased over the centuries.[2]

The mass media may have contributed in two ways to the manner in which people deal with violence. Since these approaches are diametrically opposed, it is scientifically sound to study *both* hypotheses in the same project. They are: (1) The mass media in general, and TV in particular, have helped most people master violence. They have made us see it in its naked forms, and helped those who were potentially violence-prone to better cope with their internalized aggression and external precipitants. (2) The media in general, and TV in particular, have *increased* our tolerance for violence. They have made us more inclined to act out, and to believe that we might get away with it. Constant reading about violence, together with the visual impact of violent shows, make us more violence-prone.

The null hypothesis, which has not been investigated, is that such exposure really makes no difference. There is a certain propensity to violence in man (and in woman) that can increase or decrease over time, but so far—to the best of our knowledge—it has remained relatively constant throughout the centuries. The vast majority of human beings have a pretty well-constructed psychological defense mechanism which is not easily shattered by external events. By stimulating the perceptual apparatus alone, it is almost impossible to stimulate a person to behave in a way contrary to his belief system.[3]

A few studies have shown that children, when watching TV for a long time, become more temporarily aggressive than do control groups which have not watched TV (Stein and Friedrich 1975; Leibert and Neale 1973). Hendry and Patrick (1977) investigated the frequency of television viewing in a sample of 2,302 fifteen-year-olds in twelve comprehensive schools. Their subjects were divided into two groups, high-frequency and low-frequency viewers, according to their own estimate of viewing time. The general picture which emerged (with some overlap of scores) was that high-frequency viewers tended to be more neurotic than low-frequency viewers; they were introverted, less intelligent, had less favorable attitudes toward school, were less likely to think that sports were important, were more inclined to be bored in their leisure time, and possessed different social attitudes.

There is no question that children are affected by their social environment. But the theorist in social learning seems to believe that TV "invented" aggression. Hence, according to one group of researchers:

> Symbolic modeling occurs largely through the pictures and words provided by mass media, particularly the omnipresent television set. Limitless opportunities are provided by these media for the child to view stabbings, beatings, stompings, stranglings, muggings, and less graphic but equally destructive forms of cruelty before he has reached kindergarten age. That children acquire patterns of aggressive behavior through symbolic modeling is supported by a substantial body of research literature. The social contagion of aggressive styles propagated through the influence of symbolic modeling is dramatic. One or two salient examples are enough to spread a new behavior among populations. (Lefkowitz et al. 1977:27)

These investigators seems to ignore or deny the existence of fantasy life, so powerful a vehicle for all our emotions.

The social-learning theorists claim that aggression and its more virulent form, violence, is encased in a cultural envelope (Eisenberg 1972) in which the individual develops. Little, if any, attention is paid to the inner psychological variables which, in our opinion, also have to be considered.

> The unconscious is a powerful determinant of behavior. When the unconscious is repressed and its content denied entrance into awareness, then eventually the person's conscious mind will be partially overwhelmed by derivatives of these unconscious elements or else he is forced to keep such rapid, compulsive control over them that his personality may become severely crippled. . . . However, the prevalent parental belief is that a child must be directed from what troubles him most: his formless, nameless anxieties, and his chaotic, angry, and even violent fantasies. (Bettelheim 1976:6)

The most comprehensive review of the impact of television on youth and on children was made by Stein and Friedrich, who state in their extensive report (1975:245–46):

> The effect of violent television on behavior other than aggression is still largely unexplored. Although it appears that cooperation and other forms of positive social interaction are not reduced by violent television for young children, is this the case for older children and adolescents? Do older children who are avid fans of violent television and are frequently aggressive also have a wide repertoire of prosocial skills, or will we find a deprivation of learning? What is the relation of aggressive attitudes toward prosocial behavior? And what are the effects of violent television on such subtle but critical dimensions as the ability to tolerate frustration and irritability?
>
> Most of the violent content studied has been derived from regular television series. Yet feature-length movies are an important part of prime-time television, and they are often quite violent. Particularly for older children and adolescents, these longer films, which allow for more development of character and plot, might have more impact than the predictable adventures of most serial characters. There is little information concerning both the content and the effect of movies on television.
>
> The world view conveyed through the types of people, power relations, and actions that lead to success or failure may have insinuated itself into our thinking so much that it is difficult to pinpoint and study. More information is needed about the kinds of beliefs and attitudes about the real world that are cultivated by television fiction. The depiction of social and occupational roles, described in the chapter, are important to study, but other features of television presentations, such as the ways in which people show affection, express anger, resolve differences, and a host of other forms of human interactions, also need to be examined.
>
> Exploration of the effects of prosocial television has barely begun. Most of the current programming and research is limited to preschool children; programs for older children and adolescents need to be developed and studied. Of particular importance is the question of generalization and durability of learning. Longitudinal research and follow-up studies are needed

to assess the long-term effects of program content. More information is needed about the critical features of models, verbal content, and modes of presentation that enhance imitation and performance in natural settings as well as the development of training procedures that might be used by parents, teachers, clinicians, and rehabilitation workers. Finally, little is known about noncontent features of programs such as pace, photographic techniques, and methods of narration.

The studies described by Stein and Friedrich are usually well done. However, excess aggression between siblings and friends is a long way from violence or murder. It requires a qualitative leap which these investigators ask us to take, not just a quantitative one—a leap that we refuse to make, simply because we believe that it is unreasonable to do so and we lack the data to substantiate it.

Bettelheim (1976) has pointed out the "therapeutic" uses of fairy tales; that they can—and do—serve to channel aggression in a reasonable and socially acceptable way. Historically, man has always been the greatest enemy of his fellowman, whether during biblical days when a famous murder took place—a certain king sent a fellow tribesman to sure death so he could "have" his wife—or at the time of the Roman Empire, when men fought lions to please the crowds, cities were burned to please Caesar, and thousands were murdered to the delight of audiences. No better fate befell people in the Christian era. If people were thought to be witches, they were burned; if thought to be invaded by the devil, tortured; if of another faith, hanged. At one time a messenger who brought bad news was executed. All this violence was done to man by man outside in the open. Today, if there is a sanctioned killing in peacetime, it is done inside.

This is not to say that it is necessarily better. Nobody claims that modern violence is less severe than in prior years. Only that it has not changed as much as some people claim that it has. The psychology, affect, impulses, wishes, fantasies, and dreams of human beings are very much the same as they were in years past. People want to be healthy, happy, loving, and able to relax and play. If anything interferes with these desires, it is not accepted with as much patience as it could or should be. Impulses—be they sexual or aggressive—are close to the surface; unless solid psychological defense mechanisms are erected, they easily fall to let the animal within us take over.

Few will be so parochial as to fail to see that large-scale violence is sufficiently commonplace in the histories of other societies and that the American record, when put in a world-historical perspective, is not as remarkable as it first seems. Compare, for example, contemporary experiences of Algeria, Nigeria, Indonesia, and Venezuela, to name only a few countries where hundreds of thousands of people have been murdered (Hofstadter and Wallace 1970:7). In a comprehensive study of wars and fatal quarrels from 1820 to 1949, Richardson gave us a precise statistical statement of their causes and the approximate number of fatalities in each. To quote him (1960: IX, X): "There seems to be no evidence that wars have been becoming either more or less frequent," and he goes on to say, "There is a suggestion, but not conclusive proof, that mankind has become less war-like since 1820 to the present time."

Turning to criminal statistics, the FBI has been collecting national statistics since 1933. Its reports have received much criticism. Suffice it to say that vested police and public interests are at play, and that the statistics can be manipulated at will, so that the steadily increasing crime waves based on the Uniform Crime Reports (UCR) have been called self-serving "paper crime waves" (see the series, *Violence in America,* Graham and Gurr 1969, for details). Our conclusion must be the same: there is little substantial evidence of an increase in total violence in the modern era.

Current and Future Research Projects

Our subjects for this study came from the inner city and the suburbs. Some were black, others white; half were male and the other half female. Some were relatively young, others older. Yet most, to a certain degree, had participated in violent activities. As described in another publication (Offer, Marohn, and Ostrov 1975), violent behavior was associated in our sample with variations in the adolescents' self-image as well as in the ratings of psychotherapists and staff in general. We found that adolescent boys who engage in violent behavior had a healthier self-image and were more liked by their psychotherapists than were nonviolent youths. For the female adolescent, we found that the opposite was true. The mental-health staff initially liked the nonviolent delinquent better; this finding disappeared after thirteen weeks of hospitalization.

In discussing the occurrence of violence on our unit (measured on the ABCL), we explained the differences in attitude, self-image, and behavior in the following way:

Our unit is not operating in a vacuum. It is a part of our social system, albeit a very small part. The unit is not a foreign body. It does not deal with rare and elusive phenomena. Rather, it deals with deviant behavior among our young. As such, it can best be understood as a microcosm of society at large. In this report we have presented data from our work with juvenile delinquents. The data demonstrated that violent behavior as a phenomenon was not unexpected in our hospital culture. The younger generation participated in it, and, in some ways, condoned it. At times, our patients and staff have shown the fascination that our culture has had with violence. As Davis (1966) has said: "There is nothing peculiarly American about such images of violence as reality. They arise from an international disenchantment with the view that life is essentially decent, rational and peaceful". . . .

Bettelheim (1966) has recently suggested that violence be studied seriously, and not be stopped short of its milder form, aggression. He states that nowadays parents have learned to accept their children's instinctual desires. Parents even are more accepting and understanding of sexual behavior of their children. But in regard to violence, Bettelheim finds no such reasonable effort: "Let the parent meet with violence in his youngster, and as likely as not he will (physically) stop the child or thunder at him, thus demonstrating that violence is all right if one is older and stronger, and makes use of it under the guise of suppressing it." Similarly, mental health professionals have found it most difficult to deal therapeutically with violence; and the mental health profession in general, and we psychiatrists is particular, have been reluctant until recently to work with juvenile delinquents. Is it possible that at least one reason is a fear of looking into the potential for violence in each of us?" (Offer, Marohn, and Ostrov 1975:1185–86)

In this book we have stressed that violence, and its milder form, aggression, are phenomena—very much human phenomena—which need to be studied. Injustice, no doubt, is the occasion of a great deal of aggression. Narcissistic issues interlace with social injustice and add to aggressive manifestations. Defining "aggression" in a diffuse way, the social system can cope with aggression in children, and can teach parents, teachers, and therapists to help their children, their pupils, and their patients in dealing with it. We have to recognize that the aggressive drive is part of the human condition and we believe that to understand it is the best way to cope with it.

Since ours was primarily a psychological study, we were not set up to study the impact of three crucial variables: sex, race, and socioeconomic status.[4] As stated in chapter 2, we tried to factor out—or control for—these three variables along with age within our subject population. Although aware as researchers that there are as many difficulties in interviewing minority-group adolescents as there are with middle-class white subjects, we did not study the impact of race on our interview results.

Diagnostic problems, which have been well documented by others, include researchers who continuously rate patients from the lower social classes as more disturbed than others. The cooperation between white and black staff was another problem we did not study, nor did we examine the impact on ourselves made by the sex, race, or age of a subject.

While emphasizing that these three variables were not specifically examined in this project, we believe that their interaction with psychological variables should be studied in the future. We also think that in order to study the impact of sex or race on the working relationship between and among staff and patients, a special research project has to be designed that will encompass these various factors, and which will involve a courageous and cooperative group of people. A great deal of preparation will be necessary for such a study in order that the potential findings will be viewed constructively.

NOTES

1. The idea of an aggressive instinct can be faulted on several grounds. First, unlike the aggressive instincts found in lower animals, people are not necessarily destructive in their aggression. Nor do humans manifest specific behavior patterns with respect to specific releasers. Instead, when we deal with humans, we deal with a much more diffuse, malleable drive which can be destructive or constructive depending on the experiences and situation of the person involved. Our use of the word "aggression" is to be understood as reflecting this broader, more flexible definition.

2. However, Richardson (1960) has not taken into account the advances in modern medicine which no doubt decrease the rate of fatalities.

3. The case of *Florida* v. *Zimora* is a prime example. A fifteen-year-old adolescent murdered a next-door neighbor allegedly because the fifteen-year-old was a "TV addict" and hence not responsible for his actions. The defense argued that TV hypnotized him to act in a way that was contrary to his regular identity. The jury rejected this argument, and the boy was convicted of first-degree murder.

4. The fact that we did not study socioeconomic variables is no indication that we underestimated the role of these factors in the etiology of certain kinds of delinquency. In 1971, when our study was being conducted, 32 percent of the nation's blacks were living below the official poverty level (Census Bureau statistics); black median-family income decreased in 1974 to 58 percent of white family income (National Urban League Annual Report 1975); black teenage unemployment in 1977 (ages sixteen to nineteen) was at a 40 percent level (Labor Department figures). There is no question that economic realities of this sort have a powerful impact on human behavior. Our data reflect socioeconomic factors, even though this was not the main focus of our study; for example, the OSIQ scores reflected significant racial differences with respect to scale score patterns (see Appendix A). It is clear that the blacks in our sample describe themselves as feeling better about their families. This theme is reflected in several other instruments: on the DCL the blacks reported less parental defiance; conversely, on the OPCQ black parents, after having resolved differences in their answers, reported their children to be better adjusted than did the white parents con-

cerning their own children. The evidence seems to indicate that black families either experience or admit to less intrafamily conflict. With respect to impulsivity, our data indicate that the salient differences were not between blacks and whites per se, but between black females and males on the one hand, and white females and males on the other. Specifically, various instruments such as the ABCL, the impulsivity ratings, and teacher's rating scale, all indicate that the black females in our sample were seen to be—or actually were—more impulsive than the black males. The white males conversely were more impulsive than the white females. We cannot generalize about these findings, however, especially since there were only five black females in our sample. We can only say that whatever the cause of various psychological reactions, psychological constructs are worth studying in their own right to the extent that they help us understand human behavior and make more beneficial interventions with respect to that behavior.

Psychiatric and Legal Help for the Delinquent

Psychotherapy must compete with numerous rivals when it functions as an intervention technique with and on behalf of juvenile delinquents (see Marohn 1977b). Advocates of community change or legal interventions are often notably more successful than are proponents of psychotherapy in obtaining governmental recognition and financial backing. The recent *Task Force Report on Juvenile Delinquency and Youth Crime* (Hanna, Kharasch, and O'Bryan 1967), which was part of the President's Commission on Law Enforcement and Administration of Justice, discusses in great detail the juvenile court system, training schools, and socioeconomic causalities, while giving a detailed summary of the social science approach to the problem. It presents the best thinking of lawyers, administrators, social workers, and social scientists. It has a striking omission, from our admittedly biased point of view: no psychodynamically oriented psychiatrist, psychologist, or social worker was part of the commission. As a result, the recommendations of the task force, although full of goodwill, lack any psychological depth whatsoever. It is a pure case of social engineering. The theory runs something like this: "People can be manipulated by their environment. If we can only supply them with the right social environment, good adult role models, and sufficient food, clothing, and education, we will eliminate the phenomenon of delinquency." It is precisely that point of view with which we take issue. It ignores the foundation of modern psychology. It leaves the individual completely at the mercy of external forces, ignoring his own wishes, ambitions, dreams, fantasies, and workings of his unconscious mind. Were it so simple, we would have had much more success with our intervention methods.

The efficacy of psychotherapy has been questioned in general as well as with delinquents in particular (Emery and Marholin 1977; McCord 1968). Despite doubts and lack of support, we feel confident that in the long run the psychotherapeutic model will be shown to be as good as other intervention techniques and to be much superior to the criminal-justice system in ameliorating the problems of the criminal in society. It is true that the legal system serves different ends than do psychotherapeutic interventions. The primary goal of the law is to maintain the social order and the behavior of individuals is judged with that primary goal in mind. As now constituted, a view of man as a rational, choosing being best matches the simple deterrence model which essentially constitutes the rationale of legal responses to crime. The foundation of the legal system's response is clarity of communication: a certain act will warrant a definite punitive response. Presumably the certainty of response is the best guaranty of efficacy of deterrence. But when the smoke clears, wardens and other prison personnel are often forced to call upon mental-health professionals for help in dealing with the "rational" criminals who were not deterred despite clarity about expected punishment.

It is not our purpose to overemphasize psychological factors in the etiology of crime. Economic causes, too, must be taken into account. People often see themselves "on the outs" in this society; when they find a way to get something for themselves, they take it—which probably accounts for much of the delinquency we see today. It is also true that human beings fight back against the conditions in which they find themselves. This is not to say that there are not other kinds of determinants, but that we must also give credence to human rationality.

From another perspective, delinquency, particularly violent delinquency, is not noticeably different from deviant behavior seen elsewhere in society. There are some who see basic flaws in the fabric of our social system. A lack of morals or of human values manifests itself in terms of white-collar crime as well as in street crime. The focus on lower class delinquency in particular represents a certain anxiety associated with a desire on the part of higher classes to emphasize the defects of another (lower) class, while ignoring the pervasive distortion of values manifested by corporate crime, white-collar crime, political crime, or income-tax cheating. But it remains true that many criminals and delinquents at all social levels struggle with emotional problems. For these people punishment or economic change occurs in the context of their ongoing emotional struggles.

The effect of legal or economic interventions will be felt as filtered through their subjective appreciation of the changes wrought. Without accompanying emotional change or psychological insight, the economic or legal responses may accomplish little. A middle-class suburban adolescent who develops a depressive reaction because of real or imagined loss acts out to relieve his or her internal tensions; so does the lower class teenager who is frightened of growing up and develops severe anxiety reactions each time he or she has to cope with sexual fantasies. Their delinquency, though as serious as that of a teenager who is economically motivated, may be differently caused. Once we accept the possibility that psychological factors exist, however, we can seek them out.

That is what we have done in this monograph. We believe that we have demonstrated the importance of various psychological factors in the population which we studied, factors whose importance bears investigation among great numbers of delinquents whose criminal behavior is psychologically determined to a significant degree.

Four different subtypes and the variables that distinguish them, together with illustrative case reports, have been discussed (see chapter 3). These psychological subgroups contribute to a better understanding of adolescent delinquent behavior, regardless of age, sex, socioeconomic status, or race. The resulting psychodynamic formulations enrich psychotherapeutic interventions. Differential emphases in treatment are appropriate for different styles of delinquency. For the *impulsive delinquent,* milieu therapy with an emphasis on limit-setting and delay is crucial. The *narcissistic delinquent* must be allowed to use staff and therapist to regulate his self-esteem and suport himself in the face of narcissistic injury. The *depressed-borderline* benefits from a psychodynamically oriented individual psychotherapy that helps him see and tolerate painful affect, while the *empty-borderline* sometimes may need psychotropic medication in addition to relationships to assist or replace defective or missing psychological functions. Correct psychodynamic assessment and diagnosis is the necessary first step toward achieving better results.

How many members of the delinquent population currently in the courts can be diagnosed by this interview approach still is unknown. More careful follow-up studies are needed, both of the delinquents who have been treated by psychiatric methods and of those who have not. Only then will we be able to tell which therapy works for whom and under what circumstances—something that has as yet never been done. Our study is in the tradition of the Gluecks (1950), Jenkins and Glickman (1947), and Petersen, Quay, and Tiffany (1961). But rarely has their work been bridged with actual therapeutic methods. Is it not time that we begin to use our hard-earned research results in the "real world"? This section has represented an attempt to refine the psychological approach to delinquency even as psychotherapy fights for recognition among delinquency intervention techniques. More work is needed to extend and further refine its results.

Conclusion

No single approach has solved the problem of juvenile delinquency. We do not yet know what factors contribute to an outbreak of delinquent behavior, why specific individuals take part in delinquent activities and—most important—why others do not. Similar biopsychosociocultural backgrounds do not lead to similar end products. Our intervention methods need overhauling, our therapeutic methods need new ideas, and our prevention needs a beginning.

A study such as this does not even begin to solve any of these questions. It simply stresses our ignorance. It clearly indicates one aspect of our knowledge however: we need more evaluation and research programs. It should be required that an evaluation procedure be built into all new or ongoing programs funded on the local, state, or Federal level. Do they really achieve what they wanted to do? If yes, how? If not, why not? We would learn just as much by knowing what went wrong as by knowing what went right. Spending millions of dollars on fly-by-night programs is not enough. A potentially good program such as the Job Corps needed better evaluation in order to have been better defended by its advocates. The various training programs in the prisons need to be evaluated, as do psychotherapeutic methods. It is possible that by integrating our several approaches, and by determining *what is best for whom, under what circumstances, delivered by which professional group, and with what kind of results,* we will have achieved a beginning in understanding delinquent behavior.

In completing a long, complex, and expensive study, we ask: have we formulated a new theory on the etiology, treatment, and prevention of juvenile delinquency? The answer to that question is definitely no. We are empiricists. We believe that the first priority for investigators in the social and behavioral sciences is to collect more reliable and valid data. Our science is burdened with excess theory—which helps to build models but is, at times, far removed from real people.

It has been our goal in this study to add to the growing literature which presents empirical findings, utilizing a variety of investigative methods. Later, once a new generation of researchers has enriched our knowledge concerning youth in general and juvenile delinquency in particular, we will again build theoretical models. At the present time we need more data. We hope that the present volume, the two that preceded it (Offer 1969; Offer and Offer 1975), and the one which follows (Marohn et al. 1979) are a step in that direction.

Epilogue

It could happen that when one thinks of delinquency as a sociologic problem or thinks of it in demographic terms, one might overlook the amount of intense personal and family suffering involved in a delinquent career and a delinquent act. The human suffering that adolescent delinquents and their families experience could be overlooked, too, when delinquents are considered in psychological terms, or described in terms of variables or factors. Certainly, as we think about the delinquents whom we studied, and some of whom we have described in this book, their histories and their stories attest to suffering, confusion, self-destructive activity, boredom, confusion, and personal unhappiness.

There is a tendency in our society to think of delinquency or criminality as exciting, because it seductively holds out to each of us a sense of autonomy and independence, a picture of being "one's own person." Yet we see that our delinquents were not "free"; they were tragically unhappy. And we must not lose sight of such individual pain when we contemplate the meaning of our research.

PART IV

APPENDICES

APPENDIX A

CODE BOOK: DEFINITIONS OF MEANS,
STANDARD DEVIATIONS, OR FREQUENCY
DISTRIBUTION OF VARIABLES USED

TABLE A-1

Frequencies and Percent Distributions of Variables #1-26 Used in the Entire Study (1969-1974)

Variable #	Definition	Frequencies and Percent Distributions[a]							
		Whole Group (N = 55)	Young (N = 27)	Old (N = 28)	Male (N = 30)	Female (N = 25)	Upper White (N = 19)	Lower White (N = 19)	Black (N = 17)
		%	%	%	%	%	%	%	%
1*	Parents' interview: age in years at which subject's emotional problems first began								
	1 = 6 years or under	47	56	39	53	40	58	42	41
	2 = 7 through 10 years	27	26	29	23	32	11	32	41
	3 = 11 years or over	25	19	32	23	28	32	26	18
2	Parents' interview: age in years at which subject first had law-breaking problem								
	1 = 12 years or under	53	67	39	53	52	53	47	59
	2 = over 12 years	47	33	61	47	48	47	53	41
3	Admission questionnaire: age in years when subject was first arrested[b]								
	1 = 13.5 years or under	52	<u>69</u>	<u>33</u>	50	55	53	39	65
	2 = 14 years or over	48	<u>31</u>	<u>67</u>	50	45	47	61	35
	(no answer: 2 subjects; never arrested: 3 subjects)								
4	Admission questionnaire: number of times subject was arrested								
	1 = 4 times or less	55	40	69	57	52	67	53	44
	2 = 5 times or more	45	60	31	43	48	33	47	56
	(no answer: 4 subjects)								
5*	Admission questionnaire: did subject use non-narcotic drugs?								
	1 = yes	63	56	70	53	75	79	61	47
	2 = no	37	44	30	47	25	21	39	53

Frequencies and Percent Distributions[a]

Variable #	Definition	Whole Group (N = 55) %	Young (N = 27) %	Old (N = 28) %	Male (N = 30) %	Female (N = 25) %	Upper White (N = 19) %	Lower White (N = 19) %	Black (N = 17) %
6	Admission questionnaire: did subject use narcotics?								
	1 = yes	19	7	30	10	29	32	17	6
	2 = no	81	93	70	90	71	68	83	94
7	Background questionnaire: did subject expect to earn more money than his or her father?[c]								
	1 = yes	61	73	50	79	42	28	74	87
	2 = no	39	27	50	21	58	72	26	13
8	Background questionnaire: plans after high school								
	1 = college	35	38	31	36	33	22	32	53
	2 = other (e.g., work, armed services)	65	62	69	64	67	78	68	47
9*	Background questionnaire: self-concept								
	1 = would like to change partially or completely	56	50	62	61	50	67	53	47
	2 = would change very little	44	50	38	39	50	33	47	53
10	Background questionnaire: father's discipline								
	1 = strict	35	50	20	37	32	39	39	39
	2 = variable	33	17	48	22	45	33	33	31
	3 = lenient	33	33	32	41	23	28	28	46
	(no answer: 3 subjects)								
11	Background questionnaire: mother's discipline								
	1 = strict	35	35	35	25	46	39	26	40
	2 = variable	39	27	50	39	37	44	47	20
	3 = lenient	27	38	15	36	17	17	26	40

TABLE A-1 (continued)

Variable #	Definition	Whole Group (N = 55) %	Young (N = 27) %	Old (N = 28) %	Male (N = 30) %	Female (N = 25) %	Upper White (N = 19) %	Lower White (N = 19) %	Black (N = 17) %
						Frequencies and Percent Distributions[a]			
12*	Background questionnaire: discipline—physical punishment?								
	1 = yes	57	65	48	52	63	65	58	47
	2 = no	43	35	52	48	37	35	42	53
	(no answer: 1 subject)								
13	Semistructured interview: smoked marijuana more than once								
	1 = yes	76	73	79	42	80	89	68	69
	2 = no	24	27	21	58	20	11	32	31
	(no answer: 1 subject)								
14	Semistructured interview: taken drugs (other than marijuana or heroin) more than once?								
	1 = yes	63	57	68	52	75	84	61	36
	2 = no	37	43	32	48	25	16	39	64
	(no answer: 4 subjects)								
15*	Semistructured interview: has had heterosexual intercourse								
	1 = yes	67	52	82	50	88	68	53	82
	2 = no	33	48	18	50	12	32	47	18
16*	Therapist rating scale: emotional experience[d,e]								
	1 = excellent	2	–	4	4	–	–	–	7
	2 = good	39	52	26	29	50	47	39	27
	3 = fair	52	36	67	57	46	47	61	47
	4 = poor	8	12	4	11	5	5	–	20

Frequencies and Percent Distributions[a]

Variable #	Definition	Whole Group (N = 55) %	Young (N = 27) %	Old (N = 28) %	Male (N = 30) %	Female (N = 25) %	Upper White (N = 19) %	Lower White (N = 19) %	Black (N = 17) %
17*	Therapist rating scale: emotional expressiveness								
	1 = excellent	21	20	22	14	29	42	6	13
	2 = good	23	20	26	18	29	26	33	7
	3 = fair	37	32	41	46	25	21	50	40
	4 = poor	19	28	11	21	17	11	11	40
18	Therapist rating scale: relationship with therapist								
	1 = excellent	35	40	30	32	38	42	39	20
	2 = good	46	40	52	50	42	42	39	60
	3 = fair	15	40	15	18	13	11	17	20
	4 = poor	4	4	4	–	8	5	6	–
19	Therapist rating scale: patient's psychological sophistication								
	1 = excellent	4	–	7	–	8	11	–	–
	2 = good	10	8	11	–	21	26	–	–
	3 = fair	46	44	48	57	33	42	50	49
	4 = poor	40	48	33	43	37	21	50	53
20*	Likability of patient according to therapist (number of millimeters from rating scale given to therapists). Median = 33 out of possible 132 mm.	56[f]	76	15	36	29	5	39	80

TABLE A-1 (*continued*)

Variable #	Definition	Whole Group (N = 55) %	Young (N = 27) %	Old (N = 28) %	Male (N = 30) %	Female (N = 25) %	Upper White (N = 19) %	Lower White (N = 19) %	Black (N = 17) %
21*	Therapist rating scale: patient's overall psychological health								
	1 = excellent	–	–	–	–	–	–	–	–
	2 = good	21	16	26	11	33	26	22	13
	3 = fair	46	32	59	54	37	42	44	53
	4 = poor	33	52	15	36	29	32	33	33
22	Teacher rating scale: leadership[d]								
	1. actively seeks leadership	5	11	–	3	8	5	5	6
	2. occasionally seeks leadership	14	7	21	7	24	16	16	12
	3. sometimes takes leadership	13	15	11	17	8	16	11	12
	4. cooperative, but seldom leads	51	44	57	50	52	53	47	53
	5. negative	16	22	11	23	8	11	21	18
23*	Teacher rating scale: initiative and creativity								
	1. actively creative	7	11	4	10	4	5	11	5
	2. original in some areas	38	33	43	23	56	58	42	12
	3. little or no creative work	36	44	29	40	32	16	37	59
	4. conforms	18	11	25	27	8	21	11	24
24	Teacher rating scale: social sensitivity								
	1. deeply concerned	–	–	–	–	–	–	–	–
	2. generally concerned	5	7	4	3	8	5	5	6
	3. somewhat concerned	35	22	46	27	44	47	26	29
	4. usually self-centered	42	48	36	47	36	26	37	65
	5. seems indifferent to needs of others	18	22	14	23	12	21	32	–

Frequencies and Percent Distributions[a]

Frequencies and Percent Distributions[a]

Variable #	Definition	Whole Group (N = 55)	Young (N = 27)	Old (N = 28)	Male (N = 30)	Female (N = 25)	Upper White (N = 19)	Lower White (N = 19)	Black (N = 17)
		%	%	%	%	%	%	%	%
25	Teacher rating scale: responsibility								
	1. thoroughly dependable	4	7	–	3	4	5	5	–
	2. conscientious	15	19	11	10	20	16	11	18
	3. usually dependable	29	22	36	17	44	37	32	18
	4. somewhat dependable	36	33	39	47	24	26	32	53
	5. unreliable	16	19	14	23	8	16	21	12
26	Teacher rating scale: industry								
	1. eager and interested	5	7	4	7	4	5	11	–
	2. prepares assigned work	13	19	7	13	12	16	5	18
	3. completes assigned work	36	33	39	16	60	37	32	41
	4. seldom completes assigned work	42	37	46	57	24	37	47	41
	5. indolent	4	4	4	7	–	5	5	–

[a]Percents do not always sum to 100 because of rounding errors; numbers underscored once indicate that the groups in question differed significantly in percent distribution at the .05 level according to a chi-square test. If a number is underscored twice it means that differences were significant at the .01 level.
[b]One subject's admission questionnaire was lost.
[c]Three subjects' background questionnaires missing.
[d]For detailed definitions of scale points, see pp. 84-85.
[e]Three patients were not rated according to Therapist Rating Scale.
[f]Means given, not percentages.
*Variable used in factor analysis.

TABLE A-2

Means and Standard Deviations of Variables #27-130 Used in the Entire Study (1969-1974)

Variable #	Definition	Means and Standard Deviations[a]							
		Whole Group (N = 55)	Young (N = 27)	Old (N = 28)	Male (N = 30)	Female (N = 25)	Upper White (N = 19)	Lower White (N = 19)	Black (N = 17)
27*	Mean likability rating according to staff during subject's first three days of hospitalization (higher score = less liked)	56.67 (9.07)	57.49 (8.99)	55.88 (9.24)	57.05 (9.28)	56.21 (8.99)	55.54 (10.76)	56.67 (9.97)	57.92 (5.71)
28*	Mean likability rating according to staff during subject's 13th week of hospitalization (higher score = less liked)	51.69 (13.04)	53.39 (13.57)	49.99 (12.51)	54.67 (13.15)	47.93 (12.14)	51.73 (14.87)	54.76 (11.93)	47.76 (11.77)
29*	Rorschach: number of responses (R)[c]	28.94 (9.73)	28.08 (7.49)	29.75 (11.51)	28.83 (9.30)	29.08 (10.45)	29.32 (9.32)	30.42 (12.50)	26.75 (5.89)
30	Rorschach: whole card responses (R)	8.57 (9.02)	6.96 (4.51)	10.07 (11.67)	7.10 (3.69)	10.42 (12.81)	11.42 (14.15)	7.74 (4.53)	6.19 (2.32)
31	Rorschach: major details (D)	18.28 (8.00)	17.69 (5.63)	18.82 (9.77)	18.70 (7.33)	17.75 (8.46)	18.00 (6.34)	19.05 (11.18)	17.69 (5.16)
32	Rorschach: small or uncommon details (Dd)	3.22 (3.60)	3.46 (3.81)	3.00 (3.44)	3.07 (3.69)	3.42 (3.54)	3.05 (3.46)	3.68 (4.45)	2.87 (2.68)
33*	Rorschach: movement (M)	4.04 (3.27)	3.31 (2.31)	4.71 (3.88)	3.63 (2.91)	4.54 (3.67)	4.42 (3.06)	5.16 (3.89)	2.25 (1.77)
34	Rorschach: color (C)	0.70 (1.06)	1.04 (1.22)	0.39 (0.79)	0.57 (0.90)	0.87 (1.23)	0.47 (0.91)	0.79 (1.18)	0.87 (1.09)
35	Rorschach: form-color (FC)	1.72 (2.21)	1.23 (1.31)	2.18 (2.75)	1.43 (1.59)	2.08 (2.80)	1.79 (2.12)	2.26 (2.83)	1.00 (1.15)
36*	Rorschach: shading (Y)	3.31 (4.34)	2.39 (3.06)	4.18 (5.16)	2.63 (2.85)	4.17 (5.64)	3.89 (4.50)	4.11 (5.46)	1.69 (1.58)
37	Rorschach: texture (T)	0.28 (0.49)	0.19 (0.49)	0.36 (0.49)	0.27 (0.52)	0.29 (0.46)	0.32 (0.48)	0.26 (0.45)	0.25 (0.58)

Means and Standard Deviations[a]

Variable #	Definition	Whole Group (N = 55)	Young (N = 27)	Old (N = 28)	Male (N = 30)	Female (N = 25)	Upper White (N = 19)	Lower White (N = 19)	Black (N = 17)
38	Rorschach: vista (V)	0.56 (1.08)	0.58 (1.07)	0.54 (1.11)	0.63 (1.00)	0.46 (1.18)	0.68 (1.11)	0.84 (1.34)	0.06 (0.25)
39	Rorschach: human content (H)	6.24 (3.80)	5.31 (2.84)	7.11 (4.39)	5.37 (3.46)	7.33 (4.00)	6.21 (3.57)	7.84 (4.47)	4.37 (2.19)
40	Rorschach: animal content (A)	13.13 (4.67)	12.89 (3.56)	13.36 (5.57)	13.57 (4.83)	12.58 (4.51)	13.58 (3.85)	12.58 (5.53)	13.25 (4.68)
41	Rorschach: anatomical content (An)	1.09 (1.51)	1.42 (1.60)	0.79 (1.37)	1.10 (1.52)	1.08 (1.53)	0.42 (0.69)	1.00 (1.37)	2.00 (1.93)
42	Rorschach: sexual content (Sx)	0.24 (1.27)	0.50 (1.82)	.00 (.00)	0.07 (0.37)	0.46 (1.87)	.00 (.00)	.00 (.00)	0.81 (2.29)
43	Rorschach: popular responses (P)	5.91 (2.17)	5.42 (2.16)	6.36 (2.13)	5.73 (2.39)	6.13 (1.89)	6.63 (1.86)	5.68 (2.58)	5.31 (1.85)
44	Rorschach: white space (S)	2.41 (2.01)	2.61 (2.04)	2.21 (2.01)	2.43 (1.89)	2.37 (2.20)	2.37 (2.39)	2.63 (1.61)	2.19 (2.07)
45	Rorschach: affective ratio (Afr)	0.66 (0.21)	0.66 (0.18)	0.66 (0.23)	0.67 (0.24)	0.65 (0.16)	0.66 (0.19)	0.64 (0.19)	0.69 (0.25)
46*	Rorschach: form percent (F%)	65.07 (18.19)	68.92 (16.37)	61.50 (19.33)	68.77 (15.12)	60.46 (20.83)	61.58 (19.82)	60.16 (18.26)	75.06 (12.03)
47*	Rorschach: good-form percent (F+%)	74.31 (12.47)	72.54 (14.17)	75.96 (10.64)	71.63 (11.20)	77.68 (13.37)	77.42 (10.11)	73.37 (12.69)	71.75 (14.59)
48	Rorschach: time for first response (T/IR)[d]	16.93 (14.41)	18.78 (19.17)	15.21 (7.81)	19.51 (18.18)	13.71 (6.50)	14.16 (7.35)	19.16 (21.93)	17.58 (8.68)

TABLE A-2 *(continued)*

		Means and Standard Deviations[a]							
Variable #	Definition	Whole Group (N = 55)	Young (N = 27)	Old (N = 28)	Male (N = 30)	Female (N = 25)	Upper White (N = 19)	Lower White (N = 19)	Black (N = 17)
49	Rorschach: chromatic time for first response (chrom T/IR)[d]	17.26 (14.83)	18.23 (19.01)	16.36 (9.76)	19.81 (18.39)	14.08 (7.85)	14.89 (8.83)	18.95 (21.93)	18.07 (9.76)
50	Rorschach: achromatic time for first response (achrom T/IR)[d]	16.47 (16.13)	18.97 (21.63)	14.14 (8.13)	19.11 (20.23)	13.17 (7.94)	13.26 (7.69)	19.37 (23.86)	16.83 (11.89)
51	Rorschach: number of different content categories used	9.07 (2.91)	9.39 (2.65)	8.79 (3.15)	9.53 (3.00)	8.50 (2.75)	9.21 (3.65)	9.05 (2.95)	8.94 (1.88)
52	Rorschach: number of rejected cards	0.07 (0.26)	0.04 (0.20)	0.11 (0.31)	0.10 (0.31)	0.04 (0.20)	0.11 (0.31)	.00 (.00)	0.13 (0.34)
53	Rorschach: movement-to-color ratio (M/C)	1.99 (2.64)	1.47 (1.55)	2.48 (3.30)	1.94 (2.31)	2.06 (3.05)	1.74 (1.37)	2.19 (2.21)	2.06 (4.04)
54[a]	Rorschach: form-color to color-form plus pure color ratio (F/CF+C)	1.34 (1.60)	0.87 (0.92)	1.76 (1.97)	1.63 (1.97)	0.96 (0.87)	1.18 (1.33)	1.91 (2.17)	0.84 (0.77)
55[a]	Impulsivity index (see p. 97)	110.00 (34.89)	116.75 (31.54)	103.73 (37.20)	105.05 (37.72)	116.19 (30.64)	108.42 (30.43)	113.74 (35.60)	107.44 (40.51)
56	Hostility score on Elizur content rating scale	5.14 (5.05)	5.19 (5.33)	5.09 (4.87)	5.38 (4.90)	4.83 (5.32)	4.84 (5.47)	5.53 (5.30)	5.03 (4.49)
57*	Total IQ on WAIS or WISC[e]	102.15 (14.40)	97.74 (15.58)	107.68 (11.43)	100.70 (12.03)	105.32 (16.72)	113.00 (10.94)	104.84 (9.61)	89.12 (11.56)
58	Information score on WAIS or WISC	9.51 (2.86)	8.63 (2.88)	10.36 (2.61)	9.43 (2.79)	9.60 (3.00)	11.00 (2.54)	10.05 (2.15)	7.23 (2.59)
59	Comprehension	10.65 (3.29)	9.22 (2.55)	12.04 (3.37)	10.17 (2.67)	11.24 (3.89)	12.00 (3.09)	11.11 (3.46)	8.65 (2.37)

TABLE A-2 *(continued)*

Variable #	Definition	Means and Standard Deviations[a]							
		Whole Group (N = 55)	Young (N = 27)	Old (N = 28)	Male (N = 30)	Female (N = 25)	Upper White (N = 19)	Lower White (N = 19)	Black (N = 17)
60	Arithmetic	9.13 (3.38)	7.89 (3.62)	10.32 (2.69)	8.63 (3.01)	9.72 (3.76)	11.42 (3.10)	8.47 (2.85)	7.29 (2.89)
61	Similarities	11.73 (2.74)	10.59 (2.39)	12.82 (2.64)	11.20 (2.66)	12.36 (2.75)	13.00 (2.36)	12.05 (2.12)	9.94 (2.93)
62	Vocabulary	10.29 (3.14)	9.15 (3.20)	11.39 (2.70)	10.07 (2.80)	10.56 (3.54)	11.89 (2.90)	10.79 (2.20)	7.94 (3.01)
63	Picture completion	11.04 (3.25)	10.85 (3.33)	11.21 (3.22)	10.97 (3.22)	11.12 (3.35)	11.63 (3.13)	12.79 (2.66)	8.41 (2.29)
64	Picture arrangements	9.64 (1.98)	9.78 (1.97)	9.50 (2.03)	9.43 (1.87)	9.88 (2.13)	10.68 (1.77)	9.21 (2.07)	8.94 (1.71)
65	Block design	11.24 (3.39)	10.56 (3.61)	11.89 (3.08)	10.97 (3.56)	11.56 (3.22)	12.84 (2.79)	12.16 (2.75)	8.41 (2.98)
66	Object assembly	10.78 (2.99)	10.00 (3.09)	11.54 (2.73)	10.27 (2.73)	11.40 (3.21)	12.58 (1.92)	11.32 (2.77)	8.18 (2.43)
67	Digit symbol[f]	10.72 (3.22)	9.78 (3.66)	11.67 (2.42)	9.60 (2.90)	12.13 (3.10)	12.22 (3.37)	10.32 (2.47)	9.89 (3.35)
68*	Offer Self-Image Questionnaire (OSIQ) scale score 1:[g] impulse control	2.78 (0.87)	3.02 (1.01)	2.56 (0.68)	2.72 (0.92)	2.84 (0.83)	2.69 (0.85)	2.60 (0.89)	3.08 (0.87)
69	OSIQ scale score 2: emotional tone	2.89 (0.83)	2.98 (0.95)	2.80 (0.72)	2.59 (0.77)	3.25 (0.78)	2.96 (0.82)	2.97 (0.76)	2.77 (0.95)
70	OSIQ scale score 3: body and self-image	2.94 (0.72)	3.04 (0.80)	2.86 (0.65)	2.89 (0.69)	3.01 (0.77)	2.90 (0.67)	2.82 (0.77)	3.14 (0.73)

TABLE A-2 (continued)

Variable #	Definition	Means and Standard Deviations[a]							
		Whole Group (N = 55)	Young (N = 27)	Old (N = 28)	Male (N = 30)	Female (N = 25)	Upper White (N = 19)	Lower White (N = 19)	Black (N = 17)
71	OSIQ scale score 4: social attitudes	2.48 (0.77)	2.62 (0.76)	2.36 (0.78)	2.33 (0.80)	2.66 (0.71)	2.47 (0.68)	2.52 (0.87)	2.45 (0.81)
72	OSIQ scale score 5: morals	2.64 (0.59)	2.66 (0.58)	2.63 (0.61)	2.69 (0.67)	2.58 (0.49)	2.51 (0.55)	2.65 (0.54)	2.78 (0.68)
73	OSIQ scale score 6: sexual attitudes	2.67 (0.64)	2.74 (0.69)	2.61 (0.59)	2.58 (0.71)	2.78 (0.53)	2.70 (0.65)	2.45 (0.61)	2.87 (0.63)
74	OSIQ scale score 7: family relations	3.24 (0.79)	3.26 (0.75)	3.23 (0.85)	2.99 (0.78)	3.56 (0.70)	3.40 (0.67)	3.37 (0.86)	2.91 (0.79)
75	OSIQ scale score 8: external mastery	2.56 (0.58)	2.69 (0.65)	2.44 (0.50)	2.53 (0.67)	2.59 (0.48)	2.51 (0.51)	2.48 (0.63)	2.70 (0.62)
76	OSIQ scale score 9: vocational and educational goals	2.17 (0.66)	2.26 (0.68)	2.09 (0.64)	2.12 (0.74)	2.23 (0.56)	2.27 (0.51)	2.35 (0.79)	1.84 (0.56)
77	OSIQ scale score 10: psychopathology	2.83 (0.75)	2.95 (0.79)	2.72 (0.70)	2.64 (0.65)	3.06 (0.81)	2.73 (0.81)	2.82 (0.74)	2.96 (0.72)
78	OSIQ scale score 11: superior adjustment	2.83 (0.56)	2.91 (0.57)	2.75 (0.54)	2.84 (0.58)	2.08 (0.54)	2.79 (0.45)	2.77 (0.65)	2.93 (0.58)
79*	OSIQ total score	2.74 (0.43)	2.84 (0.45)	2.64 (0.41)	2.63 (0.47)	2.86 (0.36)	2.72 (0.39)	2.74 (0.48)	2.75 (0.45)
80	Adolescent behavior check list (ABCL) weighted total: violence toward property[h]	8.51 (12.07)	11.83 (15.94)	5.33 (4.99)	10.52 (15.08)	6.10 (6.47)	4.19 (4.62)	10.66 (17.96)	10.95 (8.41)
81*	ABCL weighted total: violence toward others	22.46 (24.22)	30.76 (29.53)	14.45 (14.07)	24.69 (26.33)	19.77 (21.63)	8.83 (8.00)	24.05 (30.08)	35.91 (21.77)

Means and Standard Deviations[a]

Variable #	Definition	Whole Group (N = 55)	Young (N = 27)	Old (N = 28)	Male (N = 30)	Female (N = 25)	Upper White (N = 19)	Lower White (N = 19)	Black (N = 17)
82	ABCL weighted total: violence toward self	7.61 (29.41)	4.74 (11.39)	10.39 (39.85)	3.75 (8.29)	12.25 (42.68)	3.91 (8.91)	12.81 (48.07)	5.95 (13.37)
83*	ABCL weighted total: antisocial behavior (not violent)	613.52 (373.82)	749.62 (393.51)	482.29 (306.56)	736.69 (362.95)	465.72 (336.91)	454.47 (282.44)	581.13 (351.41)	827.49 (403.75)
84*	Delinquency checklist: total score[i]	57.82 (31.27)	54.41 (30.01)	61.11 (32.63)	52.80 (29.73)	63.84 (32.60)	65.21 (27.89)	55.42 (34.14)	52.23 (31.76)
85	Delinquency checklist: parental defiance score	8.69 (4.95)	8.04 (4.85)	9.32 (5.06)	7.57 (4.59)	10.04 (5.12)	10.89 (4.15)	9.84 (4.55)	4.94 (4.22)
86	Delinquency checklist: delinquency role score	15.11 (8.09)	14.48 (7.56)	15.71 (8.66)	13.90 (7.92)	16.56 (8.21)	15.74 (7.43)	14.74 (9.61)	14.82 (7.35)
87	Delinquency checklist: drug usage score	5.45 (5.16)	4.07 (4.21)	6.79 (5.69)	3.57 (4.27)	7.72 (5.29)	8.32 (5.09)	5.00 (5.31)	2.77 (3.35)
88	Delinquency checklist: assaultive behavior score	2.02 (2.79)	2.56 (3.57)	1.50 (1.64)	2.23 (2.14)	1.76 (3.43)	1.32 (1.34)	1.74 (2.16)	3.12 (4.12)
89	OSIQ item scores: distance between father and child[j]	71.65 (13.59)	75.77 (13.26)	68.86 (13.34)	72.29 (15.24)	70.95 (11.85)	69.28 (14.38)	72.97 (11.47)	74.37 (16.42)
90	OSIQ item scores: distance between mother and child[j]	71.74 (16.71)	78.68 (16.51)	67.02 (15.44)	74.50 (16.55)	68.70 (16.79)	64.83 (18.20)	77.97 (13.31)	74.81 (15.18)
91*	OSIQ item scores: distance between father and mother[j]	54.44 (13.64)	57.39 (14.78)	52.20 (12.54)	54.20 (12.82)	54.71 (14.80)	51.78 (10.59)	53.35 (12.69)	61.83 (18.96)
92*	OSIQ: difference between father's and mother's distance to resolution[j] (smaller score = father tends to win)	5.00 (18.89)	3.76 (22.00)	6.20 (18.61)	4.72 (19.19)	5.62 (21.18)	8.44 (18.77)	1.53 (17.02)	5.39 (27.47)

TABLE A-2 (continued)

Variable #	Definition	Means and Standard Deviations[a]							
		Whole Group (N = 55)	Young (N = 27)	Old (N = 28)	Male (N = 30)	Female (N = 25)	Upper White (N = 19)	Lower White (N = 19)	Black (N = 17)
93	OSIQ: father's total adjustment score[k]	3.38 (0.54)	3.27 (0.49)	3.46 (0.57)	3.39 (0.51)	3.37 (0.57)	3.47 (0.50)	3.41 (0.54)	3.14 (0.60)
94	OSIQ: mother's total adjustment score[k]	3.41 (0.53)	3.33 (5.54)	3.47 (0.53)	3.53 (0.56)	3.28 (0.48)	3.42 (0.51)	3.58 (0.50)	3.08 (0.52)
95*	OSIQ: average parents' (father and mother) total adjustment score[k]	3.39 (0.44)	3.30 (0.40)	3.47 (0.47)	3.46 (0.46)	3.32 (0.43)	3.44 (0.42)	3.49 (0.44)	3.11 (0.44)
96	Revealed differences procedure: number of acts initiated by wife (subject's mother)[l]	304.33 (132.25)	318.61 (157.25)	293.63 (112.35)	321.45 (131.65)	285.50 (133.69)	280.50 (110.12)	323.31 (164.54)	320.00 (111.40)
97*	Revealed differences procedure: number of acts initiated by husband (subject's father)[l]	307.33 (125.30)	329.83 (156.58)	290.46 (95.77)	343.05 (126.17)	268.05 (114.81)	294.28 (100.08)	301.56 (149.88)	348.25 (130.62)
98	Revealed differences procedure: percentage of acts initiated by wife (subject's mother)[l]	48.57 (7.66)	47.94 (6.79)	49.04 (8.36)	47.05 (7.37)	50.25 (7.81)	47.78 (6.37)	50.75 (8.32)	46.00 (8.77)
99	Revealed differences procedure: percentage of acts initiated by husband (subject's father)[l]	49.55 (7.63)	49.72 (6.92)	49.42 (8.27)	51.09 (7.00)	47.85 (8.11)	50.61 (6.40)	47.69 (8.06)	50.87 (9.48)
100*	Revealed differences procedure:[l] tendency re compromise over concession: (1 = did not emphasize compromise; 2 = could not make a judgment; 3 = compromise)	2.69 (0.68)	2.56 (0.78)	2.79 (0.59)	2.59 (0.80)	2.80 (0.52)	2.83 (0.51)	2.69 (0.70)	2.37 (0.92)
101*	Revealed differences procedure:[l] tendency to add new information rather than repeat (see #100)	2.17 (0.96)	2.00 (0.97)	2.29 (0.95)	2.00 (0.98)	2.35 (0.93)	2.39 (0.92)	2.13 (0.96)	1.75 (1.03)
102	Revealed differences procedure:[l] judged warmth (see #100)	2.57 (0.67)	2.67 (0.59)	2.50 (0.72)	2.50 (0.67)	2.65 (0.67)	2.67 (0.69)	2.56 (0.63)	2.37 (0.74)

Means and Standard Deviations[a]

Variable #	Definition	Whole Group (N = 55)	Young (N = 27)	Old (N = 28)	Male (N = 30)	Female (N = 25)	Upper White (N = 19)	Lower White (N = 19)	Black (N = 17)
103	Revealed differences procedure:[1] judged decision reaching (see #100)	2.17 (0.93)	2.06 (0.94)	2.25 (0.94)	2.09 (0.97)	2.25 (0.91)	2.44 (0.86)	2.13 (0.96)	1.63 (0.92)
104*	Revealed differences procedure:[1] husband's positive affect	64.98 (14.65)	59.17 (15.61)	69.33 (12.50)	61.14 (16.95)	69.20 (10.48)	71.39 (11.45)	61.31 (15.76)	57.87 (14.58)
105[m]	Revealed differences procedure:[1] wife's positive affect	59.55 (15.66)	57.33 (18.18)	61.21 (13.66)	53.77 (14.70)	65.90 (14.48)	62.44 (15.39)	58.63 (15.27)	54.87 (17.71)
106*	Revealed differences procedure:[1] difference in positive affect between husband and wife	5.57 (13.09)	1.83 (13.84)	8.37 (12.03)	7.45 (15.46)	3.50 (9.83)	9.17 (13.59)	2.69 (12.48)	3.25 (12.76)
107*	Staff rating: degree of subject's depression (lower = more of the trait)[n]	2.75 (0.69)	2.84 (0.73)	2.66 (0.65)	2.99 (0.57)	2.45 (0.71)	2.76 (0.59)	2.56 (0.79)	2.95 (0.64)
108*	Staff rating: degree of subject's impulsiveness (lower = more of the trait)[n]	2.72 (1.14)	2.40 (1.12)	3.02 (1.09)	2.55 (0.84)	2.91 (1.41)	3.45 (0.97)	2.58 (1.19)	2.05 (0.77)
109	Primary mental abilities: spatial relations score[o] (no data: 25 subjects)	31.40 (10.89)	28.29 (10.88)	35.46 (9.85)	38.17 (10.66)	36.25 (9.70)	33.33 (7.00)	36.10 (10.99)	22.63 (11.53)
110	Concealed figures score[o] (no data: 21 subjects)	20.82 (7.52)	18.65 (6.04)	23.93 (8.53)	18.35 (6.13)	24.36 (8.11)	24.61 (5.84)	22.45 (6.83)	14.10 (5.99)
111	Rod and frame test score[o] (no data: 20 subjects)	56.03 (54.25)	63.70 (61.50)	45.80 (42.71)	63.05 (65.44)	45.50 (30.20)	29.71 (14.63)	42.55 (29.27)	107.70 (74.79)
112	Size estimation test: number of looks/trial[o] (no data: 20 subjects)	6.99 (4.07)	6.67 (3.30)	7.42 (5.01)	7.56 (4.93)	6.14 (2.14)	7.80 (5.09)	6.36 (2.39)	6.55 (4.11)
113	Size estimation test: time/trial[o] (no data: 20 subjects)	16.36 (7.78)	17.67 (9.49)	14.61 (4.36)	16.17 (5.10)	16.65 (10.86)	14.38 (4.55)	19.27 (12.33)	15.93 (3.58)

TABLE A-2 (continued)

Variable #	Definition	Whole Group (N = 55)	Young (N = 27)	Old (N = 28)	Male (N = 30)	Female (N = 25)	Upper White (N = 19)	Lower White (N = 19)	Black (N = 17)
					Means and Standard Deviations[a]				
114	Size estimation test: size/trial° (no data: 20 subjects)	44.24 (2.42)	44.64 (2.46)	43.71 (2.34)	44.37 (2.42)	44.06 (2.51)	44.05 (2.45)	44.84 (2.45)	43.86 (2.48)
115	Schematizing test: lag score°	0.014 (0.020)	0.009 (0.020)	0.020 (0.019)	0.015 (0.022)	0.012 (0.017)	0.008 (0.027)	0.012 (0.011)	0.024 (0.013)
116	Schematizing test: percent accuracy° (no data: 22 subjects)	56.82 (12.19)	55.58 (13.03)	58.50 (11.20)	52.90 (12.62)	62.85 (8.88)	59.85 (10.88)	60.36 (6.52)	48.11 (15.69)
117	Color/word test: regressed time to read colors only° (no data: 21 subjects)	−2.32 (17.32)	4.52 (19.56)	−10.98 (8.46)	3.25 (19.06)	−10.28 (10.72)	−9.17 (9.28)	1.66 (22.08)	3.46 (18.64)
118	Color/word test: color/word interference score° (no data: 21 subjects)	12.71 (27.27)	24.87 (30.21)	−2.69 (11.15)	15.90 (31.84)	8.16 (19.19)	8.25 (18.26)	17.97 (36.27)	13.22 (28.43)
119*	Video interview with staff:[p] interviewee's opinion of patient (1 = positive; 2 = neutral; 3 = negative)	1.83 (0.40)	1.91 (0.33)	1.74 (0.45)	1.83 (0.38)	1.82 (0.43)	1.78 (0.40)	1.96 (0.36)	1.74 (0.42)
120*	Video interview with staff:[p] interviewee's description of patient's character (1 = active; 4 = passive)[q]	2.37 (0.45)	2.30 (0.44)	2.44 (0.45)	2.39 (0.50)	2.34 (0.38)	2.42 (0.51)	2.40 (0.37)	2.27 (0.47)
121*	Video interview with staff:[p] interviewee's opinion of patient's future (1 = optimistic; 2 = pessimistic)	1.38 (0.35)	1.39 (0.37)	1.37 (0.35)	1.40 (0.39)	1.37 (0.31)	1.34 (0.33)	1.44 (0.36)	1.37 (0.38)
122	Video interview with staff:[p] interviewee rated soft/loud (1 = soft; 6 = loud)[q]	3.41 (0.66)	3.40 (0.63)	3.42 (0.70)	3.43 (0.63)	3.38 (0.70)	3.20 (0.70)	3.50 (0.69)	3.56 (0.54)
123	Video interview with staff:[p] interviewee rated warm/cold (1 = warm; 6 = cold)[q]	3.51 (0.71)	3.52 (0.65)	3.50 (0.77)	3.55 (0.72)	3.46 (0.70)	3.49 (0.76)	3.66 (0.67)	3.35 (0.69)

TABLE A-2 (continued)

Variable #	Definition	Means and Standard Deviations[a]							
		Whole Group (N = 55)	Young (N = 27)	Old (N = 28)	Male (N = 30)	Female (N = 25)	Upper White (N = 19)	Lower White (N = 19)	Black (N = 17)
124	Video interview with staff:[p] interviewee rated passive/active (1 = passive; 6 = active)[q]	4.04 (0.71)	4.10 (0.65)	3.97 (0.78)	4.05 (0.74)	4.02 (0.70)	4.04 (0.56)	4.07 (0.93)	4.00 (0.64)
125	Video interview with staff:[p] interviewee rated unlikable/likable (1 = unlikable; 6 = likable)[q]	3.80 (0.59)	3.86 (0.59)	3.74 (0.59)	3.86 (0.55)	3.73 (0.64)	3.73 (0.58)	3.85 (0.49)	3.84 (0.72)
126*	Video interview with staff:[p] interviewee rated cheerful/depressed (1 = cheerful; 6 = depressed)[q]	3.32 (0.60)	3.26 (0.65)	3.39 (0.53)	3.19 (0.49)	3.48 (0.69)	3.35 (0.59)	3.24 (0.69)	3.39 (0.53)
127	Follow-up interview: number of months out of hospital (no data: 7 subjects)	21.20 (11.79)	17.04 (7.75)	23.32 (14.27)	21.39 (14.04)	19.05 (8.96)	21.11 (13.98)	19.50 (9.34)	20.07 (11.97)
128	Follow-up interview: number of times arrested (no data: 7 subjects)	1.69 (2.51)	1.78 (2.25)	1.48 (2.65)	<u>2.35</u> (2.93)	<u>0.77</u> (1.34)	1.11 (2.26)	2.21 (2.91)	1.73 (2.22)
129	Follow-up interview: number of months institutionalized in correctional facility (no data: 7 subjects)	1.49 (3.46)	1.78 (3.70)	1.04 (3.06)	2.04 (4.05)	0.64 (2.17)	1.58 (3.81)	1.57 (3.63)	1.00 (2.65)
130	Follow-up interview: number of months institutionalized in mental hospital (no data: 7 subjects)	0.76 (2.47)	0.83 (2.60)	0.64 (2.23)	0.69 (2.35)	0.77 (2.51)	0.47 (1.84)	1.36 (3.45)	0.47 (1.81)

[a] Numbers underscored once indicate that the means in question differed significantly at the .05 level using analysis of variance. Numbers underscored twice indicate that differences were significant at the .01 level.

[b] Variable used in factor analysis was late minus early likability.

[c] One patient excluded because number of responses was less than 10.

[d] One subject's time for first response scores was not recorded.

[e] Wechsler 1949, 1955.

[f] One subject inadvertently was not given the Digit Symbol Test.

[g] Two subjects were not given the OSIQ; for comparisons with normal and disturbed groups, see OSIQ Manual (Offer et al. 1977).

[h]See p. 21 for description of ABCL.

[i]See p. 19 for description of DCL.

[j]Sum of absolute value of differences between subjects' scores score on 41 items common to OPCQ and OSIQ.

No data (1 parent only): 10 subjects; parents unable to complete task: 1 subject.

[k]Parents' estimate of how well adjusted the child felt himself or herself to be; no data: 11 subjects as above.

[l]See Bales (1955) for definition of these categories; no data (1 parent only): 10 subjects; parents unable to complete task: 1 subject; tape incomprehensible: 1 subject; tape lost: 1 subject; percent acts by husband and wife do not add to 100 because experimenter's instructions to subjects were part of total number of acts initiated.

[m]In factor analysis, "104" and "105" were added to form a parents' positive-affect score.

[n]Ratings done individually by senior staff on a scale from 1 to 6; score for each subject represents mean across raters.

[o]For definition of these variables, see Ostrov (1975).

[p]Score is mean rating across three staff members for each subject; see p. 85 for description.

[q]Intervening scale points were not defined.

[*]Variable used in factor analysis.

TABLE A-3

Frequencies and Percent Distributions of Variables #131-33 Used in the Entire Study (1969-1974)

Variable #	Definition	Frequencies and Percent Distributions[a]							
		Whole Group (N = 55)	Young (N = 27)	Old (N = 28)	Male (N = 30)	Female (N = 25)	Upper White (N = 19)	Lower White (N = 19)	Black (N = 17)
		%	%	%	%	%	%	%	%
131	Follow-up interview: drug use								
	1 = none[b]	39	27	50	37	41	44	36	36
	2 = marijuana only	28	41	17	37	18	17	14	57
	3 = psychedelics, speed, phenobarb, uppers, downers, but not heroin	26	23	29	17	36	28	50	–
	4 = heroin	7	9	4	8	5	11	–	7
	(no data: 9 subjects)								
132	Follow-up interview: alcohol use								
	1 = none, or not to the point of drunkenness	85	82	88	72	100	78	86	93
	2 = to the point of drunkenness	15	18	12	28	–	22	14	7
	(no data: 8 subjects)								
133	Follow-up interview: feeling about self[c]								
	1 = very positive	18	14	22	21	15	11	8	39
	2 = positive	61	67	57	67	55	67	61	54
	3 = neutral	9	5	13	4	15	6	23	–
	4 = negative	9	14	4	15	11	8	8	8
	5 = very negative	2	–	4	4	–	6	–	–
	(no data: 11 subjects)								

[a] Percents do not always sum to 100 because of rounding errors; if chi-square comparison between groups significant at less than .05 level then numbers are underlined.

[b] For chi-square comparison among groups, categories #3 and #4 were collapsed.

[c] Because of small cell sizes, no chi-square comparison among groups was performed.

APPENDIX B

RELIABILITIES OF VARIOUS INSTRUMENTS USED

TABLE B-1

Reliability of Various Instruments Used to Study Fifty-five Juvenile Delinquents

ABCL Reliability:[a] *Scale* (weighted total 13-week score)	No. of Items	Reliability Coefficient
1. Violence toward self	5	.513
2. Violence toward others	19	.743
3. Violence toward property	17	.636
4. Nonviolent antisocial behavior	127	.825

Likability Scales: *Scale* (average across raters used in analyses in text)	No. of Raters	Reliability Coefficient
1. Early	8[d]	.550
2. Late	8	.772

Videotape "Global" Rating:[b] *Scale* (average across raters used in analyses in text)		
1. Cheerful/depressed	2	.676
2. Passive/active	2	.682
3. Warm/cold	2	.773
4. Soft/loud	2	.665
5. Likable/unlikable	2	.700
6. Anxious/calm[c]	2	.406
7. Trusting/suspicious[c]	2	.453

Staff Rating of Subjects' Impulsivity and Depression: *Scale* (average across raters used in analyses in text)		
1. Impulsivity	7	.902
2. Depression	7	.719

[a] Reliability was calculated using a formula given by Winer (1971) which adjusts the reliability rating for anchor points.

[b] Because these data were rated along discrete, six-point scales, reliability was calculated using a formula presented by Cohen, 1968 for the analysis of nonparametric data.

[c] These variables were not used in further analyses.

[d] While all staff rated subjects' likability, for analytic purposes only those staff who rated all fifty-five subjects were used to calculate the reliability of this rating; there were eight such staff.

APPENDIX C

FACTOR ANALYSIS

TABLE C-1

Factor Loadings on Variables Composing Four Factors of a Five-Factor
Solution Generated by a Factor Analysis of 43 Variables

Factor	Variable Name and Definition	Loading on Factor[a]	Communality
1.	*Impulsive*		
	Therapist rating: overall health, poor	.689	.503
	ABCL: violence toward others, high	.658	.577
	Teacher rating: social sensitivity, poor	.639	.625
	Staff rating of impulsivity: impulsive	.620	.619
	ABCL: nonviolent, high	.532	.528
	Self-image from background Q: like to change	.529	.348
	Early likability: not likable	.496	.379
2.	*Narcissistic*		
	OSIQ total score: well adjusted	.784	.656
	OSIQ impulse control: well adjusted	.733	.616
	DCL total score: low	.730	.628
	Video interview: interviewee depressed	.516	.325
3.	*Depressed Borderline*		
	Staff rating of depression: depressed	.827	.702
	Background Q: physical punishment? Yes	.580	.508
	Teacher rating: initiative, high	.455	.288
	Power score, father vs. mother: father tends to dominate	.434	.339
	Change in likability: becomes more likable	.418	.362
	Use narcotics? Yes[b]	.403	.260
4.	*Empty Borderline*		
	Video interview: passive	.740	.591
	Therapist rating: emotional expressiveness, low	.672	.476
	Therapist rating: emotional experience, low	.609	.408
	Parents' OSIQ: total adjustment score, low	.591	.458
	Video interview: what kind of person? Negative[b]	.423	.534
	Video interview: pessimistic	.408	.278

[a]Absolute values of loadings are given because direction of variables is arbitrary. Variables are listed only if their primary loading is on the factor in question and if they loaded .40 or more on that factor.

[b]These variables were not stably associated with this factor across factor solutions, but were associated with this factor in the five-factor solution. They were not used to generate subjects' factor scores.

REFERENCES

Adkins, W. R. 1964. The Relationship of 3 Cognitive Controls to Reports of Effective and Ineffective Life Behavior. *Dissertation Abstracts* 24:3419–3420.

Aichorn, A. 1935 (1925). *Wayward Youth.* New York: Viking Press.

Ainslie, G. 1975. Specious Reward: A Behavioral Theory of Impulsiveness and Impulse Control. *Psychological Bulletin* 82:463–496.

Alexander, F., and Staub, H. 1956 (1931). *The Criminal, the Judge and the Public; a Psychological Analysis.* New York: Collier Books.

Altus, W. D., and Clark, J. H. 1949. Subtest Variation on the Wechsler-Bellevue for Two Institutionalized Behavior Problem Groups. *Journal of Consulting Psychology* 13:444–447.

Andry, R. G. 1957. Faulty Paternal and Maternal Child Relationships, Affection, and Delinquency. *British Journal of Delinquency* 8:34, 1957.

Anthony, J. 1969. The Reaction of Adults to Adolescents and Their Behavior. In *Adolescence,* ed. G. Caplan and S. Lebovici. New York: Basic Books, Inc.

Arieti, S. 1967. *The Intrapsychic Self: Feeling, Cognition and Creativity in Health and Mental Illness.* New York: Basic Books, Inc.

Arnold, W. R. 1971. Race and Ethnicity Relative to Other Factors in Juvenile Court Dispositions. *American Journal of Sociology* 77:211–227.

Baittle, B., and Kobrin, S. 1964. On the Relationship of a Characterological Type of Delinquent to the Milieu. *Psychiatry* 27:6–16.

———, and Offer, Daniel. 1971. On the Nature of Adolescent Rebellion. In *Annals of Adolescent Psychiatry,* Vol. I, ed. S. C. Feinstein, P. Giovacchini and A. Miller. New York: Basic Books, Inc.

Bales, R. F. 1970. *Personality and Interpersonal Behavior.* Holt, Rinehart and Winston, New York.

Bandura, A. 1973. *Aggression: A Social Learning Analysis.* Englewood Cliffs, New Jersey: Prentice-Hall, Inc.

———, and Walters, R. H. 1959. *Adolescent Aggression.* New York: Ronald Press.

Barndt, R. J., and Johnson, D. M. 1955. Time Orientation in Delinquents. *Journal of Abnormal and Social Psychology* 51:343–345.

Beck, S. J. et al. 1961. *Rorschach's Test: I. Basic Processes.* (3rd ed.) New York: Grune and Stratton.

Bettelheim, B. 1966. Violence: A Neglected Mode of Behavior. In the *Annals of the American Academy of Political and Social Science* 364:50–59.

———. 1976. *The Uses of Enchantment.* New York: Alfred A. Knopf.

Bird, Brian. 1957. A Specific Peculiarity of Acting Out. *Journal American Psychoanalytic Association* 5:630–647.

Blank, L. 1958. The Intellectual Functioning of Delinquents. *Journal of Social Psychology* 47:9–14.

Block, H. A., and Niederhoffer, A. 1958. *The Gang: A Study in Adolescent Behavior.* New York: The Philosophical Library.

Block, Jack. 1971. *Lives through Time.* Berkeley, Cal.: Bancroft Books.

Blos, P. 1962. *On Adolescence.* New York: Free Press.

Bock, R. D. 1963. Programming Univariate and Multivariate Analysis of Variance. *Technometrics* 5:95–117.

Borland, B. L., and Heckman, H. K. 1976. Hyperactive Boys and Their Brothers: A 25-Year Follow-Up Study. *Archives of General Psychiatry* 33:669–675.

Bowlby, J. et al. 1966. *Maternal Care and Mental Health: A Reassessment of Its Effects.* New York: Schocken Books.

REFERENCES

Boynton, P. L., and Walsworth, B. M. 1943. Emotionality Test Scores of Delinquent and Nondelinquent Girls. *Journal of Abnormal and Social Psychology* 38:87–92.

Broverman, D. M. 1960a. Dimensions of Cognitive Style. *Journal of Personality* 28: 167–185.

———. 1960b. Cognitive Style and Intra-Individual Variation in Abilities. *Journal of Personality* 28:240–256.

——— et al. 1968. The Roles of Activation and Inhibition in Sex Differences in Cognitive Abilities. *Psychological Review* 75:23–50.

Browning, C. J. 1960. Differential Impact of Family Disorganization on Male Adolescents. *Social Problems* 8:37–44.

Buben, J. 1975. Adolescent and Young Adult Rorschach Responses. In *From Teenage to Young Manhood,* D. Offer and J. B. Offer. New York: Basic Books, Inc.

Campbell, S. B. 1973. Cognitive Styles in Reflective, Impulsive, and Hyperactive Boys and Their Mothers. *Perceptual and Motor Skills* 36:747–752.

———, and Douglas, V. I. 1972. Cognitive Styles and Responses to the Threat of Frustration. *Canadian Journal of Behavioural Science* 4:30–42.

Carroll, H. M., and Curran, F. J. 1940. A Follow-Up Study of Three Hundred Court Cases from the Adolescent Ward of Bellevue Hospital. *Mental Hygiene* 24:621–638.

Cerney, M., and Shevrin, H. 1974. The Relations between Color Dominated Responses on the Rorschach and Explosive Behavior in a Hospital Setting. *Bulletin of the Menninger Clinic* 38:430–444.

Clark, J. P., and Tifft, L. L. 1966. Polygraph and Interview Validation of Self-Reported Deviant Behavior. *American Sociological Review* 31:516–523.

Cleckley, H. 1964. *The Mask of Sanity.* 4th ed. St. Louis, Mo.: C. V. Mosby.

Cloward, R. A., and Ohlin, L. E. 1960. *Delinquency and Opportunity.* Glencoe, Ill.: The Free Press.

Cohen, A. K. 1971. *Delinquent Boys.* Glencoe, Ill.: The Free Press.

Cohen, J. 1957. Factor-Analytically Based Rationale for the Wechsler Adult Intelligence Scale. *Journal of Consulting Psychology* 21:451–457.

———. 1968. Weighted Kappa: Nominal Scale Agreement with Provision for Scaled Disagreement or Partial Credit. *Psychological Bulletin* 70:213–220.

Conger, J. J., and Miller, W. C. 1966. *Personality, Social Class and Delinquency.* New York: John Wiley and Sons.

Cox, Rachel D. 1970. *Youth into Maturity.* New York: Mental Health Materials Center.

Cronback, L. J., and Gleser, G. C. 1965. *Psychological Tests and Personnel Decision.* Urbana, Ill.: University of Illinois Press.

Davids, A., Kidder, C., and Reich, M. 1962. Time Orientation in Male and Female Juvenile Delinquents. *Journal of Abnormal and Social Psychology* 64:239–240.

Davis, D. B. 1966. Violence in American Literature. *The Annals of the American Academy of Political and Social Science* 364:28–36.

Deutsch, Helene. 1967. *Selected Problems of Adolescence.* Psychoanalytic Study of the Child Monographs, No. 3, New York: International Universities Press.

Docter, R. F., and Winder, C. L. 1954. Delinquent vs. Nondelinquent Performance on the Porteus Qualitative Maze Test. *Journal of Consulting Psychology* 18:71–73.

Douvan, E., and Adelson, J. B. 1966. *The Adolescent Experience.* New York: John Wiley and Sons.

Drake, D. M. 1970. Perceptual Correlates of Impulsive and Reflective Behavior. *Developmental Psychology* 2:202–214.

Engel, M. 1959. The Stability of the Self-Concept in Adolescence. *Journal of Abnormal and Social Psychology* 58:211–215.

Eisenberg, L. 1972. The Human Nature of Human Nature. *Science* 176:123–128.

Eissler, K. R., ed. 1949. *Searchlights on Delinquency.* New York: International Universities Press.

Emery, R. E., and Marholin, D. II. 1977. An Applied Behavior Analysis of Delinquency: The Irrelevancy of Relevant Behavior. *American Psychologist* 32:860–874.

REFERENCES

Erikson, E. H. 1950. *Childhood and Society.* New York: W. W. Norton and Company.
———. 1959. Identity and the Life Cycle. *Psychological Issues.* 1:1–171 New York: International Universities Press.
———. 1968. *Identity: Youth and Crisis.* New York: W. W. Norton and Company.
Erikson, K. 1962. Notes on the Sociology of Deviance. *Social Problems* 9:307.
Erikson, R. V., and Roberts, A. H. 1966. A Comparison of Two Groups of Institutionalized Delinquents on Porteus Maze Test Performance. *Journal of Consulting Psychology* 30:567.
———, and Roberts, A. H. 1971. Some Ego Functions Associated with Delay of Gratification in Male Delinquents. *Journal of Consulting and Clinical Psychology* 36:378–382.
Eskin, L. D. 1960. "A Study of Some Possible Connections between Criminal Behavior and Perceptual Behavior." Ph.D dissertation, New York University (Xerox).
Fabianic, D. A. 1972. "Self-Report Delinquency Questionnaire: An Evaluation." Ph.D dissertation, University of Iowa (Xerox).
Feuer, Lewis S. 1969. *The Conflict of Generations: The Character and Significance of Student Movements.* New York: Basic Books, Inc.
Field, J. G. 1960. The Performance-Verbal IQ Discrepancy in a Group of Sociopaths. *Journal of Clinical Psychology* 16:321–322.
Fine, P., and Offer, D. 1965. Periodic Outbursts of Antisocial Behavior. *Archives of General Psychiatry* 13:240–251.
Finn, J. D. 1972. *Multivariance, Univariate and Multivariate: Analysis of Variance, Covariance and Depression, Version V.* Buffalo, N.Y.: National Educational Resources.
Finney, B. C. 1955. Rorschach Test Correlates of Assaultive Behavior. *Journal of Projective Techniques* 19:6–16.
Fisher, G. M. 1961. Discrepancy in Verbal and Performance IQ in Adolescent Sociopaths. *Journal of Clinical Psychology* 17:60.
Fontana, A. F. 1966. Family Etiology of Schizophrenia: Is a Scientific Methodology Possible? *Psychological Bulletin* 6:214–227.
Fooks, G., and Thomas, R. R. 1957. Differential Qualitative Performance of Delinquents on the Porteus Maze. *Journal of Consulting Psychology* 21:351–353.
Foulds, G. A. 1951. Temperamental Differences in Maze Performance." *British Journal of Psychology* 42:209–217.
Fountain, Gerard. 1961. Adolescent into Adult: An Inquiry. *Journal of the American Psychoanalytic Association* 9:417–433.
Freud, A. 1958. Adolescence. *Psychoanalytic Study of the Child* 13:255–278.
———. 1965. Dissociality, Delinquency, Criminality. In *Normality and Pathology in Childhood: Assessments of Development.* New York: International Universities Press.
Freud, S. 1958 (1905). Three Essays on the Theory of Sexuality. In *The Complete Psychological Works of S. Freud,* ed. J. Strachey. Vol. 7. London: The Hogarth Press.
———. 1958 (1911). Formulations on the Two Principles of Mental Functioning. In *The Complete Psychological Works of S. Freud,* ed. J. Strachey. Vol. 12. London: The Hogarth Press.
———. 1958 (1920). Beyond the Pleasure Principle. In *The Complete Psychological Works of S. Freud,* ed. J. Strachey. Vol. 18. London: The Hogarth Press.
Friedenberg, E. Z. 1959. *The Vanishing Adolescent.* Boston: Beacon Press.
Friedlander, K. 1945. Formation of the Anti-Social Character. *The Psychoanalytic Study of the Child* 1:189–203.
———. 1960. *The Psycho-Analytical Approach to Juvenile Delinquency: Theory, Case Studies, Treatment.* New York: International Universities Press.
Garber, B. 1972. *Follow-Up Study of Hospitalized Adolescents.* New York: Brunner/Mazel.
Gardner, R. W. 1951. Impulsivity as Indicated by Rorschach Test Factors. *Journal of Consulting Psychology* 15:464–468.

REFERENCES

————. 1970. Scores for the Cognitive Control of the Extensiveness of Scanning. *Perceptual and Motor Skills* 31:330.

———— et al. 1959. Cognitive Control: A Study of Individual Consistencies in Cognitive Behavior. *Psychological Issues* 1(4):1–186.

————, Jackson, D. N., and Messick, S. J. 1960. Personality Organization in Cognitive Controls and Intellectual Abilities. *Psychological Issues* 2(4):1–149.

————, and Long, R. I. 1960. The Stability of Cognitive Controls. *Journal of Abnormal and Social Psychology* 61:485–487.

————, and Moriarty, A. 1968. *Personality Development at Preadolescence*. Seattle, Wn.: University of Washington Press.

Gerbner, G. 1976. Living with Television: The Violence Profile. *Journal of Communication* 173–194.

————. 1978. A Sociological Perspective on TV Research. American Psychiatric Association Annual Meeting, Atlanta, Ga.

Gill, H. S. 1966. Delay of Response and Reaction to Color on the Rorschach. *Journal of Projective Techniques and Personality Assessment* 30:545–552.

Glover, E. 1960. *The Roots of Crime. Selected Papers on Psychoanalysis*. Vol. II New York: International Universities Press.

Glueck, S., and Glueck, E. T. 1962. *Family Environment and Delinquency*. Boston: Houghton Mifflin.

————, and Glueck, E. T. 1940. *Juvenile Delinquents Grown Up*. New York: Commonwealth Fund.

————, and Glueck, E. T. 1934. *One Thousand Juvenile Delinquents*. Cambridge, Mass.: Harvard University Press.

————, and Glueck, E. T. 1956–57. Early Detection of Juvenile Delinquents. *Journal of Criminal Law, Criminology, and Police Science* 47:174–182.

————, and Glueck, E. T. 1970. *Toward a Typology of Juvenile Offenders*. New York: Grune and Stratton.

————, and Glueck, E. T. 1950. *Unraveling Juvenile Delinquency*. New York: The Commonwealth Fund.

Gold, M. 1966. Undetected Delinquent Behavior. *The Journal of Research in Crime and Delinquency* 3:27–46.

Goldfarb, W. 1945. Effects of Psychological Deprivation in Infancy and Subsequent Stimulation. *American Journal of Psychiatry* 102:18–33.

Gough, H. G., and Peterson, D. R. 1952. The Identification and Measurement of Predispositional Factors in Crime and Delinquency. *Journal of Consulting Psychology,* 16:207–212.

Graham, H. D., and Gurr, T. R. 1969. *Violence in America: Historical and Comparative Perspectives*. Washington, D.C.: U.S. Government Printing Office.

Grinker, R. R. Sr., and Werble, B. 1977. *The Borderline Patient*. New York: J. Aronson.

Gross, M. D., and Wilson, W. C. 1974. *Minimal Brain Dysfunction*. New York, Brunner/Mazel.

Haggard, E. A. 1973. Some Effects of Geographic and Social Isolation in Natural Settings. In *Men in Isolation and Confinement*, ed. J. E. Rasmussen. Chicago: Aldine Publishing Co.

Hall, G. S. 1904. *Adolescence: Its Psychology and Its Relation to Physiology, Anthropology, Sociology, Sex, Crime, Religion and Education*. New York: D. Appleton and Company.

Hanna, K. M., Kharasch, L. B., and O'Bryan, J. 1967. *Task Force Report: Juvenile Delinquency and Youth Crime*. Washington, D.C.: Commission on Law Enforcement and Administration of Justice.

Hare, R. D. 1965. Psychopathy, Fear Arousal and Anticipated Pain. *Psychological Reports* 16:499–502.

————. 1966. Psychopathology and Choice of Immediate versus Delayed Punishment. *Journal of Abnormal Psychology* 71:25–29.

————. 1970. *Psychopathy: Theory and Research*. New York: John Wiley and Sons.

Harrison, A., and Nadelman, L. 1972. Conceptual Tempo and Inhibition of Movement in Black Preschool Children. *Child Development* 43:657–668.

REFERENCES

Hartmann, E. et al. 1968. *Adolescents in a Mental Hospital.* New York: Grune and Stratton.

Hartmann, H. 1953. Contribution to the Metapsychology of Schizophrenia. *The Psychoanalytic Study of the Child* 8:177–198.

Hatfield, J. S., Ferguson, L. R., and Alpert, R. 1967. Mother-Child Interaction and the Socialization Process. *Child Development* 38:365–414.

Healy, W., and Bronner, A. F. 1936. *New Light on Delinquency and Its Treatment.* New Haven, Conn.: Yale University Press.

Heine, H. 1887. Gedanken und Einfalle. In *Sämtliche Werke* 4(1). Leipzig.

Hendry, L. B., and Patrick, H. 1977. Adolescents and Television. *Journal of Youth and Adolescence* 6:325–337.

Henry, W. E. 1956. *The Analysis of Fantasy.* New York: John Wiley and Sons, Inc.

Herrick, C. J. 1956. *The Evolution of Human Nature.* Austin, Texas: University of Texas Press.

Hetherington, E. M., Stouwie, R. J., and Ridberg, E. H. 1971. Patterns of Family Interaction and Child Rearing Attitudes Related to Three Dimensions of Juvenile Delinquency. *Journal of Abnormal Psychology* 78:160–176.

Hewitt, L. E., and Jenkins, R. L. 1946. *Fundamental Patterns of Maladjustment: The Dynamics of Their Origin.* Springfield, Ill.: State of Illinois.

Hofstadter, R., and Wallace, M., eds. 1970. *American Violence.* New York: Alfred A. Knopf.

Hollingshead, A. B. 1965 (unpublished). Two-Factor Index of Social Position. New Haven, Conn.

Holtzman, W. H. 1950. Validation Studies of the Rorschach Test: Impulsiveness in the Normal Superior Adult. *Journal of Clinical Psychology* 6:348–351.

Holzman, P. S. 1969. Perceptual Aspects of Psychopathology. In *Neurobiological Aspects of Psychopathology,* ed. J. Zubin and C. Shagass. New York: Grune and Stratton.

———. 1954. The Relation of Assimilation Tendencies in Visual, Auditory, and Kinesthetic Time-Error in Cognitive Attitudes of Leveling and Sharpening. *Journal of Personality* 22:375–394.

———, and Gardner, R. W. 1959. Leveling and Repression. *Journal of Abnormal and Social Psychology* 59:151–155.

———, and Rousey, C. 1971. Disinhibition of Communicated Thought: Generality and Role of Cognitive Style. *Journal of Abnormal Psychology* 77:263–274.

Howard, K. I., and Gordan, R. A. 1963. Empirical Note on the 'Number of Factors Problem' in Factor Analysis. *Psychological Reports* 12:247–250.

Hurwitz, I. et al. 1972. Neuropsychological Function of Normal Boys, Delinquent Boys, and Boys with Learning Problems. *Perceptual and Motor Skills* 35:387–394.

Hutt, M. L. 1969. *The Hutt Adaptation of the Bender-Gestalt Test.* 2d ed. New York: Grune and Stratton.

Israel, N. R. 1969. Leveling-Sharpening and Anticipatory Cardiac Response. *Psychosomatic Medicine* 31:499–509.

Jacob, T. 1975. Family Interaction in Disturbed and Normal Families: A Methodological and Substantive Review. *Psychological Bulletin,* 1975, 82, 33–65.

Jenkins, R. L., and Blodgett, E. 1960. Prediction of Success or Failure of Delinquent Boys from Sentence Completion. *American Journal of Orthopsychiatry* 30:741–756.

———, and Glickman, S. 1947. Patterns of Personality Organization among Delinquents. *The Nervous Child* 6:329–339.

Johnson, A. M. 1949. Sanctions for Superego Lacunae of Adolescents. In *Searchlights on Delinquency,* ed. K. R. Eissler. New York: International Universities Press.

———, and Szurek, S. A. 1952. The Genesis of Antisocial Acting Out in Children and Adults. *Psychoanalytic Quarterly* 21:323–343.

Johnston, M. H. 1973 (unpublished). Word Association in Schizophrenic Children. University of Chicago (Xerox).

Kagan, J. 1965. Impulsive and Reflective Children: Significance of Conceptual Tempo. In *Learning and the Educational Process,* ed. J. D. Krumholtz. Chicago: Rand, McNally.

REFERENCES

————, and Moss, H. A. 1962. *Birth to Maturity: A Study in Psychological Development.* New York: John Wiley and Sons, Inc.

————, Pearson, L., and Welch, L. 1966. Conceptual Impulsivity and Inductive Reasoning. *Child Development* 37: 583–594.

———— et al. 1964. Information Processing in the Child: Significance of Analytic and Reflective Attitudes. *Psychological Monographs* 78:(1, whole no. 578).

Katz, J. M. 1971. Reflection-Impulsivity and Color-Form Sorting. *Child Development* 42:745–754.

Kawi, A. A., and Pasamanick, B. 1958. Association of Factors of Pregnancy with Reading Disorders in Childhood. *Journal of the American Medical Association* 166:1420–1423.

Keniston, Kenneth. 1968. *Young Radicals: Notes on Committed Youth.* New York: Harcourt Brace, Jovanovich, Inc.

Keough, B. K., and Donlon, G. M. 1972. Field Dependence, Impulsivity, and Learning Disabilities. *Journal of Learning Disabilities* 5:331–336.

Kiell, N. 1964. *The Universal Experience of Adolescence.* New York: International Universities Press.

Kingsley, L. 1960. Wechsler-Bellevue Patterns of Psychopaths. *Journal of Consulting Psychology* 24:373.

Kissel, S. 1966. Juvenile Delinquency and Psychological Differentiation: Differences between Social and Solitary Delinquents. *Journal of Clinical Psychology* 22:442.

Klein, G. S. 1954. Need and Regulation. *Nebraska Symposium on Motivation* ed. M. R. Jones. Lincoln, Neb.: University of Nebraska Press.

————. 1958. Cognitive Control and Motivation. In *Assessment of Human Motives,* ed. G. Lindzey. New York: Holt, Rinehart and Winston.

Kohut, H. *The Analysis of Self.* 1971. New York: International Universities Press.

Kulik, J. A., Stein, K. B., and Sarbin, T. R. 1968*a.* Dimensions and Patterns of Adolescent Antisocial Behavior. *Journal of Consulting and Clinical Psychology* 32:375–382.

————, ————, ————. 1968*b.* Disclosure of Delinquent Behavior Under Conditions of Anonymity and Non-Anonymity. *Journal of Consulting and Clinical Psychology* 32:506–509.

La Barba, R. C. 1965. Relationship of Color Responses on the Rorschach to Qualitative Scores on the Porteus Maze Test. *Perceptual and Motor Skills* 21:61–62.

Lander, B. 1954. *Towards an Understanding of Juvenile Delinquency: A Study of 8,464 Cases of Juvenile Delinquency in Baltimore.* New York: Columbia University Press.

Lefkowitz, Monroe M. et al. 1977. Growing Up to be Violent. In *Theories of Aggression,* ed. Robert Maxwell, M.D. New York: Pergamon Press, Inc.

Levy, V. 1972. Field-Independence and Typologies of Delinquency. Ph.D. dissertation, University of Southern California (Xerox).

Lewis, D. O., and Balla, D. A. 1976. *Delinquency and Psychopathology.* New York: Grune and Stratton.

Liebert, R. M., et al. 1973. *The Early Window: The Effect of Television on Children and Youth.* New York: Pergamon Press.

Lippert, W. W., Jr., and Senter, R. J. 1966. Electrodermal Responses in the Sociopath. *Psychonomic Science* 4:25–26.

Lombroso, C. T. et al. 1966. Ctenards in Healthy Youths. *Neurology* 6:1152–1158.

Lorenz, K. 1966. *On Aggression.* New York: Harcourt Brace Jovanovich, Inc.

McCandless, B. R., Persons, W. S., III, and Roberts, A. 1972. Perceived Opportunity, Delinquency, Race, and Body Build among Delinquent Youths. *Journal of Consulting and Clinical Psychology* 38:281–287.

McCord, W. 1968. Delinquency: Psychological Types. In *International Encyclopedia of the Social Sciences,* vol. 4, ed. D. L. Sills. New York: Macmillan, Free Press.

————, McCord, J., and Zola, I. K. 1959. *Origins of Crime.* New York: Columbia University Press.

McCorkle, L. W., Elias, A., and Bixby, F. L. 1958. *The Highfields Story: An Experi-*

mental Treatment Project for Youthful Offenders. New York: Holt, Rinehart and Winston.
Main, Sir Henry. 1963. *Ancient Law.* Boston: Beacon Press.
Mann, L. 1973. Differences between Reflective and Impulsive Children in Tempo and Quality of Decision Making. *Child Development* 44:274–279.
Manne, S. H., Kandel, A., and Rosenthal, D. 1962. Differences between Performance IQ and Verbal IQ in a Severely Sociopathic Population. *Journal of Clinical Psychology* 18:73–77.
Marohn, R. C. 1974. Trauma and the Delinquent. *Adolescent Psychiatry* 3:354–361.
———. 1977a. The "Juvenile Impostor": Some Thoughts on Narcissism and the Delinquent. *Adolescent Psychiatry* 5:186–212.
———. 1977b. Sin, Symptom or Social Deviance—A Psychiatric Perspective on Juvenile Delinquency. Paper Presented at the Symposium "Critical Issues in Adolescent Mental Health." Washington, D.C.
——— et al. 1979. *Adolescent Behavior—A Psychotherapeutic Perspective.* Forthcoming monograph.
Marohn, R. C. et al. 1973. A Hospital Riot: Its Determinants and Implications for Treatment. *American Journal of Psychiatry* 130:631–636.
———, Offer, D., and Ostrov, E. 1971. Juvenile Delinquents View Their Impulsivity. *American Journal of Psychiatry* 128:418–424.
Martinson, R. 1974. What Works?—Questions and Answers about Prison Reform. *The Public Interest* 35:22–54.
Masterson, J. F. 1967. *The Psychiatric Dilemma of Adolescence.* Boston: Little, Brown and Co.
———. 1972. *Treatment of the Borderline Adolescent: A Developmental Approach.* New York: John Wiley and Sons.
Matza, D. 1964. *Delinquency and Drift.* New York: John Wiley and Sons.
Mednick, S. A., and Christansen, K. O. (eds.) 1977. *Biosocial Bases of Criminal Behavior.* New York: Halsted Press.
Merton, R. K. 1938. Social Structure and Anomie. *American Sociological Review* 3:672–682.
———. 1957. *Social Theory and Social Structure.* Rev. ed. Glencoe, Ill.: Free Press.
Misch, R. C. 1954. The Relationship of Motoric Inhibition to Developmental Level and Ideational Functioning: An Analysis by Means of the Rorschach Test. Ph.D. dissertation, Clark University (Xerox).
Mischel, W. 1961a. Preference for Delayed Reinforcement and Social Responsibility. *Journal of Abnormal and Social Psychology* 62:1–7.
———. 1961b. Father Absence and Delay of Gratification: Cross-Cultural Comparisons. *Journal of Abnormal and Social Psychology* 63:116–124.
———, and Gilligan, C. 1964. Delay of Gratification, Motivation for the Prohibited Gratification, and Responses to Temptation. *Journal of Abnormal and Social Psychology* 69:411–417.
———, and Metzner, R. 1962. Preference for Delayed Reward as a Function of Age, Intelligence, and Length of Delay Interval. *Journal of Abnormal and Social Psychology* 64:425–431.
Monahan, T. P. 1957. Family Status and the Delinquent Child: A Reappraisal and Some New Finding. *Social Forces,* 35:250–258.
Morris, H. H., Escoli, P. J., and Wexler, R. 1956. Aggressive Behavior Disorders in Childhood: A Follow-Up Study. *American Journal of Psychiatry* 112:991–997.
Morris, N., and Hawkins, G. 1970. *The Honest Politician's Guide to Crime Control.* Chicago: The University of Chicago Press.
Moustakas, C. E., Siegel, I. E., and Schalock, H. D. 1956. An Objective Method for the Measurement and Analysis of Child-Adult Interaction. *Child Development,* 27:109–134.
Murray, C. A. 1976. The Link Between Learning Disabilities and Juvenile Delinquency, Current Theory and Knowledge. Washington, D.C.: LEAA.
Nixon, R. E. 1962. *The Art of Growing.* New York: Random House.

REFERENCES

Nye, F. I. 1958. *Family Relationships and Delinquent Behavior*. New York: John Wiley and Sons.

——, and Short, J. F., Jr. 1957. Scaling Delinquent Behavior. *American Sociological Review* 22:326–331.

Offer, D. 1969. *The Psychological World of the Teenager*. New York: Basic Books, Inc.

——, Marohn, R. C., and Ostrov, E. 1975. Violence among Hospitalized Delinquents. *Archives of General Psychiatry* 32:1180–1186.

——, and Offer, J. B. 1975. *From Teenage to Young Manhood: A Psychological Study*. New York: Basic Books, Inc.

——, Ostrov, E., and Howard, K. 1977. *The Offer Self-Image Questionnaire for Adolescents: A Manual*. Chicago: Michael Reese Hospital.

——, and Sabshin, M. 1974. *Normality: Theoretical and Clinical Concepts of Mental Health*. New York: Basic Books, Inc.

——, and ——. 1963. The Psychiatrist and the Normal Adolescent. *AMA Archives of General Psychiatry* 9:427–432.

Oltman, P. K. 1968. Portable Rod-and-Frame Apparatus. *Perceptual and Motor Skills* 26:503–506.

Ostrov, E. 1974. Patterns of Cognitive Control Functioning in a Group of Adolescent Delinquents. Ph.D. dissertation, University of Chicago.

——, Offer, D., and Marohn, R. C. 1976. Hostility and Impulsivity in Normal and Delinquent Rorschach Responses. In *Mental Health in Children*, Vol. II ed. D. V. Siva Sankar. Westbury, N.Y.: PJD Publications, Ltd.

——, ——, ——, and Rosenwein, T. 1972. The Impulsivity Index: Its Application to Juvenile Delinquency. *Journal of Youth and Adolescence* 1:179–196.

Otteson, J. P., and Holzman, P. S. 1976. Cognitive Controls and Psychopathology. *Journal of Abnormal Psychology* 85:125–139.

Paine, R. S., Werry, J. S., and Quay, H. C. 1968. A Study of Minimal Cerebral Dysfunction. *Developmental Medicine and Child Neurology* 10:505–520.

Palermo, D. S., and Jenkins, J. J. 1964. *Word Association Norms*. Minneapolis, Minn.: University of Minnesota.

Persons, R. W. 1967. Relationship between Psychotherapy with Institutionalized Boys and Subsequent Community Adjustment. *Journal of Consulting Psychology* 31: 137–141.

Peterson, D. R. 1961. Behavior Problems of Middle Childhood. *Journal of Consulting Psychology* 25:205–209.

——, Quay, H. C., and Cameron, G. R. 1959. Personality and Background Factors in Juvenile Delinquency as Inferred from Questionnaire Responses. *Journal of Consulting Psychology* 23:395–399.

——, ——, and Tiffany, T. L. 1961. Personality Factors Related to Juvenile Delinquency. *Child Development* 32:355–372.

Porteus, S. D. 1942. *Qualitative Performance in the Maze Test*. New York: The Psychological Corp.

——. 1945. Q-Scores, Temperament, and Delinquency. *The Journal of Social Psychology* 21:81–103.

Powers, E., and Witmer, H. 1951. *An Experiment in the Prevention of Delinquency*. New York: Columbia University Press.

Quay, H. C. 1964. Personality Dimensions in Delinquent Males as Inferred from the Factor Analysis of Behavior Ratings. *Journal of Research in Crime and Delinquency* 1:33–37.

——. 1965a. Personality and Delinquency. In *Juvenile Delinquency: Research and Theory*, ed. H. C. Quay. Princeton, N.J.: D. Van Nostrand Co., Inc.

——. 1965b. Psychopathic Personality as Pathological Stimulation-Seeking. *American Journal of Psychiatry* 122:180–183.

——. 1966. Personality Patterns in Preadolescent Delinquent Boys. *Educational Psychology Measurement* 26:99–110.

——, and Quay, L. C. 1965. Behavior Problems in Early Adolescence. *Child Development* 36:215–220.

210

————, and Werry, J. S., eds. 1972. *Psychopathological Disorders of Childhood*. New York: John Wiley and Sons.

————, Peterson, D. R., and Consalvi, L. 1960. Interpretation of Three Personality Factors in Juvenile Delinquency. *Journal of Consulting Psychology* 24:555.

Reckless, W. C., Dinitz, S., and Murray, E. 1956. Self-Concept as an Insulator Against Delinquency. *American Sociological Review*, 21:744–746.

————, and ————. 1967. Pioneering with Self-Concept as a Vulnerability Factor in Delinquency. *Journal of Criminal Law, Criminology and Police Science* 58:515–523.

Redl, F. 1966. Ego Disturbances and Ego Support and the Phenomenon of Contagion and "Shock Effect." In *When We Deal with Children*. New York: Free Press.

Richardson, L. F. 1960. *Statistics of Deadly Quarrels*. Chicago: Quadrangle Books.

Robbertse, P. M. 1955. Personality Structure of Socially Adjusted and Socially Maladjusted Children, According to the Rorschach Test. *Psychological Monographs* 69 (No. 19, Whole No. 404):1–20.

Roberts, A. H., and Erikson, R. V. 1968. Delay of Gratification, Porteus Maze Test Performance, and Behavioral Adjustment in a Delinquent Group. *Journal of Abnormal Psychology* 73:449–453.

————, ————, Riddle, M., and Bacon, J. G. 1974. Demographic Variables, Base Rates, and Personality Characteristics Associated with Recidivism in Male Delinquents. *Journal of Consulting and Clinical Psychology* 42:833–41.

Robins, L. N. 1966. *Deviant Children Grown-up: A Sociological and Psychiatric Study of Sociopathic Personality*. Baltimore, Md.: Williams and Wilkins.

Romanella, A. E. 1967. Emotions in Adolescence and Response to Color on the Rorschach. *Dissertation Abstracts* 28 (I-B):344.

Rorschach, H. 1942. *Psychodiagnostics, a Diagnostic Test Based on Perception*. Translated by P. Lemkau and B. Kronenburg. Bern: Huber.

Rosenberg, M. 1965. *Society and the Adolescent Self-Image*. Princeton, N.J.: Princeton University Press.

Rosenthal, R. 1966. *Experimenter Effects in Behavioral Research*. New York: Appleton-Century-Crofts.

Routh, D. K., and Roberts, R. D. 1972. Minimal Brain Dysfunction in Children: Failure to Find Evidence for a Behavioral Syndrome. *Psychological Reports* 31:307–14.

Sanders, R., and Cleveland, S. E. 1953. The Relationship between Certain Examiner Personality Variables and Subjects' Rorschach Scores. *Journal of Projective Techniques* 17:34–50.

Schachtel, E. G. 1950. Some Notes on the Use of the Rorschach Test. In *Unraveling Juvenile Delinquency*, ed. S. Glueck and E. Glueck. New York: The Commonwealth Fund.

————. 1966. *Experiential Foundations of Rorschach's Test*. New York: Basic Books, Inc.

Schaefer, E. S., 1964. An Analysis of Consensus in Longitudinal Research on Personality Consistency and Change: Discussion of Papers by Bayley, Macfarlane, Moss, Kagan, and Murphy. *Vita Humana*, 7:143–146.

Schafer, R. 1948. *The Clinical Application of Psychological Tests*. New York: International Universities Press, Inc.

Schlesinger, H. J. 1954. Cognitive Attitudes in Relation to Susceptibility to Interference. *Journal of Personality* 22:354–374.

Schuessler, K. E., and Cressey, D. R. 1950. Personality Characteristics of Criminals. *American Journal of Sociology* 55:476–484.

Schwartz, G., and Puntil, J. E. 1977. Summary and Policy Implication of the Youth and Society. In *Illinois Reports*. Chicago: Chicago Institute for Juvenile Research.

Shapiro, D. 1965. *Neurotic Styles*. New York: Basic Books, Inc.

————. 1960. A Perceptual Understanding of Color Response. In *Rorschach Psychology*, ed. M. A. Rickers-Ovsiankina. New York: John Wiley and Sons.

Shaw, C. R. 1930. *The Jack Roller*. Chicago: University of Chicago Press.

————, and McKay, H. D. 1969 (1932). *Juvenile Delinquency and Urban Areas*. Chicago, University of Chicago Press.

REFERENCES

Shipe, D. 1971. Impulsivity and Locus of Control as Predictors of Achievement and Adjustment in Mildly Retarded and Borderline Youth. *American Journal of Mental Deficiency* 76: 12–22.

Shore, M. F., and Massimo, J. L. 1969. Five Years Later: A Follow-Up Study of Comprehensive Vocationally Oriented Psychotherapy. *American Journal of Orthopsychiatry* 39:769–773.

———, and ———. 1966. Comprehensive Vocationally Oriented Psychotherapy for Adolescent Delinquent Boys. A Follow-Up Study. *American Journal of Orthopsychiatry* 36:609–615.

———, and ———. 1973. After Ten Years: A Follow-Up Study of Comprehensive Vocationally Oriented Psychotherapy. *American Journal of Orthopsychiatry* 43: 128–132.

Short, J. F., Jr., and Nye, F. I. 1957. Reported Behavior as a Criterion of Deviant Behavior. *Social Problems* 5:207–213.

———, and Strodtbeck, F. L. 1965. *Group Process and Gang Delinquency*. Chicago: University of Chicago Press.

Shulman, H. M. 1929. *A Study of Problem Boys and Their Brothers*. A Report to the New York State Crime Commission.

Shybut, J. 1968. Delay of Gratification and Severity of Psychological Disturbances among Hospitalized Psychiatric Patients. *Journal of Consulting and Clinical Psychology* 32:462–468.

Siddle, D. A. T. et al. 1976. Skin Conductance Recovery in Anti-Social Adolescents. *British Journal of Social and Clinical Psychology* 15: 425–428.

Siegman, A. W. 1961. The Relationship between Future Time Perspective, Time Estimation, and Impulse Control in a Group of Young Offenders, and in a Control Group. *Journal of Consulting Psychology* 25:470–475.

Siipola, E., and Taylor, V. 1952. Reactions to Ink Blots under Free and Pressure Conditions. *Journal of Personality* 21:22–47.

Singer, J. L., Wilensky, H., and McCraven, V. 1956. Delaying Capacity, Fantasy and Planning Ability: A Factorial Study of Some Basic Ego Functions. *Journal of Consulting Psychology* 20:375–383.

Slocum, W., and Stone, C. L. 1963. Family Culture Patterns and Delinquent-Type Behavior. *Management and Family Living*, 25:202.

Spiegel, J. P. 1971. Toward a Theory of Collective Violence. In *Dynamics of Violence*, ed. J. Fawcett. Chicago: American Medical Association.

Stein, A. H., and Friedrich, L. K. 1975. The Impact of Television on Children and Youth. In *Review of Child Development Research* vol. 5, ed. E. Mavis Hetherington. Chicago: University of Chicago Press.

Stein, K. B., Sarbin, T. R., and Kulik, J. A. 1968. Future Time Perspective: Its Relation to the Socialization Process and the Delinquent Role. *Journal of Consulting and Clinical Psychology* 32:257–264.

———, ———, and ———. 1971. Further Validation of Antisocial Personality Types. *Journal of Consulting and Clinical Psychology*, 36:177–182.

Storment, C. T., and Finney, B. C. 1953. Projection and Behavior: A Rorschach Study of Assaultive Mental Hospital Patients. *Journal of Projective Techniques* 17:349–360.

Strodtbeck, F. 1951. Husband-Wife Interaction Over Revealed Differences. *American Sociological Review*, 16:468–473.

Stroop, J. R. 1935. The Basis of Ligon's Theory. *American Journal of Psychology* 47:499–504.

Sutherland, E. H. and Cressey, D. R. 1955. *Principles of Criminology*. 5th ed. New York: J. B. Lippincott.

Sykes, G. M., and Matza, D. 1957. Techniques of Neutralization. *American Sociological Review* 22:664–670.

Taintor, Z. et al. 1978. Personal Communication.

Thrasher, F. 1936. *The Gang*. 2nd ed. Chicago: University of Chicago Press.

Thurstone, L. L. 1944. *A Factorial Study of Perception*. Chicago: University of Chicago Press.

REFERENCES

———, and Thurstone, T. G. 1963. *Primary Mental Abilities*. Chicago: Science Research Associates.

Tiffany, T. L., Peterson, D. R., and Quay, H. C. 1961. Types and Traits in the Study of Juvenile Delinquency. *Journal of Clinical Psychology* 17:19–24.

Tinbergen, N. 1968. On War and Peace in Animals and Men. An Ethologist's Approach to the Biology of Aggression. *Science* 160:1411–18.

Townsend, J. K. 1967. The Relationship between Rorschach Signs of Aggression and Behavioral Aggression in Emotionally Disturbed Boys. *Journal of Projective Techniques* 31:13–22.

Vaillant, G. E., and McArthur, C. C. 1972. Natural History of Male Psychologic Health: I. The Adult Life Cycle from 18–50. *Seminars in Psychiatry* 4:415–427.

Vane, J. R., and Eisen, V. W. 1954. Wechsler-Bellevue Performance of Delinquent and Non-Delinquent Girls. *Journal of Consulting Psychology* 18:221–225.

Verrill, B. V. 1958. An Investigation of the Concept of Impulsivity. Ph.D. dissertation, University of Houston (Texas) (Xerox).

Walls, R. T., and Smith, T. S. 1970. Development of Preference for Delayed Reinforcement in Disadvantaged Children. *Journal of Educational Psychology* 61:118–123.

Warren, M. Q. 1976. Intervention with Juvenile Delinquents. In M. K. Rosenheim, ed. *Pursuing Justice for the Child*. Chicago: The University of Chicago Press.

——— et al. 1966. Interpersonal Maturity Level Classification: Juvenile Diagnosis and Treatment of Low, Middle and High Maturity Delinquents. California Youth Authority (Mimeo).

Wechsler, D. 1955. *Manual for the Wechsler Adult Intelligence Scale*. New York: The Psychological Corporation.

———. 1944. *The Measurement of Adult Intelligence*. Baltimore, Md.: Williams and Wilkins.

———. 1949. *Wechsler Intelligence Scale for Children: Manual*. New York: The Psychological Corporation.

Weeks, H. A. and Smith, M. 1939. Juvenile Delinquency and Broken Homes in Spokane, Washington. *Social Forces,* 18:48–55.

Weintraub, S. A. 1973. Self-Control as a Correlate of an Internalizing-Externalizing Symptom Dimension. *Journal of Abnormal Child Psychology* 1:292–307.

Weiss, G., Ninde, K., Weary, J. S., et al. 1971. Studies on the Hyperactive Child. VIII. Five-Year Follow-Up. *Archives of General Psychiatry* 24:409–414.

Wender, P. H. 1971. *Minimal Brain Dysfunction in Children*. New York: Wiley-Interscience.

———, Pedersen, F. A., and Waldrop, M. F. 1967. A Longitudinal Study of Early Social Behavior and Cognitive Development. *American Journal of Orthopsychiatry* 37:691–696.

Werner, E. et al. 1968. Reproductive and Environmental Casualties: A Report on the 10-Year Follow-Up of the Children of the Kauai Pregnancy Study. *Pediatrics* 42:112–127.

Wheeler, S., Cottrell, L. S., Jr., and Romasco, A. 1967. Juvenile Delinquency: Its Prevention and Control. In *Task Force Report: Juvenile Delinquency and Youth Crime*. Washington, D.C.: Commission on Law Enforcement and Administration of Justice.

Wiens, A. N., Maturazzo, J. D., and Garver, K. D. 1959. Performance and Verbal IQ in a Group of Sociopaths. *Journal of Clinical Psychology* 15:191–193.

Williams, J. R., and Gold, M. 1972. From Delinquent Behavior to Official Delinquency. *Social Problems* 20:209–229.

Winer, B. J. 1971. *Statistical Principles in Experimental Design*. 2nd ed. New York: McGraw-Hill Book Co.

Winnicott, D. W. 1958. The Antisocial Tendency. In *Collected Papers*. New York: Basic Books, Inc.

———. 1973. Delinquency as a Sign of Hope. In *Adolescent Psychiatry,* vol. 2, ed. S. Feinstein and P. Giovacchini. New York: Basic Books, Inc.

REFERENCES

Witkin, H. A. 1969. Social Influence in the Development of Cognitive Style. In *Handbook of Socialization Theory and Research,* ed. D. A. Goslin. Chicago: Rand McNally and Co.

————, Dyk, R. B., Faterson, H. F. et al. 1962. *Psychological Differentiation.* New York: John Wiley and Sons.

————, Lewis, H. B., Hertzman, M. et al. 1954. *Personality through Perception.* New York: Harper and Bros.

Wolfensberger, W. P. et al. 1962. Rorschach Correlates of Activity Level in High School Children. *Journal of Consulting Psychology* 26:269–272.

Wolfgang, Marvin E. 1967. The Culture of Youth. In *Task Force Report: Juvenile Delinquency and Youth Crime.* Washington, D.C.: Commission on Law Enforcement and Administration of Justice.

Wright, C. 1944. The Qualitative Performance of Delinquent Boys on the Porteus Maze Test. *Journal of Consulting Psychology* 8:24–26.

Zern, D., Kenney, H. J., and Kvaraceus, W. C. 1974. Cognitive Style and Overt Behavior in Emotionally Disturbed Adolescents. *Exceptional Children* 41:194–195.

AUTHOR INDEX

SUBJECT INDEX

Adolescent adaptations, 16, 17, 51, 98
Adolescent/adult relationships, 158–60; *see also* Delinquents: parents and
Adolescent Behavior Check List (ABCL), 17, 21–22, 42, 43, 47, 97–98, 105–9, 166, 169
Adolescent character disorders, 6–7
Adolescent coping mechanisms, 17, 30, 137, 155–59, 172
Adolescents: delinquent, 7, 13–18, 28, 81–96, 114, 156, 175 (*see also* Delinquents); disturbed, 3, 6, 29, 59, 81, 84, 114, 147; normal, 8, 16, 24, 81–96, 114, 138, 156–59
Aggression, 59, 90, 155–58, 163–68; depression and, 158; humor and, 158
Alcohol. *See* Drug usage
Algeria, 166
Antisocial behavior, 21–22, 51, 97, 105–10, 139, 144
Anxiety responses, 59, 77–78, 142–44, 155, 172
Australia, 83
Automatization test, 149–50

Bale's interaction categories, 25
Behavorial science, 3, 87, 175
Behavior problems, 3, 6, 13, 36–37, 151, 164
Bender-Gestalt Test, 24–25
Bio-psycho-social research, 3, 8
Block Design subtest, 114, 118, 122
Brain damage and dysfunction, 6, 17–18, 145–52
Brazil, 83

California Youth Authority, 41
Children's Embedded Figures Test, 150

Civil War, 5
Cognitive style functioning, 21, 112–32, 142, 149–51; studies of, 8, 35, 98, 112–14
Color reactivity, 102, 104, 107, 110, 117
Color/word test, 119, 123–25
Communication patterns, 5, 31, 87–91, 154
Concealed Figures Test, 116, 119, 122
Countertransference, 34–36
Crime: nonviolent, 4; rates of, 4, 15, 41, 156; violent, 4, 32; *see also* Violence/nonviolence

Data analysis: multivariate, 27, 85, 92, 104–5, 119–22, 126; univariate, 92
Delinquency: acting out and, 7, 28–29, 36–37, 80, 139–40; broken homes and, 89, 147; chronic, 6, 17, 53, 156; definitions of, 3–5, 14, 29–30, 114, 155–56, 159; diagnosis of, 6, 14, 168; discipline and, 89–90; ego development and, 138–39; environment and, 113, 138, 161, 163, 170; etiology of, 5–7, 31, 81, 128, 145–47, 160, 171, 174–75; motor functioning and, 149; neuropsychological deficits and, 149; neuroticism and, 28–29, 130, 137, 163; peer groups and, 29–30, 85, 95, 139; prevention of, 174–75; problems of, 3, 15; psychology of, 7, 28; studies of, 3–6, 13–16, 28–31, 40–41, 87–91, 95, 145–57, 175 (*see also* Research projects); superego and, 157–58; treatment of, 4–8, 16, 28–30, 36–40, 44, 57–59, 64–66, 71–72, 146–47, 171–74; understanding of, 3, 6–7, 31, 39, 138, 154–55; value systems of, 30
Delinquency Check List (DCL), 19, 21, 47, 118–20, 124–27, 131, 168
Delinquent/disturbed contrast, 125–26, 129, 132, 136